SAGE Brief Guide to
CORPORATE SOCIAL RESPONSIBILITY

SAGE Brief Guide to

CORPORATE SOCIAL RESPONSIBILITY

Los Angeles | London | New Delhi
Singapore | Washington DC

Los Angeles | London | New Delhi
Singapore | Washington DC

FOR INFORMATION:

SAGE Publications, Inc.
2455 Teller Road
Thousand Oaks, California 91320
E-mail: order@sagepub.com

SAGE Publications Ltd.
1 Oliver's Yard
55 City Road
London EC1Y 1SP
United Kingdom

SAGE Publications India Pvt. Ltd.
B 1/I 1 Mohan Cooperative Industrial Area
Mathura Road, New Delhi 110 044
India

SAGE Publications Asia-Pacific Pte. Ltd.
33 Pekin Street #02-01
Far East Square
Singapore 048763

Printed in the United States of America

Library of Congress Cataloging-in-Publication Data

Sage brief guide to corporate social responsibility.

p. cm.
Includes bibliographical references and index.

ISBN 978-1-4129-9722-5 (pbk.)

1. Social responsibility of business. I. Sage Publications, inc.

HD60.S225 2012
658.4′08—dc22
2011009897

This book is printed on acid-free paper.

11 12 13 14 15 10 9 8 7 6 5 4 3 2 1

Senior Executive Editor: Lisa Cuevas Shaw

Development Editor: Julie Nemer

Editorial Assistant: MaryAnn Vail

Production Editor: Eric Garner

Typesetter: C&M Digitals (P) Ltd.

Proofreader: Laura Webb

Cover Designer: Gail Buschman

Marketing Manager: Helen Salmon

Permissions Editor: Karen Ehrmann

CONTENTS

PREFACE

Commerce is by its very nature a normative enterprise. It is concerned with creating value for owners and other constituencies, ranging from the firm's immediate stakeholders, such as employees, customers, and suppliers, to the entire society within which the business operates. But what particular value do we expect modern businesses to bring to our society?

The concept of corporate social responsibility (CSR) refers to the general belief held by many that modern businesses have a responsibility to society that extends beyond the stockholders or investors in the firm. That responsibility, of course, is to make money or profits for the owners. These other societal stakeholders typically include consumers, employees, the community at large, government, and the natural environment. There are many ways in which companies may manifest their CSR in their communities and abroad. Most of these initiatives would fall in the category of discretionary, or philanthropic, activities, but some border on improving some ethical situation for the stakeholders with whom they come into contact.

As we think about the importance of CSR/CSP in the new millennium, it is useful to review the results of the millennium poll on CSR that was sponsored by Environics, International, the Prince of Wales Business Leaders Forum, and the Conference Board. This poll included 1,000 persons in 23 countries on six continents. The results of the poll revealed how important citizens of the world now thought CSR really was. The poll found that in the 21st century, companies would be expected to do all the following: demonstrate their commitment to society's values on social, environmental, and economic goals through their actions; fully insulate society from the negative impacts of company actions; share the benefits of company activities with key stakeholders, as well as shareholders, and demonstrate that the company can be more profitable by doing the right thing. This "doing well by doing good" approach will reassure stakeholders that new behaviors will outlast good intentions. Finally, it was made clear that CSR/CSP is now a global expectation that requires a comprehensive, strategic response.

This *Brief Guide to Corporate Social Responsibility* is designed to provide students and practitioners with a quick reference guide to this important topic. While corporate social responsibility is certainly gaining increased respect and attention, the research in this area is still ever-evolving and the key terminology is constantly in flux. With entries covering key terms such as "Strategic Corporate Responsibility" alongside others such as "Corporate Social Responsibility," "Corporate Citizenship," and "Global Business Citizenship," this volume aims to provide readers with an introduction to these ever-evolving concepts and the relationships between them.

FORMAT

This guide to corporate social responsibility provides key terms and concepts related to CSR in a short, easy-to-use format. It is intended to act as a companion for business courses or as a reference for students and practitioners who would like to learn more about the basics of CSR.

The text is divided into five sections that contain important keywords that relate to those sections: *Corporate Social Responsibility and Related Terms; Corporate Social Responsibility on the Global Stage; Corporate Governance, Stakeholders, and Shareholders; Corporate Social Responsiveness: Public Affairs and Public Relations, Politics, and Philanthropy; and Measuring Corporate Social Performance and Implications for Financial Performance.* Each keyword entry is a comprehensive essay written by a business scholar, and entries address such critical topics as strategic philanthropy, corporate moral agency, triple bottom line, corporate social performance, and social audits. In the back of the book, you will also find three appendixes. Appendix A, Problematic Practices, includes entries on businesses and industries that have engaged in problematic practices that raise questions about their commitment to corporate social responsibility. A correlation table in this appendix also provides suggested pairings between the problematic practices and the entries in the text, so that instructors have an idea of which concepts are illustrated in the problematic practices entries. Appendix B provides a directory of

CSR-related organizations and Internet links, and Appendix C provides a directory of online CSR information sources and publications.

ACKNOWLEDGMENTS

We would like to acknowledge and thank Robert Kolb, editor of SAGE's award-winning *Encyclopedia of Business Ethics and Society,* whose contributions provided the foundation for this companion text.

—The Editors of SAGE

PART I

Corporate Social Responsibility and Related Terms

CORPORATE SOCIAL RESPONSIBILITY (CSR)

The concept of corporate social responsibility (CSR) refers to the general belief held by many that modern businesses have a responsibility to society that extends beyond the stockholders or investors in the firm. That responsibility, of course, is to make money or profits for the owners. These other societal stakeholders typically include consumers, employees, the community at large, government, and the natural environment. The CSR concept applies to organizations of all sizes, but discussions tend to focus on large organizations because they tend to be more visible and have more power. And, as many have observed, with power comes responsibility.

DEVELOPMENT OF THE CSR CONCEPT

The concept of CSR has a long and varied history. It is possible to trace evidences of the business community's concern for society for centuries. Formal writings on CSR, or social responsibility (SR), however, are largely a product of the 20th century, especially the past 50 years. In addition, though it is possible to see footprints of CSR thought and practice throughout the world, mostly in developed countries, formal writings have been most evident in the United States, where a sizable body of literature has accumulated. In recent years, the continent of Europe has been captivated with CSR and has been strongly supporting the idea.

A significant challenge is to decide how far back in time we should go to begin discussing the concept of CSR. A good case could be made for about 50 years because so much has occurred during that time that has shaped theory, research, and practice. Using this as a general guideline, it should be noted that references to a concern for SR appeared earlier than this, and especially during the 1930s and 1940s. References from this earlier period worth noting included Chester Barnard's 1938 publication, *The Functions of the Executive,* J. M. Clark's *Social Control of Business* from 1939, and Theodore Kreps's

Measurement of the Social Performance of Business from 1940, just to mention a few. From a more practical point of view, it should be noted that as far back as 1946 business executives (the literature called them businessmen in those days) were polled by *Fortune* magazine asking them about their social responsibilities.

In the early writings on CSR, the concept was referred to more often as just SR rather than CSR. This may have been because the age of the modern corporation's prominence and dominance in the business sector had not yet occurred or been noted. The 1953 publication by Howard R. Bowen of his landmark book *Social Responsibilities of the Businessman* is argued by many to mark the beginnings of the modern period of CSR. As the title of Bowen's book suggests, there apparently were no *businesswomen* during this period, or at least they were not acknowledged in formal writings.

Bowen's work proceeded from the belief that the several hundred largest businesses at that time were vital centers of power and decision making and that the actions of these firms touched the lives of citizens at many points. Among the many questions raised by Bowen, one is of special note here. Bowen asked, what responsibilities to society may businessmen reasonably be expected to assume? This question drove much subsequent thought and is still relevant today. Bowen's answer to the question was that businesspeople should assume the responsibility that is desirable in terms of the objectives and values of society. In other words, he was arguing that it is society's expectations that drive the idea of SR.

Bowen went on to argue that CSR or the "social consciousness" of managers implied that businesspeople were responsible for the consequences of their actions in a sphere somewhat wider than that covered by their profit-and-loss statements. It is fascinating to note that when Bowen referenced the *Fortune* article cited earlier, it reported that 93.5% of the businessmen agreed with this idea of a wider SR. Because of his early and seminal work, Bowen might be called the "father of corporate social responsibility."

If there was scant evidence of CSR definitions in the literature in the 1950s and before, the decade of the 1960s marked a significant growth in attempts to formalize or more accurately state what CSR means. One of the first and most prominent writers in this period to define CSR was Keith Davis, then a professor at Arizona State University, who later extensively wrote about the topic in his business and society textbook, later revisions, and articles. Davis argued that SR refers to the decisions and actions that businesspeople take for reasons that are at least partially beyond the direct economic or technical interest of the firm.

Davis argued that SR is a nebulous idea that needs to be seen in a managerial context. Furthermore, he asserted that some socially responsible business decisions can be justified by a long, complicated process of reasoning as having a good chance of bringing long-run economic gain to the firm, thus paying it back for its socially responsible outlook. This has often been referred to as the enlightened self-interest justification for CSR. This view became commonly accepted in the late 1970s and 1980s.

Davis became well known for his views on the relationship between SR and business power. He set forth his now-famous *Iron Law of Responsibility,* which held that the social responsibilities of businesspeople needed to be commensurate with their social power. Davis's contributions to early definitions of CSR were so significant that he could well be argued to be the runner-up to Bowen for the "father of CSR" designation.

The CSR concept became a favorite topic in management discussions during the 1970s. One reason for this is because the respected economist Milton Friedman came out against the concept. In a 1970 article for the *New York Times Magazine,* Friedman summarized his position well with its title—"The Social Responsibility of Business Is to Increase Its Profits." For many years since and continuing today, Friedman has maintained his position. In spite of Friedman's classic opposition, the CSR concept has continued to be accepted and has continued to grow.

A landmark contribution to the concept of CSR came from the Committee for Economic Development (CED) in its 1971 publication *Social Responsibilities of Business Corporations.* The CED got into this topic by observing that business functions by public consent, and its basic purpose is to serve constructively the needs of society to the satisfaction of society. The CED noted that the social contract between business and society was changing in substantial and important ways. It noted that business is being asked to assume broader responsibilities to society than ever before. Furthermore, the CED noted that business assumes a role in contributing to the quality of life and that this role is more than just providing goods and services. Noting that business, as an institution, exists to serve society, the future of business will be a direct result of how effectively managements of businesses respond to the expectations of the public, which are always changing. Public opinion polls taken during this early period by Opinion Research Corporation found that about two thirds of the respondents thought business had a moral obligation with respect to achieving social progress in society, even at the possible expense of profitability.

The CED went on to articulate a three-concentric-circles definition of SR that included an inner, an intermediate, and an outer circle. The *inner circle* focused on the basic responsibility business had for its economic function—that is, providing products, services, jobs, and economic growth. The *intermediate circle* focused on responsibilities business had to exercise its economic activities in a sensitive way by always being alert to society's changing social values and priorities. Some early arenas in which this sensitivity were to be expressed included environmental conservation; relationships with employees; and meeting the expectations of consumers for information, fair treatment, and protection from harm. The CED's *outer circle* referred to newly emerging and still ambiguous responsibilities that business should be involved in to help address problems in society, such as urban blight and poverty.

What made the CED's views on CSR especially noteworthy was that the CED was composed of businesspeople and educators and, thus, reflected an important practitioner view of the changing social contract between business and society and businesses' newly emerging social responsibilities. It is helpful to note that the CED may have been responding to the times in that the late 1960s and early 1970s was a period during which social movements with respect to the environment, worker safety, consumers, and employees were poised to transition from special interest status to government regulation. In the early 1970s, we saw the creation of the Environmental Protection Agency, the Consumer Product Safety Commission, and the Equal Employment Opportunity Commission. Thus, it can be seen that the major initiatives of government social regulation grew out of the changing climate with respect to CSR.

Another significant contributor to the development of CSR in the 1970s was George Steiner, then a professor at UCLA. In 1971, in the first edition of his textbook, *Business and Society,* Steiner wrote extensively on the subject. Steiner continued to emphasize that business is fundamentally an economic institution in society but that it does have responsibilities to help society achieve its basic goals. Thus, SR goes beyond just profit making. Steiner also noted that as companies became larger their social responsibilities grew as well. Steiner thought the assumption of social responsibilities was more of an attitude, of the way a manager approaches his or her decision-making task, than a great shift in the economics of decision making. He held that CSR was a philosophy that looks at the social interest and the enlightened self-interest of business over the long-run rather than just the old narrow, unrestrained short-run self-interest of the past.

Though Richard Eells and Clarence Walton addressed the CSR concept in the first edition of their book *Conceptual Foundations of Business* (1961), they elaborated on the concept at length in their third edition, which was published in 1974. In this book they dedicated a whole chapter to recent trends in corporate social responsibilities. Like Steiner, they did not focus on definitions, per se, but rather took a broader perspective on what CSR meant and how it evolved. Eels and Walton continued to argue that CSR is more concerned with the needs and goals of society and that these extend beyond the economic interest of the business firm. They believed that CSR was a concept that permits business to survive and function effectively in a free society and that the CSR movement is concerned with business's role in supporting and improving the social order.

In the 1970s, we initially found mention increasingly being made to CSP as well as CSR. One major writer to make this distinction was S. Prakash Sethi. In a classic 1975 article, Sethi identified what he called dimensions of CSP and, in the process, distinguished between corporate behavior that might be called social obligation, SR, or social responsiveness. In Sethi's schema, social obligation was corporate behavior in response to market forces or legal constraints. The criteria here were economic and legal only. SR, in contrast, went beyond social obligation. He argued that SR implied bringing corporate behavior up to a level where it is congruent with the prevailing social norms, values, and expectations of society. Sethi went on to say that while social obligation is proscriptive in nature, SR is prescriptive in nature. The third stage in Sethi's model was social responsiveness. He regarded this as the *adaptation* of corporate behavior to social needs. Thus, anticipatory and preventive action is implied.

Some of the earliest empirical research on CSR was published in the mid-1970s. First, in 1975, Bowman and Haire conducted a survey striving to understand CSR and to ascertain the extent to which companies were engaging in CSR. Though they never really defined CSR in the sense we have been discussing, the researchers chose to measure CSR by counting the proportion of lines devoted to SR in the annual reports of the companies they studied. While not providing a formal definition of CSR, they illustrated the kinds of topics that represented CSR as opposed to those that were strictly business in nature. The topics they used were usually subheads to sections in the annual report. Some of these subheads were as follows: corporate responsibility, SR, social action, public service, corporate citizenship, public responsibility, and social responsiveness. A review of their topical approach indicates that they had a good idea of what CSR generally meant, given the kinds of definitions we saw developing in the 1970s.

Another research study in the mid-1970s was conducted by Sandra Holmes in which she sought to determine executive perceptions of CSR. Like Bowman and Haire, Holmes had no clear definition of CSR. Rather, she chose to present executives with a set of statements about CSR, seeking to find out how many of them agreed or disagreed with the statements. Like the Bowman and Haire list of "topics," Holmes's statements addressed the issues that were generally believed to be what CSR was all about during this time period. For example, she sought executive opinions on businesses' responsibilities for making a profit, abiding by regulations, helping to solve social problems, and the short-run and long-run impacts on profits of such activities. Holmes further added to the body of knowledge about CSR by identifying the outcomes that executives expected from their firms' social involvement and the factors executives used in selecting areas of social involvement.

In 1979, Archie B. Carroll proposed a four-part definition of CSR, which was embedded in a conceptual model of CSP. Like Sethi's earlier article, Carroll sought to differentiate between CSR and CSP. His basic argument was that for managers or firms to engage in CSP they needed to have (1) a basic *definition* of CSR, (2) an understanding/enumeration of the *issues* for which a SR existed (or, in modern terms, stakeholders to whom the firm had a responsibility, relationship, or dependency), and (3) a specification of the *philosophy or pattern of responsiveness* to the issues.

At that time, Carroll noted that previous definitions had alluded to businesses' responsibility to make a profit, obey the law, and to go beyond these activities. Also, he observed that, to be complete, the concept of CSR had to embrace a full range of responsibilities of business to society. In addition, some clarification was needed regarding that component of CSR that extended beyond making a profit and obeying the law. Therefore, Carroll proposed that the SR of business encompassed the economic, legal, ethical, and discretionary expectations that society had of organizations at a given point in time.

A brief elaboration of this definition is useful. First, and foremost, Carroll argued that business has a responsibility that is *economic* in nature or kind. Before anything else, the business institution is the basic economic unit in society. As such it has a responsibility to produce goods and services that society

7

wants and to sell them at a profit. All other business roles are predicated on this fundamental assumption. The economic component of the definition suggests that society *expects* business to produce goods and services and sell them at a profit. This is how the capitalistic economic system is designed and functions.

He also noted that just as society expects business to make a profit (as an incentive and reward) for its efficiency and effectiveness, society expects business to obey the law. The law, in its most rudimentary form, represents the basic rules of the game by which business is expected to function. Society expects business to fulfill its economic mission within the framework of legal requirements set forth by the society's legal system. Thus, the *legal* responsibility is the second part of Carroll's definition.

The next two responsibilities represented Carroll's attempt to specify the nature or character of the responsibilities that extended beyond obedience to the law. The *ethical* responsibility was claimed to represent the kinds of behaviors and ethical norms that society expected business to follow. These ethical responsibilities extended to actions, decisions, and practices that are beyond what is required by the law. Though they seem to be always expanding, they nevertheless exist as expectations over and beyond legal requirements.

Finally, he argued there are *discretionary* responsibilities. These represent voluntary roles and practices that business assumes but for which society does not provide as clear cut an expectation as in the ethical responsibility. These are left to individual managers' and corporations' judgment and choice; therefore, they were referred to as discretionary. Regardless of their voluntary nature, the expectation that business perform these was still held by society. This expectation was driven by social norms. The specific activities were guided by businesses' desire to engage in social roles not mandated, not required by law, and not expected of businesses in an ethical sense, but which were becoming increasingly strategic. Examples of these voluntary activities, during the time in which it was written, included making philanthropic contributions, conducting in-house programs for drug abusers, training the hard-core unemployed, or providing day care centers for working mothers. These discretionary activities were analogous to the CED's third circle (helping society). Later, Carroll began calling this fourth category *philanthropic,* because the best examples of it were charitable, humanistic activities business undertook to help society along with its own interests.

Though Carroll's 1979 definition included an economic responsibility, many today still think of the economic component as what the business firm *does for itself* and the legal, ethical, and discretionary (or philanthropic) components as what business *does for others*. While this distinction represents the more commonly held view of CSR, Carroll continued to argue that economic performance is something business does for society as well, though society seldom looks at it in this way.

EXAMPLES OF CSR IN PRACTICE

There are many ways in which companies may manifest their CSR in their communities and abroad. Most of these initiatives would fall in the category of discretionary, or philanthropic, activities, but some border on improving some ethical situation for the stakeholders with whom they come into contact. Common types of CSR initiatives include corporate contributions (or philanthropy), employee volunteerism, community relations, becoming an outstanding employer for specific employee groups (such as women, older workers, or minorities), making environmental improvements that exceed what is required by law, and so on.

Among the 100 Best Corporate Citizens identified in 2005 by *Business Ethics* magazine, a number of illuminating examples of CSR in practice are provided. Cummins, Inc., of Columbus, Indiana, has reduced diesel engine emissions by 90% and expects that within 10 years the company will be at zero or close to zero emissions. In addition, the engine maker underwrites the development of schools in China, is purchasing biodiverse forest land in Mexico, and funds great architecture in its local community. Cummins also publishes a sustainability report that is available to the public.

Xerox Corporation, Stamford, Connecticut, is a multinational corporation that places high value on its communities. One of its most well-known community development traditions has been its Social Service Leave Program. Employees selected for the program may take a year off with full pay and work for a community nonprofit organization of their choice. The program was begun in 1971, and by 2005, more than 460 employees had been granted leave, translating into about half a million volunteer service hours for the program.

Green Mountain Coffee Roasters, Waterbury, Vermont, was a pioneer in an innovative program designed to help struggling coffee growers by paying them "fair trade" prices, which exceed regular market prices. The company has also been recognized for offering microloans to coffee-growing families and underwriting business ventures that diversify agricultural economics.

Another example of CSR in practice is the Chick-fil-A restaurant chain based in Atlanta, Georgia. Founder and CEO Truett Cathy has earned an outstanding reputation as a businessman deeply concerned with his employees and communities. Through the WinShape Centre Foundation, funded by Chick-fil-A, the company operates foster homes for more than 120 children, sponsors a summer camp, and has hosted more than 21,000 children since 1985. Chick-fil-A has also sponsored major charity golf tournaments.

In the immediate aftermath of Hurricane Katrina in 2005, judged to be the worst and most expensive ever in terms of destruction, hundreds of companies made significant contributions to the victims and to the cities of New Orleans, Biloxi, Gulfport, and the entire Gulf Coast. These CSR efforts have been noted as one of the important ways by which business can help people and communities in need.

As seen in the examples presented, there are a multitude of ways that companies have manifested their corporate social responsibilities with respect to communities, employees, consumers, competitors, and the natural environment.

CSR IN THE NEW MILLENNIUM

As we think about the importance of CSR/CSP in the new millennium, it is useful to review the results of the millennium poll on CSR that was sponsored by Environics, International, the Prince of Wales Business Leaders Forum, and the Conference Board. This poll included 1,000 persons in 23 countries on six continents. The results of the poll revealed how important citizens of the world now thought CSR really was. The poll found that in the 21st century, companies would be expected to do all the following: demonstrate their commitment to society's values on social, environmental, and economic goals through their actions; fully insulate society from the negative impacts of company actions; share the benefits of company activities with key stakeholders, as well as shareholders, and demonstrate that the company can be more profitable by doing the right thing. This "doing well by doing good" approach will reassure stakeholders that new behaviors will outlast good intentions. Finally, it was made clear that CSR/CSP is now a global expectation that requires a comprehensive, strategic response.

—Archie B. Carroll

Further Readings

Ackerman, R. W. (1973). How companies respond to social demands. *Harvard Business Review, 51*(4), 88–98.

Ackerman, R. W., & Bauer, R. A. (1976). *Corporate social responsiveness.* Reston, VA: Reston.

Asmus, P. (2005). 100 Best corporate citizens. *Business Ethics,* Spring, 20–27.

Aupperle, K. E., Carroll, A. B., & Hatfield, J. D. (1985). An empirical investigation of the relationship between corporate social responsibility and profitability. *Academy of Management Journal, 28,* 446–463.

Backman, J. (Ed.). (1975). *Social responsibility and accountability.* New York: New York University Press.

Barnard, C. I. (1938). *The functions of the executive.* Cambridge, MA: Harvard University Press.

Bowen, H. R. (1953). *Social responsibilities of the businessman.* New York: Harper & Brothers.

Carroll, A. B. (1979). A three-dimensional conceptual model of corporate social performance. *Academy of Management Review, 4,* 497–505.

Carroll, A. B. (1991, July/August). The pyramid of corporate social responsibility: Toward the moral management of organizational stakeholders. *Business Horizons, 34,* 39–48.

Carroll, A. B. (1999). Corporate social responsibility: Evolution of a definitional construct. *Business & Society, 38*(3), 268–295.

Carroll, A. B., & Buchholtz, A. K. (2006). *Business and society: Ethics and stakeholder management* (6th ed.). Cincinnati, OH: South-Western/Thomson.

Committee for Economic Development (CED). (1971, June). *Social responsibilities of business corporations.* New York: Author.

Davis, K. (1960, Spring). Can business afford to ignore social responsibilities? *California Management Review, II,* 70–76.

Davis, K. (1973). The case for and against business assumption of social responsibilities. *Academy of Management Journal, 16,* 312–322.

Davis, K., & Blomstrom, R. L. (1966). *Business and its environment.* New York: McGraw-Hill.

Drucker, P. F. (1984). The new meaning of corporate social responsibility. *California Management Review, XXVI,* 53–63.

Eels, R., & Walton, C. (1974). *Conceptual foundations of business* (3rd ed.). Homewood, IL: Richard D. Irwin.

Epstein, E. M. (1987). The corporate social policy process: Beyond business ethics, corporate social responsibility, and corporate social responsiveness. *California Management Review, XXIX,* 99–114.

Frederick, W. C. (1960). The growing concern over business responsibility. *California Management Review, 2,* 54–61.

Frederick, W. C. (1978). *From CSR₁ to CSR₂: The maturing of business and society thought.* Working Paper No. 279, Graduate School of Business, University of Pittsburgh.

Friedman, M. (1962). *Capitalism and freedom.* Chicago: University of Chicago Press.

Griffin, J. J. (2000). Corporate social performance: Research directions for the 21st century. *Business & Society, 39*(4), 479–491.

Griffin, J. J., & Mahon, J. F. (1997). The corporate social performance and corporate financial performance debate: Twenty-five years of incomparable research. *Business & Society, 36,* 5–31.

Harrison, J. S., & Freeman, R. E. (1999, October). Stakeholders, social responsibility, and performance: Empirical evidence and theoretical perspectives. *Academy of Management Journal, 1999,* 479–485.

Husted, B. W. (2000). A contingency theory of corporate social performance. *Business & Society, 39*(1), 24–48.

Jones, T. M. (1980, Spring). Corporate social responsibility revisited, redefined. *California Management Review, 1980,* 59–67.

Manne, H. G., & Wallich, H. C. (1972). *The modern corporation and social responsibility.* Washington, DC: American Enterprise Institute for Public Policy Research.

McGuire, J. W. (1963). *Business and society.* New York: McGraw-Hill.

Parket, I. R., & Eilbirt, H. (1975, August). Social responsibility: The underlying factors. *Business Horizons, XVIII,* 5–10.

Preston, L. E. (1975). Corporation and society: The search for a paradigm. *Journal of Economic Literature, XIII,* 434–453.

Preston, L. E., & Post, J. E. (1975). *Private management and public policy: The principle of public responsibility.* Englewood Cliffs, NJ: Prentice Hall.

Rowley, T., & Berman, S. (2000). A brand new brand of corporate social performance. *Business & Society, 39*(4), 397–418.

Schwartz, M. S., & Carroll, A. B. (2003). Corporate social responsibility: A three domain approach. *Business Ethics Quarterly, 13*(4), 503–530.

Sethi, S. P. (1975, Spring). Dimensions of corporate social performance: An analytic framework. *California Management Review, XVII,* 58–64.

Steiner, G. A. (1971). *Business and society.* New York: Random House.

Swanson, D. L. (1995). Addressing a theoretical problem by reorienting the corporate social performance model. *Academy of Management Review, 20,* 43–64.

Wartick, S. L., & Cochran, P. L. (1985). The evolution of the corporate social performance model. *Academy of Management Review, 10,* 758–769.

Wood, D. J. (1991). Corporate social performance revisited. *Academy of Management Review, 16,* 691–718.

STRATEGIC CORPORATE
SOCIAL RESPONSIBILITY

Strategic corporate social responsibility is the attempt by companies to link those largely discretionary activities explicitly intended to improve some aspect of society or the natural environment with their strategics and core business activities. While corporate social responsibility has historically referred to a firm's economic, legal, ethical, and discretionary responsibilities to society, strategic corporate social responsibility, in general, represents discretionary activities that form a company's community relations function or foundation, including corporate philanthropy, volunteerism, and multisector collaborations. Corporate social responsibility can be compared with the mere general concept of corporate responsibility, which is a company's complete set of responsibilities to its stakeholders, societies where it operates, and the natural environment, as manifested through its operating practices.

Corporate social responsibility represents the direct efforts by a company to improve aspects of society by the firm as compared with the integral responsibilities that every firm has with respect to primary stakeholders such as employees, customers, investors, and suppliers. The use of the term *strategic* implies that the discretionary socially oriented activities of the firm are intended to have direct or indirect benefits for the firm—that is, to somehow help the firm achieve its strategic and economic objectives. There is a wide range of ways in which companies can use corporate social responsibility activities strategically. These ways range from helping local schools improve so that, long term, the workforce will be better educated, to improving local conditions in the community so that it will be easier to recruit and retain employees, to improving the firm's reputation among customers so that they will continue to use the company's products and services, as well as numerous other examples.

Sometimes termed *enlightened self-interest,* strategic corporate social responsibility initiatives are closely linked to strategic philanthropy and cause marketing. They attempt to help achieve a company's core mission and strategies by providing a socially beneficial foundation for enhanced economic value added. This benefit to the firm happens through improved reputation from the social desirability that key stakeholders, such as customers and employees, feel for being affiliated in some way with a company perceived to be more socially responsible or, more directly, through increased use of the company's products and services that are tied to donations to specific charitable organizations.

Some observers object to strategic corporate social responsibility on the grounds that the company cannot or should not both be doing moral or social good while also profiting financially. Other observers see no necessary conflict in what is called doing well and doing good, because for companies that are under increasing pressure for good short-term results, strategic corporate social responsibility represents a way for them to attempt to meet the needs of multiple stakeholders, particularly investors and societal stakeholders, including customers, employees, and investors concerned with corporate responsibility, simultaneously.

There is significant and growing evidence from a large number of research studies that companies that are more socially responsible, or more responsible in general to all their stakeholders, perform at the same level or somewhat better than less responsible companies. This empirical evidence suggests that there are no necessary trade-offs between profitability in terms of financial performance and responsibility, even explicitly socially beneficial activities. Companies with good corporate social responsibility records, according to employee and consumer surveys, may find it easier to recruit and retain employees, attract and keep new customers, and even attract investors concerned about issues of corporate responsibility, also called socially responsible or ethical investors.

—Sandra Waddock

Further Readings

Gourville, J. T., & Kasturi Rangan, V. (2004). Valuing the cause marketing relationship. *Harvard Business Review, 47*(1), 38–57.

Lantos, G. P. (2001). The boundaries of strategic corporate social responsibility. *Journal of Consumer Marketing, 18*(7), 595–630.

Phillips, R. (2000). The corporate community builders: Using corporate strategic philanthropy for economic development. *Economic Development Review, Summer,* 7–11.

STRATEGIC PHILANTHROPY

Strategic philanthropy is an approach by which corporate or business giving and other philanthropic endeavors of a firm are designed in such a way that it best fits with the firm's overall mission, goals, and values. This implies that the business has a carefully articulated strategy and that it understands how to integrate its philanthropic initiatives with this strategy in actual practice. A major characteristic of strategic philanthropy is that the motivation is not solely altruistic. To understand how strategic philanthropy has become an everyday practice, it is useful to trace this concept as it has unfolded in business history.

BEGINNINGS OF CORPORATE PHILANTHROPY

The concept of philanthropy evolved through business history even before the broader corporate social responsibility movement had taken shape. The concept of business responsibility that prevailed in the United States during most of its history was fashioned after the traditional, or classical, *economic model* of the firm. Dominant in the late 1800s and early 1900s, the economic model of the firm thought of the marketplace as the primary determinant of what business firms did in their communities and in society. The pattern of corporate philanthropy in Europe and other parts of the Western world paralleled its development in the United States. Unfortunately, though the marketplace did a reasonably good job in deciding what goods and services should be produced, it did not fare as well in ensuring that business always acted generously, fairly, and ethically. In addition, business created many social problems and the view was developing that business had some responsibility for these social problems that extended beyond just producing goods and services.

Years later, when laws began to be passed constraining business practices, it might be said that a *legal model* emerged. Society's expectations of business changed from being strictly economic in nature to encompassing issues that previously had been at business's discretion. Over time, a *social model* of the firm emerged. What this social model did, in effect, is embrace both the economic and legal emphases and add yet another layer of expectations by society that business would assume some role in addressing social problems and issues that had arisen.

In the late 1800s and early 1900s, initial indications of business's willingness to contribute to the community were localized efforts toward meeting community needs through philanthropy, or business giving, and paternalistic practices. It is evident that businesspeople did engage in philanthropy— contributions to charity and other worthy causes—even during the periods that were dominated by the traditional economic view. Voluntary activities to improve, beautify, and uplift the community were evident. One very early example of this was the cooperative efforts between the railroads and the Young Men's Christian Association immediately after the Civil War to provide community services in areas affected by the railroads. These initiatives, in hindsight, can now be seen as early examples of strategic philanthropy, because they benefited both the communities and the railroads.

The emergence of large corporations during the late 1800s played a major role in hastening the movement away from the strict classical economic model of the firm in society. As the economy transitioned away from one dominated by small, powerless companies to large corporations with more concentrated power, questions of business responsibility began to be raised. By the 1920s, community service had become much more important for business. The most visible example of this was the Community Chest movement, which received its impetus from business.

One example of early progressive business ideology was reflected in Andrew Carnegie's 1889 essay "The Gospel of Wealth." Carnegie asserted that business must pursue profits but that business wealth should also be used for the benefit of the community. Philanthropy turned out to be one of the best ways in which firms could benefit the community. A prime example of this was Carnegie's funding and building of more than 2,500 libraries for communities.

Corporate philanthropy continued to grow into the 20th century and by the late 20th century had become one of the institutionalized ways by which businesses could aid communities, the growing number of nonprofit organizations, and other national and international groups. Today, corporate philanthropy is considered to be one of the foremost means by which companies fulfill their social responsibilities and come to be regarded as good corporate citizens.

PHILANTHROPY DEFINED

Before developing the concept of strategic philanthropy further, it is useful first to examine the concept of philanthropy itself. The word *philanthropy* has generally been defined as a concern for or love of humankind. Philanthropy has been linked to efforts to demonstrate this fondness or concern for humankind through charitable gifts, aid, or donations. Though most people would not philosophically disagree with the concept of philanthropy, throughout history some have. Friedrich Nietzsche, for example, objected to it as a concept of universal good because he thought it represented the weak parasitically living off the strong. Ayn Rand is another major philosopher who held a similar view. Political views on philanthropy have also been present. Most governments have been supportive of philanthropic efforts on the part of companies and individuals and have supported these efforts through tax incentives and tax breaks. Though the term *philanthropy* seems to imply some altruistic expression, as in "love of humankind," today the concept more nearly refers to the giving of resources for the benefit of others.

Conceptually, today, philanthropy may be seen as a part of companies' corporate social responsibility or corporate citizenship initiatives. Archie Carroll has argued that philanthropy fulfills businesses' discretionary responsibilities to be good corporate citizens. These philanthropic activities are voluntary, guided only by businesses' desire to engage in social activities that are not mandated, not required by law, and not generally expected in an ethical sense. Philanthropy is "desired/expected" in most societies. The public has an expectation that business will engage in philanthropy, in part because it has become so much a part of business tradition and in part because many believe it is part of the social contract between business and society, especially between business and the local community. Others believe business should engage in philanthropy to partially offset some of the social harm or social problems business has engendered.

By the first decade of the 2000s, philanthropic initiatives include corporate giving, matching programs in which companies match contributions given by their employees, product and service donations, employee volunteerism, partnerships with local governments and other organizations, and any other kind of community involvement on the part of the organization and its employees. These philanthropic initiatives are in response to ongoing needs in the community in areas such as education, culture and the arts, health/human

services, and civic and community activities. In addition, special needs arise
due to emergencies such as the tsunami in Southeast Asia in 2004 and
Hurricanes Katrina and Rita in the United States in 2005.

STRATEGIC PHILANTHROPY TAKES SHAPE AND EVOLVES

The concept of strategic philanthropy has evolved out of traditional forms of
business giving. Early on, corporate giving was more focused on the needs
that had arisen in the community and so philanthropy was more altruistic in
nature—more focused on an exclusive consideration of the needs of others.
With the passage of time and the heightened competition and cost pressures
that have characterized the business community in the past several decades,
corporate executives have begun looking more carefully at the kinds of
impacts philanthropic efforts might have. It has become evident that business
can not only help others but help itself at the same time, and this germ of
thought is what has produced the modern strategic philanthropy emphasis. At
the same time, corporate giving has become institutionalized and professional-
ized, and as it has been turned over to professional managers, top management
has come to view the giving function as one that should deliver more specific,
direct benefits to the company, and thus, the idea of strategic philanthropy has
been born and cultivated in a business climate that has been more driven by
profitability and accountability toward the bottom line.

Strategic philanthropy is an approach to business giving that seeks to
achieve goals for the community or recipient of the giving and for the business
itself as well. Strategic philanthropy is more focused. It does not just address
any legitimate need in the community but rather focuses on those needs or
issues that are consistent with or aligned with the firm's overall mission,
objectives, programs, or products/services. A classic example of strategic philanthropy is the Ronald McDonald Houses sponsored by McDonald's ham-
burger chain. The Ronald McDonald Houses are facilities usually built near
children's hospitals to help families who want to be close to their children who
may be receiving longer-term treatment at the hospital. The Ronald McDonald
House Charities maintains more than 200 houses in 44 countries around the
world where families can stay together for free when traveling for a sick
child's treatment and 48 rooms within hospitals for the same purpose.
McDonald's, which has long viewed children as one of its target markets, thus
is able to generously contribute to children and their families, thus enhancing
its own interest or strategy at the same time. The children and their families

win and McDonald's as a corporation wins. It should be clarified that McDonald's, as a company, initiated and sponsors the Ronald McDonald House Charities, but many other companies also contribute to the charity. In addition, each chapter also relies on individual contributions. In a sense, then, this is an ideal example of strategic philanthropy in that McDonald's gets high name recognition and publicity for the charity, even though the company is just one of the many supporters of the charity.

In using strategic philanthropy, companies strive to align their corporate giving or community relations initiatives with their own goals, objectives, or markets. The idea is to have a double impact—a positive impact on the recipients of the philanthropy and some kind of positive impact on the businesses' bottom lines or strategies. Two other examples are worthy of mention. The first is Novartis' creation of its nonprofit, Novartis Research Institute for Tropical Diseases. The nonprofit Institute allows it to focus on the discovery of new drugs for treating neglected diseases. The company benefits and the victims of neglected diseases benefit. Second is IBM's On Demand Community Program. This program permits IBM employees around the world to share the company's technology and other resources with the agencies where they sign up for volunteer service. Both parties benefit.

Strategic management expert Michael Porter has argued that the term *strategic philanthropy* has begun to be used to explain virtually any type of charitable giving that has some definable theme, focus, or approach that builds bridges between the businesses that are giving and needs in the community. Porter has been critical of strategic philanthropy, arguing that the link between the companies and the charities arc often weak, tenuous, or semantic. He suspects that most of these initiatives really do not have anything at all to do with corporate strategy but are aimed at achieving positive publicity or goodwill for the companies and for improving employees' morale. His belief is that for strategic philanthropy to be viewed as genuine or valid, it needs to effectively integrate social and economic goals in such a way so as to produce legitimate social impact in the community. Of course, his criticisms may be broadened to include any corporate citizenship initiatives on the part of business, not just philanthropy.

CAUSE-RELATED MARKETING

One of the shapes or variations that strategic philanthropy has taken on is that of cause-related marketing, or cause marketing. Many critics claim that this is more marketing than philanthropy, but others have held that it is an extreme form of strategic philanthropy in that the link between the businesses' interest and some social or public cause is tightly tied together. In cause marketing, each time a consumer uses a service or buys a product, a donation is given by the company to the charity. Thus, cause marketing has sometimes been referred to as "quid pro quo philanthropy."

One of the earliest examples of cause-related marketing was in the early 1980s when American Express Company introduced a program whereby it would contribute 1 cent to the restoration of the Statue of Liberty each time one of its credit cards was used to make a purchase. This initiative generated $1.7 million for the restoration of the historical monument and a substantial increase in the use of the company's cards. Today, American Express coordinates its philanthropic and marketing efforts with its community business program and cause-related-marketing campaign to help small business owners acquire access to the credit and resources they need to start or grow their businesses. So the company now gives a portion of credit card charges to three national nonprofit organizations specializing in community economic development when American Express Community Business Card customers use their cards. Today, many different companies have linked using their products or services to the amount they would then donate to some worthy charitable cause.

Just as Porter has been critical of strategic philanthropy, he has especially been critical of cause-related marketing. He thinks these efforts are more targeted toward improving the companies' reputations than doing good in the community and, thus, fail as authentic efforts toward strategic philanthropy. In his view, the best way to maximize philanthropy's value is to follow a path that effectively combines pure philanthropy with pure business in such a way that genuine social and economic values are created.

THE BUSINESS CASE FOR STRATEGIC PHILANTHROPY

The impetus behind the movement toward strategic philanthropy has been the expectation by CEOs and top echelon executives that for corporate giving to continue, the "business case" for it has to be established. The business case is the argument or rationale as to how the business is specifically benefiting from the philanthropic endeavors. It is the explication of reasons why business is believed to be benefited by the philanthropy. One of the leading business groups supporting the idea of strategic philanthropy is Business for Social Responsibility (BSR), a nonprofit association of firms and executives who support the idea of integrating business's social role with its economic objectives. BSR has assembled research that indicates that companies, through their philanthropic giving, may

- increase customer loyalty and enhance brand image,
- strengthen employee loyalty and productivity,
- enhance corporate reputation, and
- expand into emerging markets.

In short, specific business advantages that strengthen the companies' bottom lines are achievable through carefully designed philanthropic initiatives.

An interesting aspect of strategic philanthropy is that two firms in the same industry may decide to pursue divergent philanthropic projects and initiatives while both are focusing on the bottom-line benefits to the company as well as helping the community. In the home improvement/products industry, for example, The Home Depot supports sustainable forestry, community impact grants, and volunteerism, while Lowe's, its major competitor, supports Habitat for Humanity, sponsorship of American Red Cross disaster relief, and community college scholarships. Executives in these two firms made strategic choices to engage different philanthropics but with doubtless similar objectives in terms of strategic impact on the company's profitability and reputation.

Since strategic philanthropy is a part of corporate social responsibility initiatives, it follows that these same benefits accrue due to these efforts. Also, it can readily be seen that most of these reasons are business related, not philanthropy related. Thus, the business case is strengthened. Finally, it is worth noting that Paul Godfrey has developed and presented an analysis of literature and research that supports the idea that (a) corporate philanthropy can generate positive moral capital among stakeholders and communities, (b) this moral capital can provide business owners with insurance-like protection for a firm's relationship-based intangible assets, and (c) this protection contributes to shareholder wealth. Thus, through logic and research, he has added to the business case for corporate philanthropy, especially strategic philanthropy.

—Archie B. Carroll

Further Readings

Burlingame, D. F., & Young, D. R. (Eds). (1996). *Corporate philanthropy at the cross-roads.* Bloomington: Indiana University Press.

Business for Social Responsibility. (2005). *Issue brief: Philanthropy.* Retrieved from www.bsr.org

Carroll, A. B., & Buchholtz, A. K. (2006). Business and community stakeholders. In *Business and society: Ethics and stakeholder management* (6th ed., pp. 471–504). Mason, OH: South-Western.

Epstein, K. (2005). Philanthropy, Inc.: How today's corporate donors want their gifts to help the bottom line. *Stanford Social Innovation Review, Summer,* 21–27.

Godfrey, P. C. (2005). The relationship between corporate philanthropy and shareholder wealth: A risk management perspective. *Academy of Management Review, 30*(4), 777–798.

Logsdon, J., Reiner, M., & Burke, L. (1990). Corporate philanthropy: Strategic responses to the firm's stakeholders. *Nonprofit and Voluntary Sector Quarterly, 19*(2), 93–109.

Porter, M. E., & Kramer, M. R. (2002). The competitive advantage of corporate philanthropy. *Harvard Business Review, December,* 57–68.

Saiia, D. H., Carroll, A. B., & Buchholtz, A. K. (2003). Philanthropy as strategy: When corporate charity begins at home. *Business and Society, 42*(2), 169–201.

Smith, C. (1996). The new corporate philanthropy. *Harvard Business Review, 72*(3), 105–115.

CORPORATE CITIZENSHIP

Corporate citizenship, sometimes called corporate responsibility, can be defined as the ways in which a company's strategies and operating practices affect its stakeholders, the natural environment, and the societies where the business operates. In this definition, corporate citizenship encompasses the concept of corporate social responsibility (CSR), which involves companies' explicit and mainly discretionary efforts to improve society in some way, but is also directly linked to the company's business model in that it requires companies to pay attention to all their impacts on stakeholders, nature, and society. Corporate citizenship is, in this definition, integrally linked to the social, ecological, political, and economic impacts that derive from the company's business model; how the company actually does business in the societies where it operates; and how it handles its responsibilities to stakeholders and the natural environment. Corporate citizenship is also associated with the rights and responsibilities granted to a company or organization by governments where the enterprise operates; just as individual citizenship carries rights and responsibilities, however, companies have considerably more resources and power than do most individuals and do not have the right to vote.

While CSR has historically referred to a company's economic, legal, ethical, and discretionary responsibilities, corporate citizenship emphasizes the integral responsibilities attendant to a company's strategies and practices. There are other definitions of corporate citizenship, but they are generally consistent with the theme of integrating social, ecological, and stakeholder responsibilities into the companies' business strategies and practices. For example, the United Nations' definition states that corporate citizenship is the integration of social and environmental concerns into business policies and operations. The U.S. association Business for Social Responsibility defines it as operating a business in a manner that meets or exceeds the legal, ethical, commercial, and public expectations that society has of business. The definition of the Center for Corporate Citizenship at Boston College requires that a good corporate citizen integrate basic social values with everyday business practices, operations, and policies so that these values influence daily decision making across all aspects of the business and takes into account its impact on all stakeholders, including employees, customers, communities, suppliers, and the natural environment.

The definition of the Corporate Citizenship Unit at Great Britain's University of Warwick Business School indicates that corporate citizenship involves the study of a broad range of issues, including community investment, human rights, corporate governance, environmental policy and practice, social and environmental reporting, social auditing, stakeholder consultation, and responsible supply chain management. Australia's Deakin University's Corporate Citizenship Research claims that corporate citizenship recognizes business's social, cultural, and environmental responsibilities to the community in which the business seeks a license to operate and recognizes economic and financial obligations to shareholders and stakeholders.

BACKGROUND

The term *corporate citizenship* as applied to companies' core business practices, strategies, and impacts became popular particularly in the European Union in the mid-1990s but has been in use at least since the 1950s. The terminology evolved from earlier conceptions of business in society, particularly from the concept of CSR, which connotes doing explicit good for society mainly through philanthropy and is considered voluntary on the part of companies. Although some scholars and practicing managers do define corporate citizenship more narrowly than the definitions above, believing that discretionary activities on the part of companies to deliberately improve societies constitute corporate citizenship initiatives, most of the business associations and centers in academic environments have developed the more broad-based conception accepted here.

Typical manifestations of CSR occur through philanthropic programs, volunteer activities, in-kind giving, and community relations. In contrast, the dominant conception of corporate citizenship applies to the ways a company operates; that is, its fundamental business model, and the stakeholder, societal, and nature-related impacts that derive from the way the company does business. Although some definitions of corporate citizenship do focus more narrowly on social good activities of companies, the more business-model-based definition related to overall corporate responsibilities is widely accepted, as the definitions given above indicate.

In the 1960s, U.S. legal scholar Dow Votaw noted that companies needed to be understood not just as economic actors in society but also as political actors. Votaw focused on specific issues related to a company's corporate citizenship that retain currency today, particularly in light of the vast size and economic clout of many large multinational corporations. The issues that concerned Votaw included companies' influence and power, which are derived from a company's size and control of economic and other resources; questions about the legitimacy of firms in society and how they are to be made accountable to broader societal interests; and how companies could be sanctioned when wrongdoing occurs. Thus, deeply embedded in the notion of corporate citizenship is the idea that companies gain legitimacy through a form of social contract granted by societies typically in the form of incorporation papers. With legitimacy comes a set of rights and also responsibilities. Corporate citizenship highlights the specific arenas in which those responsibilities apply, encompassing relationships with stakeholders and impacts on the natural environment and societies.

The reach, scope, and size of many large companies have created significant pressures from different groups in society for better corporate citizenship and greater attention to the ethical values that underpin it. These pressures are highlighted by the fact that, by 2002, 51 of the world's largest economies were said not to be countries but companies. In part, it is this spectacular size and attendant power that have created much of the attention to corporate citizenship, fueled further by concerns about globalization's impacts; management practices of outsourcing key functions to developing nations to reduce costs; ethical and accounting scandals; and corporate influence on governments, communities, and whole societies.

Corporate leaders began paying significant attention to issues of corporate citizenship during the late 1990s and early 2000s, following waves of antiglobalization protests; critiques of corporate outsourcing practices; fears about climate change and other serious environmental problems said to be at least partially created by businesses; and the rise of anticorporate activism sometimes directed at specific companies and sometimes at policies of powerful global institutions such as the World Trade Organization, the World Bank, and the International Monetary Fund. Advanced communication technologies fueled the ability of activists and other critics to question corporate activities and create increasing demands for responsibility, transparency, and accountability by companies.

On the business side, numerous new activities and organizations designed to highlight good corporate citizenship emerged during the 1990s and early 2000s. At least partially in response to vocal activism about supply chain practices, many multinational corporations developed and implemented internal codes of conduct during the 1990s. Some of these companies also asked their supply chain partners to implement the codes in their operations as well. In addition to internal codes, a number of codes and sets of principles, frequently generated by multisector coalitions that included companies, governmental representatives, activists, and nongovernmental organizations (NGOs), also emerged. These codes represent what their developers consider to be a baseline or floor of ethical conduct that serves as the foundation of corporate citizenship. Prominent business ethicists Thomas Donaldson and Thomas Dunfee have labeled such foundational values hypernorms. Although still somewhat controversial as to whether they exist, hypernorms identified by Donaldson and Dunfee include basics such as respect for human dignity, basic rights, good citizenship, and, similarly, fundamental values. Such hypernorms serve as a foundation for all human values and also as a basis for good corporate citizenship. They are built on three principles, including the respect for core human values that determine a floor of practice and behavior below which it is ethically problematic, respect for local traditions, and respect for the context in which decisions are made.

During the 1990s and into the 2000s, there was a great deal of activism against certain corporate practices such as outsourcing, which frequently involved contracting with manufacturers in developing nations whose workers were subjected to abusive conditions, ecological deterioration, and poor labor standards, as well as the impact of globalization. This activism generated a flurry of development of codes of conduct that attempted to codify how such basic principles could be put into practice in companies. As the codes developed, many companies, particularly large multinational firms with brand names to protect, began demanding that their suppliers live up to the standards articulated in the codes.

Many companies developed their own codes of conduct; in addition, a number of codes emerged that were developed by multisector coalitions working from internationally agreed documents or core ethical standards. Among the most prominent, although not without its critics, was the United Nations' Global Compact's set of 10 (originally nine) principles, which were drawn from internationally agreed declarations and treaties. The Global Compact, which had nearly 2,000 members by 2005, was established in 1999 by UN Secretary-General Kofi Annan to "initiate a global compact of shared values and principles, which will give a human face to the global market." In signing onto the Global Compact, companies agree to uphold 10 fundamental principles on human rights, labor rights, environment, and anticorruption.

The Global Compact's 10 principles focus on core or foundational principles and are drawn from major UN declarations and documents that have been signed by most of the countries of the world. Documents from which the principles are drawn include the Universal Declaration of Human Rights, the International Labour Organization's Declaration on Fundamental Principles and Rights at Work, the Rio Declaration on Environment and Development, and the United Nations Convention Against Corruption. The two human rights principles require companies to support and respect the protection of internationally proclaimed human rights and make sure that they are not complicit in any human rights abuses. The four labor standards require companies to uphold the freedom of association and the effective recognition of the right to collective bargaining, eliminate all forms of forced and compulsory labor, effectively abolish child labor, and eliminate discrimination in employment. The three environmental principles require companies to support a precautionary approach to environmental challenges, undertake initiatives to promote greater environmental responsibility, and encourage the development and diffusion of environmentally friendly technologies. The corruption principle, added in 2004, requires companies to work against all forms of corruption, including bribery and extortion.

There are other important codes and principles aimed at putting corporate citizenship efforts into operating practices and strategies. These codes include the Guidelines for Multinational Enterprises of the Organisation for Economic Co-operation and Development, the Global Sullivan Principles of Corporate Social Responsibility, the Marine Stewardship Council's Principles and Guidelines for Sustainable Fishing, the Natural Step's Sustainability Principles, the UN's Norms on the Responsibilities of Transnational Corporations and Other Enterprises with regard to Human Rights, the Equator Principles (for the financial services industry), the Sustainable Forestry Principles, the Caux Principles, the Business Principles for Countering Bribery, the CERES (Coalition for Environmentally Responsible Economies) Principles, the Clean Clothes Campaign model code, the Workplace Code of Conduct of the Fair Labor Association, the Keidanren Charter for Good Corporate Behavior and the Keidanren Environment Charter, the Canadian Business for Social Responsibility Guidelines, the World Federation of the Sporting Goods Industry Model Code, and numerous others. One observer at the International Labour Organization, a division of the United Nations, counted more than 400 such principles and codes including individual company codes. Many, although certainly not all, of the core issues embedded in these codes are similar, despite differences in wording and specific focus.

These codes and principles evolved, in part, because of societal concerns about corporate practices and impacts. For example, the practice of outsourcing operations including manufacturing and production of many goods and services to low-wage developing nations became very popular among large companies starting in the 1990s and continuing to the present. This practice drew attention to the companies' corporate citizenship because many of the facilities in the developing nations were exposed in media reports as having sweatshop working conditions, abusing the human rights of workers, having poor safety standards, or employing weak environmental management. The practice of outsourcing continued into the 2000s and expanded to call and support centers, programming, and other technologically sophisticated services, which shifted from the developed nations to the developing nations. Concerns about domestic job loss for communities where the outsourcing company had facilities combined with low wages and poor conditions in some developing nations created a public focus on the implications of this type of practice for different groups of stakeholders.

Other factors fueling attention to corporate citizenship include the array of ethical scandals, accounting misrepresentations, and frauds that were uncovered in the United States in the early 2000s, as well as in Europe and elsewhere. Accompanied by accusations of corruption and undue influence in the political affairs of nations, and participation by companies in abusive regimes in certain countries, these scandals drew attention to corporate citizenship or what some believed to be lack thereof. Chief executive compensation, estimated to be on the order of 450 times that of the average worker in the early 2000s, and a wave of consolidations through mergers and acquisitions that created huge oligopolies and even near monopolies in many industries, further fanned the desire for better corporate citizenship and also fanned the flames of attention to corporate citizenship.

Pressures for ever-increasing short-term financial performance from financial markets beginning in the 1980s and continuing to the present have focused many corporate leaders' attention on short-term share prices. The attention to share price caused some observers and critics to believe that companies were failing to pay sufficient attention to other stakeholders, that is, those affected by and able to affect the company's activities. Corporate citizenship thus evolved during the 1990s and 2000s in part as a voluntary effort by many large, and therefore highly visible, transnational corporations as well as numerous smaller ones, to demonstrate their goodwill in the face of concerns about their size, short-term decision-making orientation, their power accrued through control of financial and other resources, and not always positive impacts on stakeholders, societies, and the natural environment.

CRITICISMS OF CORPORATE CITIZENSHIP AND RESPONSES

Criticism of a company's corporate citizenship can come from many sources, including activists, the media, local communities affected by company activities, customers, and sometimes nations. Some activists set up websites that attempt to foster action against a company, such as a boycott. Wal-Mart, for example, has faced significant problems in some communities because of the company's impact on local shopping districts, low wages, and discrimination against women. Some investors are also concerned about corporate responsibility or citizenship and choose their investments at least in part on the basis of how they perceive the company's corporate citizenship through what is called socially responsible investing. The Social Investment Forum in the United States estimated in 2003 that some $2.16 trillion or more than one of every nine equity investment dollars in the United States was invested in assets that employed at least one of the three main responsible investment strategies—screening investments, shareholder advocacy, and community investment. Screening investments means paying attention to particular negative practices, including poor supply chain management practices such as child labor or abusive working conditions, poor environmental practices, or harmful products such as cigarettes, which some investors wish to avoid. Some investors look for positive practices that they wish to encourage. Returns for investments in screened funds as compared with traditional funds are roughly comparable.

Shareholder advocates focus on changing corporate practices by submitting shareholder resolutions. Shareholder resolutions are aimed at changing matters of concern to activist investors and are directed to the board of directors through the annual meeting process. Shareholder resolutions can focus on a wide range of issues of concern, including environmental policies and practices, labor standards, wages, harmful products, and excessive executive compensation, to name a few areas of criticism. Some chief executives engage in dialogue with the shareholder activists and promise changes, resulting in the resolutions being withdrawn, while others come to a vote during the annual meeting process. Community investors sometimes put their money into projects that are aimed specifically at helping to improve communities, such as housing developments, retail establishments, and similar projects. They may carry a somewhat lower rate of return than traditional investments, but social investors are willing to make that trade-off when necessary.

Defining corporate citizenship as the contributions of businesses to society through the combination of core business activities, social investment and philanthropy, and participation in the public policy process, the World Economic Forum created a framework for action signed by 40 multinational companies' CEOs in 2002. This framework for action focuses on three key elements that help flesh out what corporate citizenship means in practice: the companies' commitment to being global corporate citizens as part of the way that they operate their businesses; the relationships that companies have with key stakeholders, which are fundamental to the company's success internally and externally; and the need for leadership on issues of corporate citizenship by the CEOs and boards of directors of those companies. This statement also points out the array of terminology used to signify corporate citizenship activities: triple bottom line or sustainable development, ethics, corporate responsibility, and corporate social responsibility. The statement also emphasizes key elements of managing responsibility: leadership that defines what corporate citizenship means to a company, integration into corporate strategies and practices, implementation, and transparency.

Evidence of growing interest on the part of companies in corporate citizenship can be found not only in their joining organizations such as the UN Global Compact, the World Business Council for Sustainable Development (WBCSD), and similar organizations but also in a growing acceptance of the need to manage their responsibilities explicitly. The WBCSD focuses on three pillars of corporate citizenship that have come to be called the triple bottom line—economic growth, ecological balance, and social progress through the lens of sustainable development. For example, many transnational firms with long supply chains have been exposed to criticisms by activists that practices in supply chain companies, which may not actually belong to the multinational company, are problematic, with poor labor standards, working conditions, and environmental standards.

Some companies have actively begun to manage their supply chain relationships by asking suppliers to live up to the multinational's own code of conduct and standards of practice, as well as ensuring that conditions in their own operations are managed responsibly. Such responsibility management approaches are aimed at helping companies protect their reputations for good citizenship by establishing global standards throughout their supply chain. They are supplemented by an emerging institutional framework aimed at assuring that stated and implicit corporate responsibilities are actually met.

STAKEHOLDERS AND CORPORATE CITIZENSHIP

The definition of corporate citizenship as having to do with the impacts of corporate practices and strategies on stakeholders, nature, and the natural environment links corporate citizenship integrally to the relationships that companies develop with their stakeholders. In the classic definition offered by R. Edward Freeman, stakeholders are said to be those who are affected by or who can affect a company. Stakeholders can be classified into two categories—primary and secondary. Primary stakeholders are those groups and individuals without whom the company cannot exist and typically are said to include owners or shareholders, employees, customers, and suppliers, particularly in companies with extended supply chain. Secondary stakeholders are those affected by or can affect the company's practices and strategies, but who are not essential to its existence. Secondary stakeholders typically include governments, communities where the company has facilities and operations, and activists interested in the company's activities, among numerous others. Sometimes governments or communities can be considered primary stakeholders, as when a company is in a regulated industry or when its business directly serves a given community. The environment is not a person but because all companies and indeed all of human civilization depend on its resources, it is frequently treated as if it were a stakeholder; hence, environmental management and related issues of ecological sustainability are tightly linked to concepts of corporate citizenship.

Each stakeholder group either takes some sort of risk with respect to the company, makes an investment of some sort in it, or is tied through some sort of emotional, reputational, or other means into the company's performance. Shareholders or owners, for example, invest their money in the company's shares and rightfully expect a fair return on that investment. Employees invest their knowledge, physical strength and abilities, skills, intellectual resources, and frequently also some of their emotions in the firm, and the firm invests in training and developing employees. Employees are repaid through their salaries and wages. A significant body of research exists that suggests that when employees are treated well by a company through progressive employee practices that are representative of good corporate citizenship, their productivity will be better and the company will benefit financially and in other ways. Customers trust that the products or services that they purchase will serve the purposes for which they are designed and add appropriate value. Good corporate citizenship with respect to customers, therefore, involves the creation of value-adding products and services. Problems with suppliers can result in numerous issues for companies relating to product quality, delivery, and customer service, not to mention the fact that if the supplier itself uses problematic practices, such as sweatshops or poor labor standards, the company purchasing its products will suffer from a degraded reputation. Hence, it is important for companies to manage their relationships with suppliers and distributors well, particularly because many external observers fail to differentiate between the corporate citizenship of the main company and its supply and distribution chain.

Communities are important to companies because they create local infrastructure, such as sewers, communications connections, roadways, building permits, and the like that companies need. Many companies that view themselves as good corporate citizens have extensive corporate community relations programs, including philanthropic programs, volunteer initiatives, and community-based events intended to enhance their local reputation as a neighbor of choice and sustain what is called their license to operate. Governments are important stakeholders, too, and most large companies have developed significant public affairs functions to deal with governmental relations. They also participate in the political processes of countries where they are located to the extent permissible locally, including contributing to campaigns and working through lobbyists to influence legislation.

Environmental management and sustainability have become important elements of good corporate citizenship as worries about the long-term sustainability of human civilization in nature have become more common. Many large companies have implemented environmental management programs in which they attempt to monitor and control the ways in which environmental resources are used so that they are not wasted through programs that encompass resource reduction, reuse, and recycling. A few progressive firms have begun to focus on issues of long-term ecological sustainability as well.

RESPONSIBILITY MANAGEMENT AND ASSURANCE

Most large corporations today have developed specific functions to deal with these different stakeholder groups in what are called boundary-spanning functions. Because the quality of the relationship between a company and its stakeholders is an important manifestation of the company's corporate citizenship, these boundary-spanning functions, which include position titles such as employee relations, community relations, public affairs, shareholder relations, supplier relations, and customer relations, are increasingly important.

In most large companies today there is still no one particular job title or function in which all the corporate citizenship activities reside, though some corporate community relations officers have assumed a great many of these responsibilities. A few companies have appointed individuals to positions with titles such as corporate social responsibility officer, vice president of corporate responsibility, or director of corporate citizenship. These jobs, however, are still far from common as of 2005.

In response to criticisms about their negative impacts on society, stakeholders, and nature, and questions about the credibility of their corporate citizenship, many large companies have developed corporate citizenship statements and strategies; some have even appointed managers to positions with titles such as corporate citizenship, corporate social responsibility, or corporate responsibility officer. By the early 2000s, many large corporations voluntarily began to issue social, ecological, or so-called triple-bottom-line reports, which encompass all three elements of corporate citizenship, aimed at economic, social, and ecological impacts.

Responsibility Management

Responsibility management and reporting in the early 2000s consisted of voluntary efforts on the part of companies to be more transparent about some of their practices and impacts. Because companies were able to report how, when, and what they wanted to, however, many critics still found problems with their corporate citizenship. In response, what can be called a responsibility assurance system, consisting of principles and codes of conduct, credible monitoring, verification, and certification systems to ensure that those principles were being met, and consistent reporting mechanisms began to evolve in the early 2000s.

A given company's corporate citizenship is guided by the company's vision and underpinned by its values. Responsibility management approaches begin with vision and values and are reinforced by stakeholder engagement, which helps companies to determine the concerns and interests of both internal and external stakeholders and make appropriate changes. Unlike CSR, which focuses on discretionary activities, corporate citizenship in its broadest sense represents a more integrated approach to the broad responsibilities of companies that is increasingly being accepted by leaders of global enterprises. When a company adopts a responsibility management approach as part of its corporate citizenship agenda, it also focuses on integrating the vision and values into the operating practices and strategies of the firm, typically by focusing on human resource practices and the array of management systems, corporate culture, and strategic decisions that constitute the firm. Another important aspect of responsibility management, which can be compared in its major elements to quality management, is developing an appropriate measurement and feedback system so that improvements can be made as necessary. A final element is that of transparency, as many companies managing corporate citizenship explicitly publish some sort of report that focuses on their social, ecological, and economic performance. Such reports have come to be called triple-bottom-line reports.

Responsibility Assurance

Skeptical stakeholders need reassurance that companies actually manage their stakeholder, societal, and ecological responsibilities well and were unsatisfied with voluntary internal responsibility management approaches, particularly since such approaches were still mostly in use by large branded companies concerned about their reputation, leaving most business-to-business companies and small and medium-sized enterprises to their own devices. Such critics need reassurance that stated standards are actually being met and that statements about corporate citizenship made by companies are accurate. As a result, in addition to internal and voluntary responsibility management approaches, during the early 2000s some large multinational companies began participating in an emerging and still voluntary responsibility assurance system. Responsibility assurance attempted to provide some external credibility to what companies were doing internally to manage their corporate citizenship. Responsibility assurance involves three major elements: principles and foundational values; credible monitoring, verification, and certification systems that help ensure that a company is living up to its stated values; and globally accepted standards for transparently reporting on corporate citizenship and responsibility activities.

Principles and Foundation Values

Principles and foundation values can be found in documents such as the UN Global Compact, OECD Guidelines for Multinational Corporations, and similar codes of conduct as discussed above. They provide guidance to companies about a floor of practice below which it is morally problematic to go and typically rest on core ethical principles or, as noted above, internationally agreed documents and treaties.

Credible Monitoring, Certification, and Verification Approaches

The second aspect of responsibility assurance encompasses credible monitoring, certification, and verification approaches. Because there is a great deal of skepticism about companies' actual corporate citizenship practice, many critics are unwilling to believe companies when they state that they are ensuring that their codes of conduct are actually being implemented. This skepticism increases in long global supply chains, where companies outsource manufacturing, assembly, and related low-skill work to facilities in developing nations; the outsourced work is granted to suppliers who are not actually owned by the customer or sourcing company. Although the supplier facilities are not actually part of the sourcing company, some multinationals' reputations have nonetheless been tainted when activists have uncovered problems in the suppliers' operations related to human and labor rights, environment, safety, working conditions, abuses that involve poor pay even by local standards or failure to pay overtime, and related problems. Child labor is another serious concern for some activists. It turned out that the media, activists, and ultimately the general public did not make a distinction between the supplying company manufacturing in developing nations and the customer company that was purchasing those goods—both were blamed for the use of child labor, but the multinationals were the nearer and more familiar target, so they bore the brunt of the blame. Even when the multinationals implemented their codes of conduct and asked their suppliers to live up to those codes, problems persisted.

As a result, some footwear, clothing, toy, and sports equipment multinationals and some large retailers, who were among the first companies targeted by activists for poor sourcing practices, not only asked their suppliers to implement a code of conduct but began hiring external verifiers to go into those companies and ensure that standards were actually being met. These verifiers are mostly independent agents; they include both NGOs and sometimes accounting firms attempting to develop an expertise in social, labor, and ecological monitoring. The verifiers perform three main functions in supplying companies, wherever they are found: verification that the standards of the sourcing firm are being met; monitoring of working conditions, pay, labor standards, and health, safety, and environmental standards; and certification to the external world that conditions are what the company says they are. Major companies such as Nike, Reebok, Levi Strauss, The Gap, Disney, and Mattel, and numerous others who have been spotlighted in the past, now employ external verifiers in addition to having their own codes of conduct and internal management systems.

Among the many organizations involved in the verification or social audit process are the Fair Labor Association; SAI International, which offers a set of standards called SA 8000; and the British firm AccountAbility, which offers a set of standards called AA 1000. Others include the Clean Clothes Campaign, the Worldwide Responsible Apparel Production program, the Ethical Trading Initiative, Verité, the Fairwear Foundation of the Netherlands, and the Worker Rights Consortium. Many of these independent monitoring and verification organizations are NGOs, while some social auditors are for-profit enterprises. In addition, some represent women's rights groups, some are focused on labor and human rights, and others are backed by religious groups. Some are local in scope and use local parties to actually conduct the monitoring, while the larger ones are international in scope. Concerns about this type of monitoring or responsibility audit, according to the U.S. association Business for Social Responsibility (BSR), range from issues about the effectiveness of monitors in actually uncovering abuses; lack of resolution of issues uncovered in reports by corporate headquarters; and opinions that other means of reducing poverty, corruption, and related systemic problems will be more effective than verification processes. BSR also suggests several positive reasons why companies wish to employ social auditors and verifiers, including cost reduction by using local monitors rather than in-house monitors especially when facilities are globally distributed, benefits to corporate reputation, better compliance both with the code and legal requirements, enhanced productivity and quality brought about by better working conditions, and greater transparency and related credibility with the public.

Globally Accepted Reporting Standards

The third important element of responsibility assurance is having globally accepted reporting standards that ensure that real transparency exists about corporate practices and impacts. Here, the analogy needs to be made to financial auditing and reporting. The auditing and accounting industry, at least within each nation, has long established standard practices, formats, and criteria for reporting corporate financial performance. Such standardization is important so that investors can compare one company's performance against others in the same industry or across different industries. Currently, the same cannot be said for corporate reporting about social and ecological matters, yet there are increasing demands on companies for greater transparency about their practices and impacts.

Although many companies issue triple- or multiple-bottom-line reports that focus not only on economic and financial matters but also on social and environmental ones, there is still no fully accepted reporting procedure that details what, how, and when different aspects of performance are to be reported. As a result, comparing the social or ecological performance of one company with that of others even within the same industry can be problematic. Restoring public trust in corporate citizenship ultimately will require standardization of social reports and even potentially some legal requirements that all companies issue such reports.

There are a number of initiatives aimed at developing globally accepted reporting standards that ensure social and ecological transparency, including a major initiative by the European Union to standardize CSR reporting. Indeed, the ISO organization, which sets quality and environmental standards, began to develop a set of corporate responsibility standards in 2004, which will be voluntary for companies once completed. A company called One Report helps multinationals and other companies gather and report on issues related to sustainability, which include both social and ecological elements, in a standardized format. Perhaps the most prominent of the initiatives around standardized triple-bottom-line reporting, sometimes called sustainability, reporting is that of the Global Reporting Initiative or GRI.

The GRI began in 1997 as an initiative of the CERES and became independent in 2002. Its mission is to develop globally standardized guidelines for sustainability reporting. Formed by a multistakeholder coalition, the GRI regularly gets input from businesses, accounting firms, and investment, environmental, research, human rights, and labor organizations to ensure that its standards are comprehensive, correct, and appropriate to the situation of different businesses. Linked cooperatively with the UN Global Compact, the GRI has developed specific reporting guidelines, principles for determining what to report and how, and content indicators that guide organizations in developing their own reports. In addition, because industries differ dramatically in the characteristics of what needs to be reported, the GRI also has begun developing industry-specific standards.

The GRI attempts to help companies integrate a number of complex attributes related to their corporate citizenship. These include their code of conduct, international conventions and performance standards, management systems standards, accounting for intangibles, assurance standards, and specific standards related to the company's industry. Sometimes criticized for its complexity, the GRI represents the most recognized approach to date of standardized triple-bottom-line or sustainability reporting.

CRITICISMS OF CORPORATE CITIZENSHIP

Some observers believe that corporate citizenship merely represents an effort on the part of companies to create a positive public image rather than substantive change within the corporation. Particularly when corporate citizenship is treated as discretionary or voluntary activities designed to improve aspects of society, critics believe that it does not go deep enough. Others point out that while the United Nations estimates that there are approximately 70,000 multinational corporations in the world with hundreds of thousands of subsidiaries, only a few highly visible, mostly brand-name companies are actively engaged in explicitly forwarding themselves as good corporate citizens. For example, as of 2005, about 2,000 companies had joined the UN Global Compact, while about 350, many of which had joined the Global Compact, had completed triple-bottom-line audits following the procedures of the GRI.

Another criticism of the concept of corporate citizenship focuses on the fact that citizenship is an individual responsibility involving a corresponding set of rights that relate to membership in a political entity, typically a nation-state, that involve civil, social, and political rights and responsibilities, while companies are not people. Companies, however, do bear responsibilities for their societal and ecological impacts, because they command significantly more resources than do most individuals, because they can influence the public policy process in many nations, and because when they participate in civil society or the political process, they carry more weight than do most individual citizens.

—Sandra Waddock

Further Readings

Andriof, J., & McIntosh, M. (Eds.). (2001). *Perspectives on corporate citizenship.* Sheffield, UK: Greenleaf.

Donaldson, T., & Dunfee, T. W. (1999). *Ties that bind: A social contracts approach to business ethics.* Boston: Harvard Business School Press.

Journal of Corporate Citizenship. Various articles, published 2001 to present. Sheffield, UK: Greenleaf.

Marsden, C. (2000, Spring). The new corporate citizenship of big business: Part of the solution to sustainability? *Business and Society Review, 105*(1), 9–26.

Matten, D., & Crane, A. (2004). Corporate citizenship: Towards an extended theoretical conceptualization. *Academy of Management Review, 29,* 166–179.

Matten, D., Crane, A., & Chapple, W. (2003, June). Behind the mask: Revealing the true face of corporate citizenship. *Journal of Business Ethics, 45*(1/2), 109–121.

McIntosh, M., Leipziger, D., Jones, K., & Coleman, G. (1998). *Corporate citizenship: Successful strategies for responsible companies.* London: Financial Times/Pitman.

Waddock, S. (2004, March). Companies, academics, and the progress of corporate citizenship. *Business and Society Review, 109,* 5–42.

Waddock, S. (2006). *Leading corporate citizens: Vision, values, value added* (2nd ed.). New York: McGraw-Hill.

Zadek, S. (2001). *The civil corporation: The new economy of corporate citizenship.* London: Earthscan.

SUSTAINABILITY

S*ustainability* is an evolving concept that expresses holistic thinking integrating society, economy, and ecology. This concept has been advanced to guide actions within present society to ensure continued existence and prosperity into the foreseeable future. Therefore, *sustainability* can be defined as an integrated understanding of the interconnectedness of human activity with all related man-made and naturally occurring systems. The goal of sustainability is often conflated with the approach needed to attain the goal—*sustainable development.* Understanding these two terms is an essential first step for addressing a set of global challenges embodied by sustainability. To that end, the Brundtland Commission, created through the United Nations, published a report in 1987 in which *sustainable development* is defined as seeking to meet the needs and aspirations of present society without compromising the ability to meet those of future generations.

Because of profound changes to our shared ecological systems, the question of sustainability is being considered around the world. From advancing ozone depletion, which leads to progressively higher levels of life-damaging radiation, to accelerating greenhouse gas emissions, which contribute to complex climate change, to habitat destruction, which results in decreased biodiversity, shared ecosystem resources are being depleted or damaged. Among the consequence of ecosystem damage and loss are that it can threaten and create social unrest in the future, while at the same time drive numerous species toward extinction. Abject poverty that attends the growing gaps between the rich and the poor is a proven driver of environmental degradation and fuels resource, trade, and policy disputes. This type of economic unrest has provided a source of motivation to address sustainability issues not only in organizations such as the United Nations but also at the World Bank and the World Trade Organization.

As our society wrestles with the meaning and actions implied by sustainability, it is helpful to consider that more than 400 years ago the Haudenosaunee (also known as the Iroquois) had their "Great Law," which, in part, requires that leaders consider the impact of their decisions on the seventh generation following that decision. There are other such examples of statements regarding sustainability from the past that very clearly define our collective responsibility to protect and plan for the future. Understanding the recurrence of this theme in human society helps us to understand the centrality of sustainability. It is also instructive to note that thinking about sustainability is not the same as achieving a sustainable outcome. Many civilizations have risen only to prove unsustainable, the Haudenosaunee being among them. What is very different today is the accumulating metrics and resulting data that confirm the impact of human activity on global ecosystem services, such as water cycles, carbon cycles, and resource renewal cycles to name a few. Climate scientists are in general agreement that global warming is real, and it is the product of human activity. The main questions now are as follows: How bad will the consequences be? How fast will they manifest? What can be done to mitigate some of the damage already done?

Sustainability explores how we collectively and individually move into the future while learning to understand how global ecosystem services underpin the social and economic activity on the planet. Business organizations are human society's most efficient resource concentrators, transformers, and distributors; thus, they create what might be called a "corporate ecology" and, therefore, business-oriented solutions central to any working and attainable definition of sustainability.

A few business organizations have viewed increased emphasis on sustainability as an opportunity. If environmental and social costs are included as additional performance metrics, then those firms that comply early and set new standards may be able to create a basis for competitive advantage. For instance, when the California Environmental Protection Agency found that two-stroke engines (the type often used in lawn mowers and gas-powered gardening equipment) were causing a large amount of air pollution, it began to demand more stringent emissions standards for these machines. At first, these new standards were opposed by industry, but a few innovators not only were able to meet the new standards but exceeded them and used 33% less fuel with their more efficient motors. In this case, a sustainability effort, once embraced by these companies, provided the compliant companies with a competitive advantage and achieved a social and environmental objective simultaneously. Sustainability, when pursued by businesses with creativity and purpose, can achieve financial, social, and environmental objectives in an integrated and positively reinforcing manner.

The concept of sustainability is not without its detractors. Some notable scholars, such as Julian Simon, feel that the combined mental power of more people will solve whatever environmental or social problems further human activity produces. The Cato Institute in 2002 concluded that sustainable development is a dubious solution in search of a problem or that it is simply a restatement of a commonsense position of taking care of one's own productive resources that is already well addressed by the current free market policy. It has also been argued that the cost of taking action to comply with sustainability initiatives such as the Kyoto Treaty on Climate Change would cost the U.S. economy a disproportionate amount. These arguments were central to the Bush administration's refusal to become a signatory nation to that agreement on "greenhouse gas" reduction. Some climate scientists and ecologists argue that greenhouse gas damage to ecosystems services may be irreversible and this damage has real costs now that will grow in the future. A concept as complex and far-reaching as sustainability will always present business and society with very conflicted and ambiguous trade-offs.

Because business organizations are uniquely transformative institutions in modern society, how business approaches the concept of sustainability is of primary importance. This central role of business in modern society is also discussed in such topics as corporate social responsibility, corporate citizenship, and corporate ecology. A number of management efficiency approaches have been suggested for business organizations that could make important contributions to our societal goal of sustainability. Some of these include ISO14000, triple-bottom-line accounting, the balanced scorecard approach to strategic management, natural capitalism, the natural step, industrial ecology, Zero Emissions Research Initiative (ZERI), ecological footprinting, and eco-effectiveness (cradle-to-cradle model). In the following sections, these approaches will be discussed briefly.

ISO14000

ISO stands for the International Standards Organization. It is a nongovernmental organization that has grown out of the General Agreement on Tariffs and Trade. As the World Trade Organization pursues agreements on global trade, quality standards have become increasingly important. One of the outcomes of the 1992 Rio Summit on the Environment was the creation of ISO14000 to create a comprehensive set of standards designed to address the most pressing environmental issues for organizations in a global market. As it currently stands, these standards are voluntary for organizations to abide by. However, the ISO14000 is building on up-to-date environmental health and safety standards. These are important standards and make significant contributions to our understanding of sustainability. However, the ISO does not make specific mention of sustainability and states as its primary focus the application of best practices that are geared toward helping organizations come into compliance with globally accepted standards on environmental health and safety. Depending on the application, the ISO approach to standardized reporting and efficiency measures can lead a company to improvements or to follow an industry to the lowest common denominator of acceptable practice.

TRIPLE-BOTTOM-LINE ACCOUNTING

This term and approach originated with the publication of John Elkington's 1998 book *Cannibals with Forks: Triple Bottom Line of 21st Century Business.* In it, Elkington argues that accounting practice should be expanded to include environmental and social costs as well as financial costs. Some scholars argue that corporate social responsibility, or corporate social performance, must measure the social, environmental, and economic performance of the corporation for a firm to be consistent in its approach to these commitments to good practice. There are obvious problems associated with assessing the costs to society for various corporate actions. According to Elkington, the price of a product should include the cost of the ecological services consumed in the production of the product and embodied in the use and disposal of the product. Great strides in ecological economics and research in social capital have helped create metrics to fill in these gaps. The triple-bottom-line approach would have a substantial impact on how organizations operate and may advance our understanding of sustainability. But there are many scholars and practitioners who oppose this type of approach, arguing that it confuses the division of labor and would make firms inefficient and uncompetitive.

BALANCED SCORECARD

This systematic approach to enterprise management was developed in the early 1990s, by Robert Kaplan and David Norton, as a way to remove some of the vagueness out of strategic management. This approach was not developed specifically as a tool to achieve sustainability, but it has promise as such. Like the triple bottom line, the balanced scorecard approach requires that management look beyond financial measurement; it incorporates a more holistic systems perspective into organizational management. This system uses what has been referred to as a double-loop feedback: One loop is business process focused, and one loop is strategic outcome focused. Both loops are intended to use measurements to provide managers with data on which decision making is based. The application for sustainability comes from the reliance on internal and external data collection and an inherent acceptance of a systems approach.

NATURAL CAPITALISM

In 1999, Paul Hawkins, Amory Lovins, and L. Hunter Lovins published a book proposing the redesign of industry based on biological models. They argue that the living systems of the earth are in decline and that the next industrial revolution will be driven by corporations. Natural capitalism is built around the idea that business opportunities become more abundant as entrepreneurs recognize environmental resource limitations. Those that can do more with less will prosper. The advocates of natural capitalism propose four interlinked principles to unlock and ultimately restore natural capital: (1) radically increase resource productivity; (2) adopt closed-loop systems and zero waste in industry; (3) sell services in place of selling products; and (4) recognize that natural capital is the source of future prosperity, thus that businesses will be incentivized to invest in its maintenance. This approach is not only an explicit plan for the concept of sustainability but also a vision of what sustainable business practice might look like.

THE NATURAL STEP

This approach is the outcome of a series of studies initiated by Karl-Henrik Rob, who established principles for sustainable society based on thermodynamics and natural cycles. Since 1989, the Natural Step Foundation has been refining and promoting its four-phase program. These phases are (1) aligning key decision makers and stakeholders around a common understanding of what it takes to be a sustainable society, (2) creating baseline data that detail the resources necessary for an organization to be sustainable, (3) creating a vision-driven strategic plan based on the data gathered through the study of the organizational system, and (4) recognizing that success depends on step-by-step implementation and continued support. While this approach is comprehensive and holistic, an organization's implementation of this approach seems dependent on the Natural Step Foundation and may be self-limiting because of restrictive access. Here again, as in natural capitalism, the emphasis and essence of the approach to sustainability is on systems thinking, confronting natural resource and cycles dependence, and creating strategies to support the health and continuation of these processes.

INDUSTRIAL ECOLOGY

The idea of industrial ecology, which has grown rapidly over the past decade, originated in a 1989 publication by Robert Frosch, and a book by this title was published by Graedel and Allenby in 1994. Very simply, industrial ecology is the idea that an industrial system should function like an ecosystem. There is no waste product in nature; the end of one process is the beginning of another. Some scholars have defined industrial ecology as the science of sustainability. Yet others would argue that this overreliance on science is the weakness of industrial ecology. It has been said that the answer to the question of sustainability will not be engineered; society must come to an understanding of the interdependence of natural systems and their limitations. These writers advocate caution regarding industrial ecology and suggest that technological fixes help human populations extend their overconsumption of resources, whether they are renewable or fixed in quantity. However, all would agree that industrial ecology will be at least part of the solution, because it provides the engineering solutions that can teach us to do much more with less consumption and helps eliminate waste and pollution.

ZERO EMISSIONS RESEARCH INITIATIVE (ZERI)

ZERI is a concept and a network started by Pauli and deSouza at the United Nations University in Japan. The ZERI network has more than 50 projects worldwide that are applying the ZERI sustainability ideas regarding biodiversity, waste elimination, creativity, and efficient design. ZERI is similar to the

Natural Step in that it employs systems thinking to address business, production, and consumption problems. ZERI seeks to create a global network of participants to create alternative organizations that produce goods and services in ways that alleviate poverty and reduce environmental degradation. ZERI is another holistic, systems-based approach to sustainability—one that seeks to model human organizations based on our understanding of naturally occurring systems.

ECOLOGICAL FOOTPRINT

Ecological Footprint is a tool created in 1993 by Mathis Wackernagel and William Rees to help quantify human demand on natural systems relative to the planet's ability to meet those demands. By showing that these demands are consistently in excess of the planet's ability to sustainably provide for these demands, the Global Footprint Network seeks to get business, government, and communities to adopt more sustainable behaviors. Unlike most of the other approaches presented here, the footprint concept is a tool that helps individuals and organizations get a sense of what their actions cost in terms of ecological services. This is an important place to start when considering the meaning and application of sustainability. Our current global ecological footprint overshoots ecosystem capacity by almost 20%, which can be absorbed for a time but not without damage and not indefinitely. Tools such as ecological foot printing are important for people to map our current trajectory and to be able to measure change when action is taken.

ECO-EFFECTIVENESS (CRADLE-TO-CRADLE MODEL)

This is a management consulting and sustainability model that is similar to the approach of natural capitalism. It was developed by Michael Braungart and William McDonough in 1995. The idea of eco-effectiveness is not simply doing more with less but designing products and services in ways that are systemically appropriate. Such products and services are designed to produce no waste and to support rather than disrupt natural systems. By studying the industry as a natural system, this concept seeks to design business processes that mimic metabolic systems both biological and mechanical. Like natural capitalism, this approach envisions the next industrial revolution as one where the end of a product use cycle is the beginning of the next nutrient cycle—where waste equals food and ecological intelligence drives profitability and competitive advantage.

As this brief survey of approaches for addressing sustainability illustrates, many scholars and practitioners have expressed urgency and insight about the global need for sustainability. A successful approach to sustainability will not be engineered. Simply building better, more efficient products will not on its own yield a sustainable future. Along with the efficient use of resources, sustainability requires some fundamental changes in how organizations work on all levels, from the individual action to international coordination. These are not insignificant changes. This fact alone captures the profound difficulty in even defining sustainability—sustainability will have different meanings depending on the level of analysis; ultimately they must all contain the understanding that a sustainable world cannot support irresponsible and inequitable resource use.

—David H. Saiia

Further Readings

Cyphert, D., & Saiia, D. (2004). In search of the corporate citizen: The emerging discourse of corporate ecology. *Southern Communication Journal, 69*(3), 241–256.

Doppelt, B. (2003). *Leading change toward sustainability: A change-management guide of business, government and civil society.* Sheffield, UK: Greenleaf.

Elkington, J. (1998). *Cannibals with forks: The triple bottom line of 21st century business.* Gabriola Island, British Columbia, Canada: New Society.

Frederick, W. C. (1998). Creatures, corporations, communities, chaos, complexity. *Business & Society, 37*(4), 358–390.

Hart, S. (2005). *Capitalism at the crossroads: The unlimited business opportunities in solving the world's most difficult problems.* Upper Saddle River, NJ: Wharton School Press.

Hawkins, P., Lovins, A., & Lovins, L. H. (1999). *Natural capitalism: Creating the next Industrial Revolution.* New York: Little, Brown.

Simon, J. (1996). *The ultimate resource 2.* Princeton, NJ: Princeton University Press.

CORPORATE ACCOUNTABILITY

Corporate accountability is a foundation of corporate social responsibility. Corporate social responsibilities, at the most general level, include economic duties, legal and regulatory compliance, responsiveness to ethical norms, and discretionary social welfare contributions. In addition, one of the most basic of all corporate social responsibilities is corporate accountability. It is defined as the continuous, systematic, and public communication of information and reasons designed to justify an organization's decisions, actions, and outputs to various stakeholders. According to this definition, corporate accountability is primarily a form of ethical communication directed toward those parties who are affected by corporate activities and effects.

Corporate accountability represents a corporation's social responsibility to explain its actions (past, present, and future) in an accessible, reasonable, and meaningful way to the society in which it operates. In a democratic society dependent on informed political discourse and deliberations, corporate accountability is a necessary foundation for the system of free enterprise. The appropriate level of corporate accountability underpins the legitimacy of corporate autonomy and decision making in a system of democratic capitalism. In such a system, business enterprises enjoy a high degree of economic freedom of choice and are expected to engage in activities that promote the interests of the business. This economic freedom, however, is contingent on the existence of strong accountability mechanisms.

There are various traditional institutional mechanisms, both external and internal to the corporation, designed to enhance and strengthen accountability to stakeholders. These well-known mechanisms include the annual report to shareholders, corporate governance, government regulations, corporate codes and credos, and various forms of corporate communications.

THE ANNUAL REPORT TO SHAREHOLDERS

The single most important component of corporate accountability is the annual report to shareholders. It includes three important financial statements: the balance sheet, the income statement, and the statement of cash flows.

The balance sheet provides a detailed list of corporate resources (assets) and claims to those resources (liabilities and equity). It can be compared with a photograph that summarizes the financial condition of a business entity at a *fixed point in time.* The income statement provides detailed information about revenues, expenses, gains, and losses. It is like a movie in that it explains what happened *over a period of time.* The statement of cash flows provides information about the sources and uses of cash. It consists of three categories: operating, investing, and financing. The financial statements gain credibility because they are audited by certified public accountants. According to the Financial Accounting Standards Board, the three main objectives of financial accounting are to provide information that is useful to those making investment and credit decisions; helpful to present and potential investors and creditors in assessing the amounts, timing, and uncertainty of future cash flows; and about economic resources, the claims to those resources, and the changes in them.

CORPORATE GOVERNANCE

Corporate governance is essential to corporate accountability and without which no corporation can exist. State laws demand that corporations are to be managed and directed by a board of directors. This board acts as a surrogate for the shareholders of the corporation and its primary role is to oversee management's performance in terms of increasing profits and meeting social responsibilities. As such, corporate governance is a fundamental component to corporate accountability as defined above because it provides a strong institutional forum for communication between managers and shareholders' representatives.

CORPORATE REGULATIONS

In 2002, the U.S. Congress overwhelmingly passed one of the most significant pieces of securities legislation in U.S. history, the Sarbanes-Oxley Act. One of the main purposes of passing the Sarbanes-Oxley legislation was to reestablish the credibility of the financial markets by strengthening corporate accountability. This purpose is in line with the goals of previous federal and state legislation in the United States and across the world.

Sarbanes-Oxley contains several important features relevant to corporate accountability. It established the Public Company Accounting Oversight

Board to oversee the accounting profession, thus radically limiting the profession's traditional autonomy. It requires chief executive officers and chief financial officers to certify all financial statements and assigns criminal responsibility to those executives who knowingly make a false certification while demanding enhanced corporate disclosures concerning off-balance-sheet financing. Sarbanes-Oxley contains several provisions to enhance auditor independence. It also requires corporate boards to establish independent audit boards.

CORPORATE CREDOS AND CODES OF CONDUCT

Credos and codes can potentially serve an important role in strengthening corporate accountability. By carefully defining its own ethical aspirations, a corporation can helpfully communicate the criteria by which it wants to be held and judged. While critics are quick to note the self-serving nature of many corporate credos and ethical codes, these kinds of documents often provide both outsiders and insiders specific and clear statements to use in evaluating the credibility of corporate management. Johnson & Johnson's corporate credo, for example, establishes customers as the primary stakeholder of the corporation. This credo is often cited as an exemplar.

INCREASING DEMAND FOR CORPORATE ACCOUNTABILITY

In recent years, the demand for corporate accountability has increased dramatically. This demand has been spurred by the sheer growth of corporate power and by corporate environmental disasters such as the *Exxon Valdez* oil spill of 1989 and the Union Carbide and the Bhopal, India, tragedy. Corporate ethics and audit failures such as those at Enron, WorldCom, and many other U.S. and global corporations have also contributed to the increased demand for more and better accountability. Globalization, the Internet, the greenhouse effect, the increased interconnection of the world economy, and the rising power of institutional investors have also contributed to this change. Finally, changes in ethical values, especially an expanded conception of corporate social responsibility, have altered expectations surrounding the need for a broadened conception of corporate accountability.

LIMITATIONS OF THE FINANCIAL STATEMENTS
AS AN ACCOUNTABILITY MECHANISM

At the same time that the demand for accountability has increased, the usefulness of traditional financial statements is being questioned. While financial statements remain as an important source of reliable and relevant information about corporate activities, they have come under intense scrutiny in recent years. There are several limitations associated with the traditional financial statements.

First, many items are omitted from the balance sheet. These include intangible assets, the value of human resources, and many liabilities such as pension and health care obligations. Second, investors and other interested parties question the use of historical cost as the predominant method of valuing assets. Third, there is a lack of forward-looking information in the annual report such as management's forecast of earnings per share. Fourth, the traditional annual report focuses exclusively on the financial performance of corporations and excludes information about environmental and social performance. Finally, annual reports, especially income statements, are subject to questionable accounting manipulations such as earnings management, a process whereby managers alter the timing of revenues and expenses to change investors' perceptions.

There is now convincing statistical evidence that earnings management is a frequent management technique used to make a company look better than it otherwise would have. These manipulations occur despite the requirement that all financial statements are audited by certified public accountants. Each of these limitations diminishes the usefulness of the financial statements as an accountability mechanism.

Corporate governance has also come under intense scrutiny in recent years. This criticism of corporate governance reached a climax in the wake of ethics failures, including earnings management, at Enron and Andersen.

THE BROADENING SCOPE OF CORPORATE ACCOUNTABILITY

In response to the increasing demand for corporate accountability and the limited ability of traditional solutions to the meet this need, the scope of corporate accountability has broadened considerably in at least four distinct ways.

Backward-Looking Information Versus
Forward-Looking Information

At the heart of the traditional accounting model was the historical cost principle, which states that the original cost of an asset is the most reliable valuation basis. It has long been argued that the best way to measure assets, liabilities, equities, revenues, and expenses is through the use of historical cost. The primary justification for this has been reliability. Simply put, historical cost can be documented and verified by auditors with a high degree of confidence and certainty.

Although historical cost accounting scores high in terms of reliability, it scores much lower in terms of relevance. Investors and creditors trying to predict future performance are more interested in forward-looking information such as managers' forecast of future earnings per share than backward-looking information (such as last year's earning per share).

In the United States, the Securities and Exchange Commission has taken a major step forward in this area by requiring publicly traded companies to publish a management discussion and analysis section in their annual reports. These reports, as has been documented, contain valuable information not only about past decisions but also about future events and trends. In short, corporations are being asked by regulators and other stakeholders not only to reasonably justify *past* actions, but they must now also disclose and explain anticipated *future* actions.

Hard Versus Soft Data

The second change in broadening the scope of corporate accountability is related to the first. There is an ever-increasing flow of financial data carefully audited by outside accountants. This is the hard data. But, at the same time, there is an increasing demand for soft data; that is, information that cannot necessarily be quantified in a precise and exact way but nonetheless is important for decision making. Soft data include descriptions of new products, emerging markets, anticipated layoffs, planned capital expenditures, joint ventures, research and development projects, advertising campaigns, and many other items.

Consider the recent controversy over the disclosure of stock options as just one important example. Many companies argued with some justification that there is simply no known and noncontroversial way to value these options in a reasonable manner. These companies argued that assigning a dollar value to stock options would provide misleading and unreliable information to shareholders and creditors. Despite these arguments, however, the demand for additional disclosure concerning stock options is unabated.

Although at one time it was possible for companies to legitimately meet the obligation of corporate accountability by publishing a set of numbers with almost no description accompanying the financial statements, today this is no longer the case. Justification now requires accurate verbal disclosures and descriptions as well.

The Bottom Line Versus Multiple Bottom Lines

Third, can corporate performance be measured with a single number? Is it conceivable that all of a corporation's thousands of decisions, actions, and outcomes can be summarized and evaluated through net income? Although some companies and many short-term investors continue to act as if the answer to both these questions is yes, other companies have now learned through experience that even if it was once true, it is certainly no longer the case.

Perhaps the most important of the changes that we have documented so far is the increasing recognition that corporate accountability now requires managers to justify not only purely financial outcomes but also environmental and social outcomes. Connected to this change, the list of legitimate stakeholders has also expanded to include employees, customers, local and global communities, and others. This means there is no longer such a thing as the bottom line. Today, there are multiple bottom lines. In a sense, there are as many bottom lines as there are stakeholders.

While just a few years ago the phrase multiple bottom line was more metaphor than reality, today it is more reality than metaphor. The Global Reporting Initiative (GRI) was established in 1997 as a joint venture between the Coalition for Environmentally Responsible Economies and the United Nations Environment Program. In June 2000, GRI published a set of guidelines to help companies improve on their environmental and social reporting. These guidelines were revised in 2002. One thousand global companies now use some form of triple-bottom-line accounting in line with GRI guidelines—reporting on economic, environmental, and social behaviors and outcomes. Among these companies are 3M, AT&T, General Motors, Ford, Shell, McDonald's, Dupont, Dow Chemical, Nike, Canon, Electrolux, Ericsson, France Telecom, and some other smaller companies as well.

Monologue Versus Dialogue

Finally, careful examination of a set of recently issued sustainability reports demonstrates the most radical change of all. To legitimately justify an organization's decisions and actions, corporate accountability is now viewed and described by many as a dialogue between the corporation and its stakeholders and not as a monologue on the part of management. For example, see especially AccountAbility 1000's AA1000—Principles and Measurement Standards and a U.K. company law reform proposal that would require the dialogue between corporations and their shareholders to be published online. This means that corporate accountability requires listening to a company's diverse stakeholders as well as responding to them. It also means that many companies now openly recognize that corporate accountability is an evolving and contested concept.

There is a growing awareness of dialogue as a formal component of corporate accountability. Dialogue is emerging as one of its central and most innovative aspects. Dialogue does not imply that organizations are abdicating their responsibility for decision making. But it does imply a recognition that organizations are embedded in society and rely on it for legitimacy.

CONCLUSION

Those managers committed to the capitalistic system realize that it is in their own self-interest to enhance corporate accountability. In a world of instant communication, those corporations that can justify their actions in a clear and sensible way may possess a strong competitive advantage over rivals who maintain a policy of secrecy. It makes good business sense to enhance corporate transparency.

Corporate accountability, however, should not be conceived of as a kind of game. Rather, it is a form of ethical communication among human beings on which the future growth and legitimacy of business depends. As globalization spreads, corporate accountability is becoming the linchpin of the worldwide economic system. As the notion of corporate social responsibility gains credence across the globe, corporate accountability is increasingly viewed as a crucial task for boards of directors, corporate management, business consultants, and accountants. Corporate accountability has always played an important role in the financial markets, but as the concept of corporate accountability broadens, its role in society will gain in importance.

—Moses L. Pava

Further Readings

Bradley, M., & Wallenstein, S. M. (2006). The history of corporate governance in the United States. In M. J. Epstein & K. O. Hanson (Eds.), *The accountable corporation* (pp. 45–72). Westport, CT: Praeger Perspectives.

Carroll, A. B. (1979). A three-dimensional model of corporate performance. *Academy of Management Review, 4*(4), 497–505.

Financial Accounting Standard Board (FASB). (1978). *Statement of financial accounting concepts no. 1: Objectives of financial reporting by business enterprises.* Norwalk, CT: Author.

Healy, P. M., & Whalen, J. M. (1999). A review of the earnings management literature and its implications for standard setting. *Accounting Horizons, 14*(4), 365–384.

KPMG International Survey of Corporate Sustainability Reporting 2000.

Millstein, I. (2006). A perspective on corporate governance: Rules, principles, or both. In M. J. Epstein & K. O. Hanson (Eds.), *The accountable corporation* (pp. 3–14). Westport, CT: Praeger Perspectives.

Pava, M. L., & Epstein, M. (1993). How good is MD&A as an investment tool? *Journal of Accountancy, 175,* 51–53.

Pava, M. L., & Krausz, J. (2006). The broadening scope of corporate accountability. In P. Allouche (Ed.), *Corporate social responsibility.* New York: Palgrave.

Waddock, S. (2004). Creating corporate accountability: Foundational principles to make corporate citizenship real. *Journal of Business Ethics, 50,* 313–327.

CORPORATE MORAL AGENCY

Insofar as they are capable of exhibiting intentional action, corporations may be regarded as moral agents. Agents reflectively endorse specific ends and shape the world by imposing those ends on the world. Because agents have this sort of intentional capacity, they are properly characterized as responsible for the actions they impose on the world. Persons are prototypical examples of agents and the class of persons is properly understood as subset of the class of moral agents. In U.S. law, the class "persons" includes entities other than human beings such as corporations. The courts attribute personhood to corporations on pragmatic grounds, finding this a useful convention for the purposes of corporate law. The question of whether or not there are grounds for thinking that, from a metaphysical standpoint, corporations are properly understood as moral agents is a separate matter.

FRENCH'S VIEW

A quarter-century ago, Peter French published an influential essay on the metaphysical status of the corporation. He has subsequently defended the core of that view in a series of books and essays. Despite its many critics, French's theory of corporate personhood remains the single most influential account of the metaphysical status of corporations. Corporations, as French noted, are of particular interest in comparison to other sorts of collectives or organizations because of their distinct rules of governance and hierarchical structure. In his early work on the metaphysical status of corporations, French reached three main conclusions. First, corporations exhibit intentionality. Second, corporations are capable of exhibiting rationality regarding their intentions. Third, corporations are capable of altering their intentions and patterns of behavior. As a result, he concluded that corporations are full-fledged moral persons and have the privileges, rights, and duties that are, in the normal course of affairs, accorded to moral persons. This claim received sustained criticism over the years. In particular, critics have argued that French's position is illegitimately anthropomorphic. For example, Richard De George has argued that, unlike human beings, corporations are not ends in themselves. Other critics have argued that it is absurd to suggest that corporate persons have the same emotional status as human persons. Still others have argued that corporations cannot be persons, since all persons have a soul and no corporation has a soul.

INTENTIONALITY

In his early defense of corporate personhood, French grounded his arguments in the belief-desire theory of intentionality. He argued that when the corporate act is consistent with an instantiation of established corporate policy, then it is proper to describe it as having been done by a corporate desire coupled with a corporate belief and so as a corporate intention. Critics seized on French's use of the belief-desire theory, arguing that, since he wrongly attributed distinctly human intentionality to corporations, his defense or corporate intentionality failed. For example, Manuel Velasquez argues that all attributions of intentions to corporations must be understood as metaphorical since they are not literal mental states. He denies the possibility of such an argument because he stipulates that intentions must be understood as mental states identical to those present in individual human minds. However, this is not the only way of understanding intentionality. One alternative way of understanding intentions is as commitments to future action. Such a characterization of intentions leaves open the possibility that entities other than conscious biological beings may be properly understood as intentional.

Central to the claim that corporations are moral agents is the claim that corporations have intentions. Prosecutors and judges routinely attribute intentionality to corporations. Nonetheless, the attribution of intentions to corporations has been rejected by many theorists as an untenable hypothesis. Partly in response to such criticism, French has modified his view of the metaphysical status of the corporation in two significant ways. First, French has abandoned the idea of corporate "persons" in favor of a defense of corporate "actors" or agents. This move allows French to avoid the criticism that his view is illegitimately anthropomorphic. Second, French now rejects the belief-desire theory of intentionality that he had previously embraced in favor of Michael Bratman's planning theory of intentionality. This allows him to avoid criticisms associated with the belief-desire theory of intentions.

CORPORATE INTENTIONS

Bratman's account of intentions emphasizes their future-directed nature. On his account, intentions are typically elements of plans. Bratman argues that as rational agents with complex goals most of our intentional actions will stem from deliberation and reflection prior to the time of action, that is, from planning. The plans characteristic of human agents have two essential features. First, plans are typically partial or incomplete. They need to be filled in over time. Second, plans typically have a hierarchical structure. Bratman has extended his analysis of the intentions of individuals to shared intentions of a certain type—namely, the intentions shared by two individuals who plan to engage in a joint activity. Consider two individuals who plan to take a trip together. What roles do their shared intention to take a trip together play? First, their shared intention allows for the coordination of planning. Second, their shared intentions structure relevant bargaining. Third, their shared intentions allow for the coordination of activities. On this account, shared intention is a state of affairs that consists of a web of attitudes of the individual participants. Shared intentions are not, then, mere mental states.

French has suggested that Bratman's account of intentionality will provide an adequate basis for a theory of corporate intentionality, yet French has not developed a sustained argument for that conclusion. However, Bratman's analysis of shared intentions has recently been extended to corporations by Denis Arnold. He argues that the state of affairs characteristic of shared intentions is also characteristic of corporations. Typically, corporate decisions are made in accordance with the structure previously characterized by French as a corporate internal decision (CID) structure. This well-known and essential feature of French's account of corporate moral agency includes hierarchical lines of organizational responsibility, rules of procedure, and corporate policies. A CID structure performs a normative function, that is, it tells members of the corporation how they ought to behave. When employees act in a manner consistent with the CID structure they instantiate corporate intentions. Corporate intentions are states of affairs consisting of both the intersecting attitudes of the class of agents comprising the corporation and the internal decision structure of the organization. The CID structure serves as the frame on which the attitudes of board members, executives, managers, and employees are interwoven to form corporate intentions.

Praiseworthy corporate intentions include value creation, the development of innovative technology, and respectful regard for stakeholders.

Blameworthy corporate intentions include deceptive marketing, systematic dumping of toxic chemicals into pristine natural environments, and theft from shareholders.

Arnold argues that since corporations are properly understood to have intentions, there is a basis for thinking that corporations are properly understood as agents. However, he points out that for corporations to be properly regarded as moral agents, a further condition must also be satisfied. Corporations must be capable of reflectively endorsing corporate intentions. Corporations that are capable of evaluating past decisions and existing plans, of determining whether those intentions ought to remain in place, or whether they should be modified or eliminated in favor of alternative intentions are capable of the requisite reflective endorsement and are properly understood as moral agents.

CONCLUSION

The idea that corporations are properly understood as moral agents remains unpersuasive to many theorists. First, some critics maintain that all agents must be understood as having souls. Since it is implausible to attribute a soul to a corporation, some theorists conclude that corporations cannot be understood as agents. Second, the idea that corporations are capable of reflectively endorsing intentions strikes some theorists as implausible. They argue that reflective endorsement is a quality of human persons and one that cannot reasonably be attributed to organizations.

Defenders of the view that corporations are properly understood as moral agents point out that this view has important implications regarding moral responsibility. For example, if a corporation is properly understood as a moral agent, then it is possible to praise or blame corporations and not just the directors, executives, managers, and workers of a corporation at a particular time. Punishment of the corporation, and not just corporate personnel, is thereby justified when corporate intentions are morally objectionable. In cases where corporation actions are especially pernicious as a result of corporate intentions, corporate capital punishment in the form of the dissolution of the corporation may be justified. So too, corporations that exhibit consistently praiseworthy behavior as a result of corporate intentions are justifiably rewarded independently of corporate personnel.

—Denis G. Arnold

Further Readings

Arnold, D. G. (2006). Corporate moral agency. *Midwest Studies in Philosophy, XXX,* 279–291.

Bratman, M. (1987). *Intention, plans, and practical reason.* Cambridge, MA: Harvard University Press.

Bratman, M. (1999). *Faces of intention: Selected essays on intention and agency.* Cambridge, UK: Cambridge University Press.

De George, R. (1986). Corporations and morality. In H. Curtler (Ed.), *Shame, responsibility and the corporation* (pp. 57–75). New York: Haven.

Donaldson, T. (1986). Personalizing corporate ontology: The French way. In H. Curtler (Ed.), *Shame, responsibility and the corporation* (pp. 99–112). New York: Haven.

French, P. T. (1979). The corporation as a moral person. *American Philosophical Quarterly, 16,* 207–215.

French, P. T. (1984). *Collective and corporate responsibility.* New York: Columbia University Press.

French, P. T. (1992). *Responsibility matters.* Lawrence: University Press of Kansas.

French, P. T. (1995). *Corporate ethics.* New York: Harcourt Brace.

French, P. T. (1996). Integrity, intentions, and corporations. *American Business Law Journal, 34,* 141–155.

May, L. (1987). *The morality of groups: Collective responsibility, group-based harm, and corporate rights.* South Bend, IN: University of Notre Dame Press.

Velasquez, M. G. (2003). Debunking corporate responsibility. *Business Ethics Quarterly, 13*(4), 531–562.

SOCIAL ENTREPRENEURSHIP

S ocial entrepreneurs create social value through the use of the entrepreneurship model. Social entrepreneurship relates to many business forms but fundamentally exists as a model that organizations are able to use in pursuit of goals directed toward building value for the society within which they are embedded. Organizations built on this model follow closely with the traditional path of entrepreneurship, pursuing perceived opportunities to achieve their goals. The key to understanding social entrepreneurship lies in acknowledging that it transcends traditional business model boundaries and can occur in any sector of business, such as in the private for-profit or not-for-profit sector or in the public sector.

To engage in social entrepreneurship, the organization is typically driven by a social entrepreneur. The social entrepreneur shares many similar skills with the traditional entrepreneur. These shared skills are identified as designing a mission with the core purpose to create and sustain value; pursuing new opportunities to serve the mission; engaging in continuous innovation, adaptation, and learning; acting boldly without being limited by the resources currently available; and exhibiting a level of heightened accountability to the stakeholders affected and for the outcomes as a result of the mission. The distinguishing factor for social entrepreneurs is that they create *social* value through the use of this model to create economic value.

While the entrepreneurial skill set is very similar between the traditional entrepreneur and the social entrepreneur, there is a large difference regarding their individual value orientation. Social entrepreneurs are more likely to have experienced some sort of transformative experience during their life, which pushes social improvement to the front of their core values. Most social entrepreneurs are also very active in the social sector throughout their lives, beginning at an early age. This social activism is then combined with their entrepreneurial skill set to enable them to pursue their social missions through social entrepreneurship.

Social entrepreneurship can often be confused with other business models or practices that are designed to create accountability to society within the business sector. Two other terms that are sometimes misused are *social ventures* and *social enterprises*. Both social ventures and social enterprises are the legal entities that are created as an end result of social entrepreneurship.

It is also useful to distinguish between a social venture and a social enterprise. Most frequently, the term *venture* is used to describe organizations that are the result of a venture capital investment, but with social ventures this is the result of social venture capital. The term *enterprise,* on the other hand, is typically associated not with an organization built on venture capital but with one that secured its financing through other means. Regardless of the methods of financing, both social ventures and social enterprises are two possible outcomes of social entrepreneurship. Social entrepreneurship must also be differentiated from terms such as *sustainable enterprises, corporate social responsibility,* and *business ethics.* While it is possible for a social venture, or a social enterprise, to practice social responsibility or sustainability, they are different concepts within the same theoretical sphere of social awareness.

A BRIEF HISTORY

Although social entrepreneurship has only recently received significant academic and professional attention, the fundamental concept has been in practice by individuals throughout the history of business enterprises. Some examples from the past include David Brower (the United States), Vinoba Bhave (India), Florence Nightingale (the United Kingdom), and Jean Monnet (France). David Brower was the Sierra Club's first executive director and built it into a global network designed to serve environmental issues. Vinoba Bhave founded the Land Gift movement in India, allowing the redistribution of more than 7,000,000 acres of land to the landless untouchables, individuals who were low-caste Hindus and viewed as "polluted" and separated from the rest of society. Florence Nightingale revolutionized health care through the foundation of the first school for nurses. Jean Monnet led the reconstruction of France after World War II and established methods to integrate Europe economically.

These individuals pursued their missions and extensively influenced the societies around them through creativity, leadership, and a vision of social improvement. These acts are distinguished from those of other socially conscious individuals by the entrepreneurial methods used to pursue their social goals. These social entrepreneurs paved new paths to pursue these ideas. Individuals such as these, along with countless social advocacy groups and community initiatives, have all set the foundation from which the current identity of social entrepreneurship has been derived.

Social entrepreneurship began to gain visibility and definition through the work of Bill Drayton and his founding of Ashoka in 1980. Ashoka became the first to pioneer into the concept of "social venture capital," providing funding for entrepreneurial individuals in pursuit of social change through innovation. The founding of Ashoka marked the beginning of social entrepreneurship as a functional and practical business theory. As social entrepreneurship continues to gain prominence and validity, it is becoming an increasing popular topic of academic discussion.

With the increase in practical applications of social entrepreneurship, it has become clear that it is a viable model within any of the business sectors. Social entrepreneurship is often categorized as a cross-sector model, in which the organizations applying the model often lie somewhere in the middle of the continuum that runs between the private for-profit and not-for-profit sector and the public business sector, blurring the boundaries of these traditional business sectors. However, as blurred as these boundaries may become, the legal distinctions between organizations in each of these sectors still exists, making it useful to examine the distinctions between each.

THE FOR-PROFIT SECTOR

Social entrepreneurship within the for-profit sector references organizations that are legally defined as existing to generate profit, while the organization defines its primary mission as one grounded in social improvement or development. When considering these for-profit organizations, it is important not to confuse the act of social entrepreneurship with the act of stewardship. The stewardship model describes organizations that acknowledge their responsibility to society and act on those responsibilities but still identify their primary objective as that of generating profit. For the for-profit social entrepreneur, the ultimate objective is to design a process that allows the organization to generate profit as a by-product of its improvements to society, as opposed to generating social value as a by-product of profit.

By maintaining the for-profit business model, it is easier for these organizations to achieve long-term financial sustainability. This occurs because the organization is often more successful at obtaining sustainable revenue streams. These revenue streams are more stable because the organization understands that its products must not only be socially beneficial but also just as attractive as a competitor's product, even if the competitor isn't driven by the same social standards. This is the result of consumers who may not know, or care, about the social mission behind the company.

Another variation of social entrepreneurship also occurs frequently within the for-profit sector—social intrapreneurship. Similar to social entrepreneurship, social intrapreneurship has become increasingly popular over the last decade. The distinguishing characteristic of entrepreneurship and intrapreneurship is that intrapreneurship occurs within preexisting organizations, often creating extensions of the same business or expanding into new businesses. One of the attractive features of intrapreneurship is the ability to fund these efforts through the preexisting organization. Thus, often the efforts of intrapreneurship are more successful because the risk of financial failure is smaller when the organization is backed by a secure revenue stream.

Excellent examples of for-profit social entrepreneurship can be found in organizations such as Newman's Own or Ben & Jerry's. Founded in 1978 by Ben Cohen and Jerry Greenfield, Ben & Jerry's began with a single ice cream shop. Explosive growth netted Ben & Jerry's sales of more than $155 million by the year 2000, amid rumors of Ben & Jerry's becoming the target of takeover interest. The rumors were confirmed as Ben & Jerry's was acquired by Unilever, an Anglo-Dutch corporation, in early 2000.

Nothing in the foregoing overview captures the spirit of social entrepreneurship undergirding Ben & Jerry's. In 1985, company founders Ben and Jerry institutionalized their long-standing commitment to social and environmental issues by establishing the Ben & Jerry's Foundation, funded through donation of 7.5% of the company's annual pretax profits. The company has not relegated its social and environmental action to its funding of the Foundation. At every decision point, the leadership of Ben & Jerry's has sought to provide social benefits from the ongoing operation of their primary business. Among many other initiatives, in a successful effort to divert its ice-cream waste from the local wastewater treatment facility, Ben & Jerry's began feeding a pig farm with its ice-cream waste; the company helped establish a nonprofit initiative known as "1% for Peace"; they came out against bovine growth hormone, based on concern about its adverse economic impact on family farming; introduced Rainforest Crunch ice cream through its scoop shops, with sales of the ice cream indirectly benefiting rainforest preservation efforts; and to help combat Vermont dairy farmers' losses during a period of volatile prices in the dairy industry, Ben & Jerry's paid a dairy premium totaling half a million dollars to the family farmers who supply the milk for Ben & Jerry's ice cream.

THE NOT-FOR-PROFIT SECTOR

Not-for-profit social entrepreneurship is represented by organizations that have legally defined themselves as existing for some other purpose than to generate profit, a direct inverse to for-profit organizations. However, within this model, many of these organizations are engaging in what would typically be classified as for-profit business practices to attain sustainability within their business model.

Within the not-for-profit sector, three primary types of organizations exist—public benefit, mutual benefit, and religious. The most common use of social entrepreneurship within this sector is within those designated for public benefit. This is because of the nature of the models; a public benefit not-for-profit exists to benefit the public. Both mutual benefit and religious not-for-profits are less focused on widespread social improvement and are more focused on providing services for a very specific audience. However, it is still possible for social entrepreneurship to exist in each of these types.

The social entrepreneurship model is often mistakenly associated with social activism within the not- for-profit sector; however, the two concepts are fundamentally different. Social activists pursue a social goal as their main mission but are distinguished from social entrepreneurs because they pursue these changes external to the business environment. The distinguishing factor in social entrepreneurship is that these organizations pursue their social goals while simultaneously engaging in market-driven activities. Organizations acting in this sector are typically less financially independent than those in the for-profit sector. With not-for-profit organizations, the fiscal gains through entrepreneurship act less as a method of profit generation and sustainability and more as a method of offsetting their costs or expanding their programs. While they are not as financially independent as their for-profit counterparts, the offset expenses do allow these organizations to engage in more creative opportunities that may not be possible through grants and donations alone.

However, with the expansion of revenue streams for these organizations, an issue arises with the allocation of these subsidizing revenues. Within the United States, any income a not-for-profit generates that is not substantially related to the social purpose of the organization becomes taxable. This is the result of the competition for the consumer's purchasing power. Many for-profit organizations feel that without the tax an arena is created for unfair competition. For many not-for-profit organizations, this means that becoming entrepreneurial and seeking new revenue streams may not be as effective as hoped.

Ben & Jerry's is again instructive on this point. Perhaps the company's most notable foray into social entrepreneurship has been the establishment of the PartnerShop program, a series of scoop shops that are independently owned and operated by community-based nonprofit organizations. Ben & Jerry's waives the standard franchise fees and provides additional support to help nonprofits operate strong businesses among youth and low-income folks by providing economic development and employment opportunities. It should be noted that social entrepreneurship has been around for centuries in the form of enterprises such as gift shops and thrift shops associated with churches and museums.

THE PUBLIC SECTOR

Outside of entrepreneurship in the private sector, it becomes more difficult to engage in social entrepreneurship, often because of inherent political and administrative constraints. Whereas the not-for-profit organization can be burdened with donors and grants who have predefined goals for the organization, the public organization is also held to often more stringent preestablished rules, regulations, and legislation. However, where the public sector has succeeded in engaging in social entrepreneurship, such efforts have enabled the institutions to expand beyond their previous constraints, thereby increasing the effect and reach of their mission. The driving force for entrepreneurship in the public sector has been a combination of a need for increased resources to fund specific programs and for a way to counteract the perceived inefficiencies of government programs.

Given that entrepreneurial activities such as risk taking are often looked down on by the public and government officials, social entrepreneurship often occurs much more frequently than intrapreneurship. Typically, entrepreneurship occurs when tasks are outsourced from local governments to organizations created specifically to coordinate specific tasks for the government outside of the public sector where it is able to function beyond the typical regulatory constraints. These organizations are then able to not only support the programs or entities they were designed to support through their services or products but are also able to generate extra revenue by expanding their programs to other organizations that can derive benefit from them.

There exist numerous examples of social entrepreneurship within the public sector. Following years of developing customized information technology applications for in-house use, the City of San Diego outsourced its information technology function to a stand-alone not-for-profit entity, the San Diego Data Processing Corporation. One principal goal of this initiative has been to successfully market government-specific technology applications to other California municipalities, all the while continuing to meet the technology needs of the elected officials and staff of San Diego. Product endorsements and "city stores," which sell items such as customized street signs, are becoming increasingly common; at the state and national levels, adopt-a-highway programs represent efforts by governmental agencies to engage in social entrepreneurship that serves to offset the high cost of road maintenance through revenue-generating alliances with private business enterprises.

SECURING FUNDING FOR SOCIAL ENTREPRENEURS

Similar to profit-oriented entrepreneurship, social entrepreneurship is often a process undertaken by individuals who have a vision and are pursuing that vision. Funding for these ventures can come from grants, donations, or what has been called social venture capital. Social venture capital, first defined by Ashoka, is the process of securing funding to advance the interests of the organization through investors who wish to have a stake in the organization. As such, social venture capital is often focused within the for-profit sector of social venturing; however, it is possible for social venture capital to be invested in not-for-profit sector ventures as well.

An important issue in building social venture capital has been designing a way for investors to receive feedback from the organizations they have invested in to know whether their investment has been successful or if the organization is not doing as well as it should be. In the typical venture, this can be done through simple financial analysis and benchmarking as the organization develops and evolves. With a social venture investment, this is much more difficult because of the difficulty of measuring social impact. The success with developing these social feedback tools is evident through the rising number of organizations that have been created to provide social venture capital such as Ashoka, Social Venture Partners, the Social Venture Capital Foundation, the Schwab Foundation, and others.

MEASUREMENT TOOLS FOR SOCIAL ENTREPRENEURSHIP

Regardless of the sector social entrepreneurship occurs in, it has become increasingly important to design methods to measure the impact social entrepreneurship has on its stakeholders. Much of the measurement throughout its history has relied on qualitative, case-based research. While this type of research has been able to define the areas that social entrepreneurship affects, it is less effective at measuring the actual level of impact that it has on society. The need for measurement has led to the development of tools that allow organizations to measure both financial and social impact. This is frequently called double-bottom-line (DBL) or triple-bottom-line (TBL) analysis. TBL divides the goals of an organization into three sectors—social, environmental, and financial. DBL divides the goals into two sectors—social and financial. DBL is the more often cited tool within social entrepreneurship, but both attempt to achieve the same goal of dividing the organization's impact into defined areas and measuring the effectiveness of that impact in each area.

To measure the goals of an organization using DBL, they are often redesigned in a way that allows the impact on society to be quantitatively measured. This enables the organization to track the success or failure of its social initiatives similarly to that of a financial initiative. Columbia University's Research Initiative for Social Enterprise (RISE) is one group that has contributed to this research. They have identified and analyzed several methods for identifying and measuring social impact. Their efforts have identified social impact measurement in three key areas of analysis—processes, impact, and monetization. Process analysis allows organizations to measure the correlation of their outputs with their social goals. Impact analysis allows organizations to analyze the effect these outputs have on society and compare them with the next best alternative for their resources, a method that is equivalent to measuring the opportunity costs of the organizations' operational processes. Monetization analysis allows the firm to place dollar values to its social impact and is the most effective in demonstrating a direct correlation between money invested and the social return.

One example of monetization analysis is social return on investment. This method, designed by REDF (formerly the Roberts Enterprise Development Fund), is used to develop a cost-benefit analysis of a social project. Rubicon Landscape Services used this method to analyze the impact their organization made by employing people with disabilities and economically challenged individuals. By calculating the amount of money they were saving the government in social service costs and the amount of additional tax revenue generated through their employment, they were able to measure the impact this program had on society with a precise dollar amount.

All three measurement methods enable the social entrepreneur to gauge his or her success at using the organization's resources in the most effective manner to support the social mission. In addition to the RISE project, many other organizations have also begun developing their own private and publicly available measurement tools, which provide a way for social venture capitalists to measure the impact of their investment, as well as a way for organizations to gauge their own success and make adjustments as they grow.

CRITICISM OF SOCIAL ENTREPRENEURSHIP

Critics of social entrepreneurship, and corporate social responsibility, believe the purpose of business activity is to serve the interests of stockholders, leaving social action to entities existing beyond the private for-profit sector. These critics argue that business leaders are ill equipped to make informed social decisions and that business leaders are solely responsible for acting in a manner that benefits the individuals who have employed them. This stance is grounded in the theory that economic returns and social returns are inherently at odds with one another, causing the pursuit of one return to reduce or eliminate the other.

Social entrepreneurs have found that this stance is inadequate for serving the needs of the community. Entities beyond the private for-profit sector have been unable to provide for many of the needs of the community. Social entrepreneurs have identified this gap in service as a viable business opportunity. The businesses built on these opportunities have a positive link between economic returns and social returns, both within the organization, and in its influence on its stakeholders. Thus, although many critics believe that social responsibility is counter to economic responsibility, social entrepreneurs have found a method that allows the two to act in parallel.

EDUCATION

Along with the growing number of social investment and analysis organizations, social entrepreneurship has also become increasingly popular with universities and other educational institutions. Many business schools have not only introduced social entrepreneurship into their MBA curriculum but some have also begun to build centers focused specifically on social entrepreneurship. Examples include Duke University's Center for the Advancement of Social Entrepreneurship, Columbia University's Research Initiative for Social Enterprise, and Oxford University's Skoll Centre for Social Entrepreneurship. In addition, competitions have come up to promote social entrepreneurship within these universities, such as the Global Social Venture Competition held at the University of California, Berkeley. Universities have also begun to reward competitors within traditional business plan competitions for being socially cognizant of their impact on society.

CONCLUSION

Social entrepreneurship has become an increasingly influential business model. It allows for organizations in all sectors of business to ground themselves on socially conscious missions and goals while still retaining the beneficial traits that have been previously available only to the for-profit sector. Social entrepreneurs are able to do this through recognizing and pursuing feasible business models that provide innovative products and services, allowing it to generate revenue while still serving its primary social goal. Social entrepreneurship has been given the opportunity to grow in impact and popularity due to its increased presence in the business and academic realms and will continue to expand as a viable business model as the global society continues to call for more socially conscious and accountable organizations.

—Lance Schaeffer and Craig P. Dunn

Further Readings

Barendsen, L., & Gardner, M. (2004). Is the social entrepreneur a new type of leader? *Leader to Leader, 8,* 43–51.

Clark, C., Rosenzweig, W., Long, D., & Olsen, S. (2005, November). Double bottom line project report: Assessing social impact in double bottom line ventures. *Research Initiative on Social Entrepreneurship* [Electronic version]. Retrieved from www.riseproject.org/DBL_Methods_ Catalog.pdf

Dees, J. G. (2001, May). *The meaning of "social entrepreneurship."* Durham, NC: Center for the Advancement of Social Entrepreneurship. Retrieved from www .fuqua.duke.edu/centers/case/documents/dees_sedef.pdf

Friedman, M. (1970, September 13). The social responsibility of business to increase its profits. *New York Times Magazine,* p. 32.

Harding, R. (2004). Social enterprise: The new economic engine? *Business Strategy Review, 4,* 39–43.

Mort, G. S., Weerawardena, J., & Carnegie, K. (2002). Social entrepreneurship: Towards conceptualization. *International Journal of Nonprofit and Voluntary Sector Marketing, 13,* 76–88.

Naumes, M., Kammermeyer, J., & Naumes, W. (2005, November). Social entrepreneurship: A relevant concept for business schools? Hellenic Communication Serve, LLC. Retrieved from http://helleniccomserve.com/naumes1.html

Roper, J., & Cheney, G. (2005). Leadership, learning and human resource management: The meanings of social entrepreneurship today. *Corporate Governance, 10,* 95–104.

PART II

Corporate Social Responsibility on the Global Stage

Global Business Citizenship

Global Codes of Conduct

Multinational Corporations (MNCS)

GLOBAL BUSINESS CITIZENSHIP

Global business citizenship (GBC) is an emerging theoretical framework that extends the concept of corporate social responsibility into a globalized environment. It is an alternative to prevailing frameworks in finance and economics in that it accepts the validity of stakeholder claims on firms. The GBC framework offers a process that multinational managers can use to consistently implement social responsibility and ethics within and across nations and cultures.

CONCEPT HISTORY

The GBC framework was developed to address several problems with predecessor concepts and to offer an alternative to views of the firm as merely a nexus of contracts or a tool of capital owners' interests. GBC's principal conceptual ancestor is corporate social responsibility (CSR), the obligation of corporations to use their power wisely and to respond to societal needs. Developed in the United States from the 1960s onward, CSR was built on an assumed moral base that was never adequately articulated. The dimensions and processes of CSR were never well-defined, so businesses had little guidance in identifying or exercising social responsibilities. Furthermore, CSR was typically defined in terms of a business's responsiveness to social demands, or responsibility to particular societies, with little attention paid to a company's own core values or to real cultural differences in ethics.

GBC is also a conceptual replacement for corporate citizenship (CC). Although some scholars have attempted to define corporate citizenship as a broad-based enactment of a business organization's social and ethical obligations, the term is much more commonly used to narrowly indicate firms' voluntary participation in philanthropy and community affairs.

GBC does not view the firm as consisting solely of contracts or as a single-purpose tool for shareholder value. The GBC concept is counterposed to these perspectives in several ways: (1) GBC accepts the view from traditional organization theory that firms are entities, not fictions; (2) GBC recognizes a broad range of relationships, rights, and duties between a firm and its stakeholders; and (3) GBC requires an explicit, principled, comprehensive moral foundation for firm policies and practices.

BUSINESSES AS CITIZENS

Citizenship ordinarily defines the relationship of persons and political units. Citizenship typically involves certain protections based on rights guaranteed by the polity's legal infrastructure, often including rights to liberty and rights to protection and welfare. Citizens may also have duties; Aristotle's observation that citizens participate in taxation, governance, and defense is still largely true in modern democracies.

On three counts, nation-state citizenship for persons does not provide an adequate metaphor for companies: Can businesses be citizens in the same way that persons are? If so, what is the polity of which businesses are "global" citizens? Finally, what kinds of citizens can businesses be? GBC, thus, requires attention to and expansion of the citizenship metaphor.

First, there is considerable debate over the question of whether organizations can be citizens as humans are. The issues concern who should have what rights and duties, how organizations should participate in government, and whether businesses should be thought of as citizens in any manner, given the presumed special moral standing of human beings and the overwhelming power and influence of large organizations. The GBC framework does not assume that businesses are equal to humans in moral status or that businesses should be accorded equivalent rights. Instead, businesses are thought of as secondary citizens—a convenient status for accomplishing certain human goals.

Second, in the absence of world government, to what polity do firms owe allegiance as citizens? Globalization has made nation-states increasingly irrelevant to economic activity, so older notions of firm allegiance to the "home" country no longer offer a basis for a business citizenship metaphor. To answer the question, the GBC framework relies on the idea of universal citizenship, as in the works of Rousseau and other "natural law" thinkers. To be a "citizen of the world" means to hold allegiance to the human race rather than to any particular subgroup. "Global citizen" reflects a perspective, not a legal status.

With respect to the third question, political theory—a branch of philosophy that attempts in part to answer the question, "How can we live well together?"—can be used to categorize the ways in which businesses can be citizens.

Minimalist theories, such as libertarianism, public choice theory, and agency theory, view the firm as a nexus of contracts with no independent substance and no loyalties other than those specified in its contracts. In this view, the firm can be a citizen only in the minimal sense of being law-abiding; it has no justification for considering the common good or the interests of noncontract holders, and its executives are not likely to see it as a citizen. Minimalist firms may indeed behave ethically within and beyond the demands of law, but their guiding perspective does not require that they do so.

Communitarian theories, with a focus on boundary maintenance and group identity, view the firm as an important player in the local environment, and so the firm can be a "corporate citizen" in the usual sense of a business that voluntarily "gives back" to local communities. Communitarian firms are likely to abide by the ethical principles governing their communities of allegiance, and they may or may not apply those principles when dealing with "outsiders."

Universalist theories, whether deontological or teleological, emphasize the rational consideration of others' interests as well as the interests of the whole, in addition to self-interest. In these views, firms accept responsibilities to a broader range of stakeholders as well as a general responsibility to act in ways that are consistent with universal ethical principles and that advance, or at least do not harm, human well-being.

Only from the lens of universalist political theories can firms be viewed as global business citizens. This does not imply that other lenses produce unethical, irresponsible firms. A minimalist firm may be law-abiding and ethical, but its focus is on generating wealth for capital owners and it will not hold an image of itself as a citizen. A communitarian firm is likely to be law-abiding and ethical at home, but may not extend these behaviors elsewhere. A universalist firm will attempt to consistently and responsibly exercise its rights and implement its duties to individuals, stakeholders, and societies within and across national and cultural borders.

THE GLOBAL BUSINESS CITIZENSHIP FRAMEWORK

The GBC framework is developed by considering relationships between a company's choices of global *strategy* and the degree of *ethical certainty* with respect to particular issues and environments. The framework is shown in Table 1 and the explanation follows.

Table 1 The Process of Implementing Global Business Citizenship: Ethical Certainty and Strategic Approaches

Degree of Ethical Certainty	Multidomestic Strategy	Globally Integrated Strategy
High certainty: Principles—a limited number of basic, universal ethical rules	(Ethical relativism)	Step 1: Code of conduct
Moderate certainty: Consistent norms—variations in practice consistent with principles	Step 2: Local implementation	(Ethical imperialism)
Low certainty: Incompatible norms—variations in practice inconsistent or in conflict with principles	Step 3: Problem analysis and experimentation	Step 4: Organizational and systemic learning

Source: Adapted from Wood, D. J., Logsdon, J. M., Lewellyn, P. G., & Davenport, K. (2006). *Global business citizenship: A transformative framework for ethics and sustainable capitalism.* Armonk, NY: M. E. Sharpe.

The Strategy Dimension

In international business, companies use a multidomestic strategy that tailors its operations to local conditions, or a globally integrated strategy that strives to achieve a unified approach across all units, or a hybrid model combining elements of the two.

The Ethical Certainty Dimension

The GBC framework acknowledges varying degrees of ethical certainty about what is right. A GBC firm has high certainty about its principles, such as, "It is wrong to harm innocent persons." However, there are situations where local custom demands variations in implementing principles without violating them. And there are situations where local norms are in conflict with principles, application of the principles will cause unintended negative consequences, or where local managers cannot tell whether local customs conform to or conflict with company norms. In such cases, the degree of ethical certainty is much lower.

GBC'S Hybrid Approach

Table 1 shows the nature of the hybrid approach that best allows companies to consistently and responsibly exercise rights and implement duties within and across national and cultural borders. Two cells are eliminated from the model and the remaining four cells form a process for implementing GBC.

The two eliminated cells are ethical relativism and ethical imperialism. First, a multidomestic strategic approach cannot be applied by GBC companies in situations of high ethical certainty, because once one accepts universal ethical principles, they must by definition be operative everywhere. Ethical relativism allows companies to violate those few big principles by which they aspire to operate. Second, ethical imperialism is also eliminated, because a globally integrated approach requires that identical practices occur everywhere a company does business. This can be dysfunctional because it fails to recognize and respect legitimate differences in practice that do not violate principles, and it, therefore, creates stresses and hostilities where none are necessary. The four remaining cells constitute rational steps in the hybrid process of implementing GBC.

Steps in the GBC Process

Step 1: Development of a Code of Conduct

To implement GBC, companies first accept a small, reasonably comprehensive set of ethical principles that are near-universal and easily justifiable. Principles of liberty and welfare contained in the Universal Declaration of Human Rights, or the 10 principles of the United Nations Global Compact, are examples. Principles serve as the basis for the company's code of conduct, developed from a comprehensive inventory of the company's exposures, liabilities, and stakeholder challenges.

Step 2: Local Implementation

Sometimes a company's code and policies can be implemented straightforwardly. Sometimes, however, modifications will be demanded to conform to local law or custom. An acceptance of cultural relativism does not necessarily imply acceptance of ethical relativism. Companies can often implement policies in culturally sensitive ways without violating basic principles. Doing so may involve a measure of stakeholder engagement and concentrated effort to listen and learn, but it need not involve conflict or compromises in basic values.

For example, child labor prohibition is a near-universal principle. But there are legitimately different ideas about what the age limits and constraints should be. UN guidelines say that children less than 14 years should not be employed full time. This can be construed as a minimum, with some nations having 16 years or older as the age of compulsory education. And, in some less developed cultures, a child of 12 years might legitimately be employed in a family enterprise as long as schooling continues and the child is not exploited.

Step 3: Problem Analysis and Experimentation

When the company is faced with high ethical uncertainty, managers at Step 3 of the GBC process respond with analysis and experimentation to situations in which their company's principles cannot readily be implemented, or are violated by, seem to conflict with, or do not cover observed local practices. Experimentation involves testing various ways of satisfying the demands of universal principles and the constraints of local cultures. Outcomes may range from discovering that there is no conflict after all to deciding that the company must exit the region because its principles cannot be applied.

Step 4: Organizational and Systemic Learning

In the final step in GBC implementation, the company engages in a continuous process of systematic learning from its experiences and making the results accessible to all company decision makers. In addition, the company engages in systemic learning. GBC is aimed at sustainable capitalism, not merely competitive advantage for particular firms; so GBC companies will share what they learn with other companies so that overall harms are lessened and benefits are enhanced for people, social institutions, and the earth itself. Systemic learning can happen through trade and industry associations, conferences, scholarly research and publications, and increasingly through the posting of data on the World Wide Web.

Examples

Companies that have adopted universal principles as their guiding values (Step 1) include export contractor W. E. Connor & Associates, in their role in supplier certification of child labor–free production, and computer giant Hewlett-Packard, which spearheaded industrywide supplier codes of conduct. Local implementation examples (Step 2) are plentiful on the UN Global Compact website (www.unglobalcompact.org). Experimentation (Step 3) can be seen in

Bouygues Telecom's employee experiments to find the most satisfactory way to recycle office paper and in the partnering of gold mining company AngloGold Ashanti with several global nongovernmental organizations to address the HIV/AIDS crisis among its African workforce by delivering both basic health care and HIV/AIDS drugs to employees and their families. Organizational learning (Step 4) is illustrated by clothing retailer the Gap's response to stakeholder criticisms with an extensive regional reporting of sweatshop conditions in its supply chain and a process for follow-up and improvement. Systemic learning (also Step 4) is seen in Interface Inc.'s transparency about and advocacy of its ongoing efforts to create and market environmentally friendly carpets and to reduce the company's overall "environmental footprint" or impact.

—Donna J. Wood

Further Readings

Logsdon, J. M., & Wood, D. J. (2002). Business citizenship: From domestic to global level of analysis. *Business Ethics Quarterly, 12*(2), 155–188.

Logsdon, J. M., & Wood, D. J. (2005). Global business citizenship and voluntary codes of ethical conduct. *Journal of Business Ethics, 59*(1), 55–80.

Wood, D. J., & Logsdon, J. M. (2001). Theorizing business citizenship. In J. Andriof & M. McIntosh (Eds.), *Perspectives on corporate citizenship* (pp. 83–103). London: Greenleaf.

Wood, D. J., & Logsdon, J. M. (2002). Business citizenship: From individuals to organizations. *Business Ethics Quarterly* (the Ruffin Supplement), 59–94.

Wood, D. J., Logsdon, J. M., Lewellyn, P. G., & Davenport, K. (2006). *Global business citizenship: A transformative framework for ethics and sustainable capitalism.* Armonk, NY: M. E. Sharpe.

GLOBAL CODES OF CONDUCT

A global code of conduct may be defined as a set of guidelines or principles for business practice that establish ethical standards for business and employee conduct, especially for those firms operating in the international business environment. Global codes of conduct have grown in importance as we have witnessed the rise of global business as a critical element in the world economy. This rise is one of the most significant developments in business during the past 50 years. This period has been characterized by the rapid growth of direct investment in foreign lands by the United States, Western Europe, Japan, and increasingly other Asian countries. Global business has grown by leaps and bounds as technology, communications, and competitive forces have pressured firms to seek new markets.

In recent years, there has been evidence of a backlash against global capitalism. One reason for this is the complexity of the transnational economy and the opportunity for ethical issues to arise as companies increasingly do business across cultures. It is inevitable that as the clash of cultures and ethics increases, the need for business to take more affirmative action to head off these problems also occurs.

Protests in recent years have been led by environmentalists, who are concerned about the degradation of natural resources, and by human rights activists, who are concerned about treatment of human rights and fair treatment of the world's workers. Many protestors are today being referred to as antiglobalists because they believe global capitalism has gone too far and has been creating more disadvantages than advantages. These antiglobalists argue that multinational corporations have created ethical problems with respect to consumers, employees, human rights, developing nations, and the natural environment.

It is against this backdrop that the issue of global codes of conduct have arisen and become more important in recent years. It should also be observed that global codes of conduct are just an extension of traditional codes of conduct that have been used by companies for decades before international business and global competition became a widespread and integral part of the business world.

As global ethical issues have become more of a serious concern, there has been a growing need for effective responses on the part of business to these issues. Companies have taken many different steps to help restore confidence and trust in business. Consequently, global extensions of corporate social responsibility, corporate citizenship, and business ethics initiatives have become commonplace in the past two decades. Thus, global codes of conduct have typically been embedded in broader programs aimed at improving corporate conduct around the world, especially in developing countries. In this context, global codes of conduct may be seen as just one element in business's overall global corporate social responsibility initiatives.

GLOBAL CODES OF CONDUCT DEFINED

A global code of conduct may be defined as a set of guidelines or principles for business practice that establish ethical standards for business and employee conduct. These global codes are established at a variety of different levels. Corporations may create a global code applicable to just the firm in question. Industry-wide codes of conduct may also be established. For example, industries such as shoes, apparel, forest products, mining, and paper have established industry-level codes of conduct. In addition, global codes of conduct have been established by international organizations. Some of these international organizations may be government based, nongovernmental organizations (NGOs), or other nonprofit, special-interest organizations interested in improving business ethics internationally.

Code Formats

Most global corporate codes of conduct are voluntary in nature. That is, there is no legal enforcement mechanism governing their implementation. Such codes may be expressed in a variety of different formats. In a major study of corporate codes, The Conference Board, a nonprofit, business advocacy association, has found that these codes may be formulated and distributed in several different formats. Codes may be stated as compliance codes. These are usually a set of directives that give guidance to managers as to what to do or not to do with respect to various business practices. Another form used is that of the corporate credo. These are composed of broad, general statements of business commitment to various constituencies, or stakeholders, and may embrace value statements and strategic objectives. Finally, management philosophy statements may be the format used. These are similar to corporate credos but may just explicitly summarize the company's or the CEO's approach to doing business.

In its own study, the U.S. Labor Department has differentiated among the following different kinds of code formats. *Special documents* include written codes of conduct that summarize company standards, principles, or guidelines in a number of different arenas. These special documents communicate standards to the public and to affected stakeholder groups such as suppliers, customers, competitors, and shareholders. *Circulated letters* are another format. Such letters expressly state company policies on a specific issue to affected stakeholders. *Compliance certificates,* another format, are documents that require suppliers, agents, or other contractors to agree in writing that they will comply with the company's stated standards. Finally, *purchase orders or letters of credit* are written documents that make compliance with a company's policy part of a contractual obligation on the part of suppliers or other contractors.

THREE TYPES OF GLOBAL CORPORATE CODES OF CONDUCT

Previously, it was stated that global corporate codes may be established by individual companies, industry groups, and international organizations. A more careful exploration of these three types of codes reflects details clarifying how each type is developed and used.

Corporate Global Codes of Conduct

Corporate codes of conduct are typically just one element in a company's overall ethics program. Today, many companies have ethics programs that are often managed by ethics officers. These ethics programs typically include codes of conduct, ethics training, whistle-blowing mechanisms (e.g., ethics "hotlines"), ethics audits, and responsibility for a variety of different ethics-related aspects of the business such as ethical decision-making processes, discipline of violators, board of director's oversight, corporate transparency efforts, and effective communication of company standards.

Since the creation in 1991 of the Federal Sentencing Guidelines, which reduce penalties for companies with ethics programs, most large corporations today have embraced the idea of ethics programs and codes of conduct. According to these U.S. Sentencing Guidelines, a key feature in an ethics program needs to be a statement of *compliance standards,* and this is what is typically reflected in a company's global code of conduct.

Regarding these compliance standards, companies are expected to have established a set of standards that then serve as the basis for detecting and preventing legal violations. The code of conduct states these standards. Beyond this, a set of ethical principles or guidelines are also helpful to extend beyond what is required by law or to address topics that may not be covered by the law. Other U.S. Sentencing Guidelines requirements state aspects of the code of conduct's implementation that make a difference in its effectiveness. For example, it is expected that the code of conduct's implementation will entail high-level personnel in the company (such as ethics officers); will prevent the undue delegation of inappropriate discretionary authority; will be effectively communicated; will contain systems for monitoring, auditing, and reporting; and will embrace effective enforcement. Furthermore, companies are expected to take action when offenses have been detected, thus preventing future offenses, and to keep up with industry standards. This means that companies are expected to carefully monitor industry standards and practices and make sure that it is at least keeping up with industry standards.

Beyond the fact that companies may suffer less severe penalties if they have ethics programs and codes of conduct in place, what other benefits do companies receive from global codes of conduct? Various studies have shown that companies believe that they get some of the following benefits from codes of conduct:

- Legal protection for the company
- Increased company pride and loyalty
- Increased consumer and public goodwill
- Improved loss prevention
- Reduced bribery and kickbacks

The literature on corporate codes identifies that companies create such codes for both normative and instrumental reasons. From a *normative* point of view, the corporate codes serve as principles intended to guide corporate behavior in the most ethical directions. These have been referred to as "aspirational strategies," the purpose of which has been to describe how employees and agents of the firm *ought* to behave. From an *instrumental* point of view, corporate codes have been motivated by a variety of justifications. According to Krista Bondy, Dirk Matten, and Jeremy Moon in 2004, some of these motivations are their being a part of an internal control system, their being a part of a strategy of differentiation in the marketplace, their being a signal to stakeholders concerning a company's quality and reputation, reduced insurance premiums, peer pressure within an industry, improvement of customer relations, maintenance of standards within a supply chain, and preemption of boycotts and formal accusations.

As to what subjects or topics global codes of conduct address, the following represent some of the most frequently addressed topics found in these corporate codes:

- Conflicts of interest
- Receipt of gifts, gratuities, and entertainment
- Protection of company's proprietary information
- Giving gifts, gratuities, and entertainment
- Employee discrimination
- Sexual harassment
- Kickbacks
- Bribes
- Employee conduct
- Employee theft
- Proper use of company assets
- General conduct

To make sure that corporate codes are more than platitudinous statements of aspiration, S. Prakash Sethi, an expert on this topic, believes that companies need to create codes of conduct for their multinational operations, but that it should not stop there. Sethi recommends that companies should permit their activities and practices to be monitored by external and independent sources. An example of this model would be the Mattel toy company, which Sethi has worked with, in setting up a code, standards, and monitoring procedures. In the case of Mattel, the independent reviews of the company's practices are posted on a website, where they may be viewed by others. The company would have the opportunity to correct any factual errors, but beyond this they may not alter the monitor's report. They may write their own report disputing the findings or reporting on how the company would be responding to the findings. Sethi argues that the best global codes are those voluntarily written by companies because such a code may be carefully scrutinized and evaluated by outside parties and only the company itself can be held responsible for its actions. Some corporations have taken their global codes a step further by stipulating that their business partners and suppliers also adhere to their codes.

Global Codes of Conduct

For example, on the subject of global outsourcing, some companies such as Nike, adidas-Salomon (formerly adidas), Levi Strauss & Co. (LS&Co.), and the Gap have striven to monitor not only their own companies but also those with which they do business.

Specific Corporate Examples

As reported by Tara Radin in 2003 and 2004, two different companies in different industries serve as modern exemplars of the use of global codes of conduct: Chiquita Brands International and LS&Co. Chiquita, operating primarily in Latin America, employs a values-based approach to management and monitors its global conduct through the umbrella of a corporate responsibility officer. Chiquita monitors its performance through both internal and external means. Chiquita issues annual corporate responsibility reports in which it presents and evaluates both the strengths and weaknesses of its social and ethical performance.

In contrast, LS&Co. operates almost exclusively through sourcing partners scattered throughout the world, including Latin America. LS&Co.'s initiatives have served as a model for others in developing outsourcing standards and guidelines as many companies operate throughout the world in a similar manner. LS&Co.'s *Global Sourcing Guidelines* include both regular country assessments as well as analyses of the extent to which its sourcing partners are adhering to the company's "Terms of Engagement," which were established in 1991. These Terms of Engagement represent the actual standards by which the company expects its global partners to comply. LS&Co. implements its initiatives through a corporate level director and regional compliance officers. The company conducts widespread monitoring of its suppliers, and is increasingly seeking to employ external monitors. In many respects, LS&Co.'s program is more difficult to implement because it operates through private contractors, while Chiquita, in contrast, operates as a direct employer. Both these companies have served as exemplars for other firms seeking to employ global codes of conduct. The experience of both these companies points to the critical importance of internal and external monitoring to give their codes of conduct integrity.

As it will become apparent with both industry-based corporate codes and international groups' codes, the issue of monitoring is crucial to the effectiveness of global codes, whatever the level of their implementation. Internal monitoring may occur by special teams or consultants and represent a necessary first step in developing effective code implementation. External monitoring, often made possible through a strategy and practice of corporate transparency, allows external groups to conduct their own analyses of the codes' effectiveness. External monitoring sets the stage for higher levels of accountability as NGOs and other stakeholder groups are able to independently evaluate the firms' progress and achievements.

Industry-Based Corporate Codes

Beyond the individual company level, some industries have begun initiatives to create global codes of conduct for the companies competing in that industry. This makes a lot of sense because often the firms in a given industry are identified as a group and the actions of one affect the reputations of others. Furthermore, if firms operating in an industry can agree on ethical standards, this places the member firms on a level playing field in terms of treatment of stakeholders and issues affecting the industry.

As suggested earlier, one of the first industries to recognize the common interests of those in the industry was the defense industry in the United States. Due to corporate scandals surfacing in the 1980s, companies in the defense industry saw that one way to promote common interests was through some form of self-regulation that might deter further government regulatory strictures. The various initiatives in the industry included codes of conduct and the creation of ethics programs, ethics officers, and ethics training. These efforts eventually led to the Defense Industry Initiative on Business Ethics and Conduct, which would be classified as an industry-based set of guidelines or corporate code.

Over the years, other industries have developed global corporate codes as their commercial activities became more internationalized. Industries that have moved in this direction by creating various forms of corporate codes include apparel/garments, lumber, paper, mining, banking, and manufacturing, in general. Thomas Hemphill has termed such initiatives as attempts at industry self-regulation.

In recent years, the controversy surrounding "sweatshops" and some of the questionable practices associated with them have spurred the creation of a number of different industry groups determined to set standards for the firms participating in the apparel industry. In many instances, these different associations have come into competition with each other, as each is striving to become the standard-setter for the industry. Two industry-level groups trying to regulate industry behavior with respect to sweatshops include the Fair Labor Association (FLA) and Social Accountability International (SAI).

According to its webpage, the FLA is a nonprofit organization that coordinates the work of industry, NGOs, and colleges and universities to promote adherence to international labor standards and improve working conditions worldwide. The FLA conducts independent monitoring and verification to ensure that the FLA's workplace standards are upheld where FLA company products are produced. Through public reporting, the FLA provides consumers and shareholders with trustworthy information to make responsible buying decisions. The FLA "workplace code of conduct" includes ethics standards for such categories as forced labor, child labor, harassment or abuse, nondiscrimination, health and safety, freedom of association and collective bargaining, wages/benefits, work hours, and compensation for overtime work. The FLA takes these standards one step further by expecting that signees to these standards also require its licensees and contractors, or suppliers, to abide by local laws in the country in which they are operating and with the standards set forth in the FLA code.

According to its webpage, SAI has the mission of promoting human rights for workers around the world as a standards organization, ethical supply chain resource, and programs developer. SAI promotes workers' rights primarily through its voluntary SA8000 system, which is based on the International Labour Organization (ILO) standards and UN Human Rights Conventions. SAI argues that SA8000 is widely accepted as the most viable and comprehensive international ethical workplace management system available. What is interesting about SAI and to some extent the FLA is that they both originate in specific industries that compete globally but have drawn other organizations, including governments and other nonprofits, into their networks. Thus, although they began as industry-based initiatives, they evolved to be more comprehensive in scope, membership, and affiliation.

Another example of industry-level global corporate codes is the banking industry that has developed its Equator Principles, which are a set of guidelines developed by the banking sector for dealing with social and environmental issues with respect to the financing of economic development projects. The Equator Principles truly represent a global industry set of standards for financial institutions as member banks currently come from most of the major countries of the world.

International Organizations' Global Codes

Over the years, a number of different international organizations have sought to develop global codes of conduct that would serve as overarching guidelines for multinational companies doing business across country lines. These international organizations have included faith-based groups, NGOs, and even some political entities that have sought to set standards for companies operating globally or in particular countries. Their standards have been dubbed "group based." Examples of these group-based global codes of conduct that have been developed by various international groups include, but are not limited to, the Sullivan Principles for South Africa, later renamed the Global Sullivan Principles, the Caux Principles for Business, Principles for Global Corporate Responsibility, the Global Reporting Initiative, and the UN Global Compact. A brief statement of several of these is illustrative of the types of groups putting them together.

Caux Principles

The Caux Principles were issued in 1994 by a group known as the Caux Round Table. The Round Table was composed of senior business leaders from Japan, Europe, and North America. The Caux Principles are an aspirational set of recommendations and guidelines for corporate behavior that seeks to communicate a worldwide set of standards for ethical and responsible business conduct. The Principles address the social impact of company operations on the local communities.

Principles for Global Corporate Responsibility: Benchmarks

These principles were developed by the Interfaith Center for Corporate Responsibility (United States), Taskforce on the Churches and Corporate Responsibility (Canada), and the Ecumenical Council for Corporate Responsibility (United Kingdom) in 1998. These principles are intended to provide a model framework through which stakeholders can assess corporate codes of conduct, policies, and practices related to Corporate Social Responsibility expectations. The standards include 60 principles and benchmarks that can be used to assess corporate social and ethical performance.

UN Global Compact

The Global Compact was issued by the United Nations in 1999. It includes a set of 9, later expanded to 10 principles, that endorsing companies would agree to abide by. According to its webpage, the UN Global Compact asks companies to embrace, support, and enact, within their sphere of influence, a set of core values in the areas of human rights, labor standards, the environment, and anticorruption.

Global Reporting Initiative (GRI)

A revision of the GRI was issued in 2000 by the Coalition of Environmentally Responsible Economies. GRI is an international reporting standard for voluntary use by organizations reporting on the social, environmental, and economic aspects of their products, services, and activities.

Global codes of conduct at this level have typically been created by a variety of different groups, often working in conjunction with governments and NGOs, to create standards that serve as guidelines for companies doing business in the international sphere. Many different companies have become signatories to these codes and some companies have agreed to comply with multiple codes.

CONCLUSION

Global codes of conduct are an important way by which companies and industries may strive to conduct their activities on a legal and ethical plane in the international sphere. Most codes began as domestic focused, only later to become globally focused in keeping with the increasing globalization of commerce worldwide. Such codes have been created primarily on three different levels—the level of the firm itself, the level of industry associations, and the global level at which international organizations have created principles and standards for all firms doing business in the world or a particular part of the world.

To some extent, the idea of global codes of conduct has been controversial and not supported by everyone. It is difficult enough to implement conduct codes at the domestic level but extremely difficult at the global level. Some commentators have thus been critical of the idea, thinking they represent more of an ideal than a realistic possibility. In spite of this, the trajectory of global codes continues to grow.

Global corporate codes seem to have a bright future. It is axiomatic that increased ethical conduct and practice can only follow from standards that have been expressly established, communicated, adopted, and monitored. As the trend toward corporate transparency continues, the monitoring activities that have begun will continue. It is expected that all three levels of corporate codes will continue to flourish in the future as companies, industries, and the business community strive to build and retain trust and credibility with customers, employees, countries, and other stakeholders. To date, the use of global codes of conduct has had a positive impact on international labor practices, and thus, they are expected to continue.

—Archie B. Carroll

Further Readings

Bondy, K., Matten, D., & Moon, J. (2004). The adoption of voluntary codes of conduct in MNCs: A three-country comparative study. *Business and Society Review, 109*(4), 449–477.

Carroll, A. B., & Buchholtz, A. K. (2006). Ethical issues in the global arena. In *Business & society: Ethics and stakeholder management* (6th ed., pp. 291–332). Cincinnati, OH: Southwestern.

Hemphill, T. A. (2004). Monitoring global corporate citizenship. *Journal of Corporate Citizenship, 14,* 81–95.

Kao, A. (2005). *Corporate citizenship reporting: Best practices.* New York: Research Report: The Conference Board.

Krumsiek, B. (2004). Voluntary codes of conduct for multinational corporations: Promises and challenges. *Business and Society Review, 109*(4), 583–593.

Lowry, D. (2004). A review of setting global standards: Guidelines for creating codes of conduct in multinational corporations. *Business and Society Review, 109*(1), 107–113.

Palframan, D. (2003, May). Corporate behavior standards: A worldwide call to reform. *Executive Action Report* (no. 57). New York: The Conference Board.

Radin, T. J. (2003). Chiquita Brands International, Inc: Values-based management and corporate responsibility in Latin America. In L. P. Hartman, D. G. Arnold, & R. E. Wokutch (Eds.), *Rising above sweatshops: Innovative approaches to global labor challenges* (pp. 353–384). Westport, CT: Praeger.

Radin, T. J. (2003). Levis Strauss & Co.: Implementation of global sourcing and operating guidelines in Latin America. In L. P. Hartman, D. G. Arnold, & R. E. Wokutch (Eds.), *Rising above sweatshops: Innovative approaches to global labor challenges* (pp. 249–291). Westport, CT: Praeger.

Radin, T. J. (2004). The effectiveness of global codes of conduct: Role models that make sense. *Business and Society Review, 109,* 415–447.

Reid, A. S. (2003). The internationalization of corporate governance codes of conduct. *Business Law Review,* October, 233–235.

Sethi, S. P. (2003). *Setting global standards.* Hoboken, NJ: Wiley.

Sethi, S. P., & Williams, O. F. (2000). Creating and implementing global codes of conduct: An assessment of the Sullivan principles as a role model for developing international codes of conduct—lessons learned and unlearned. *Business and Society Review, 105*(2), 169–202.

Williams, O. (Ed.). (2000). *Global codes of conduct: An idea whose time has come.* South Bend, IN: University of Notre Dame Press.

MULTINATIONAL CORPORATIONS (MNCs)

The term *multinational corporation* (MNC) can be defined and described from differing perspectives and on a number of various levels, including law, sociology, history, and strategy as well as from the perspectives of business ethics and society. Certain characteristics of MNCs should be identified at the start since they serve, in part, as their defining features. Often referred to as "multinational enterprises," and in some early documents of the United Nations they are called "transnational organizations," MNCs are usually very large corporate entities that while having their base of operations in one nation—the "home nation"—carry out and conduct business in at least one other, but usually many nations, in what are called the "host nations." MNCs are usually very large entities having a global presence and reach. Names and company logos such as those of Coca Cola, Exxon Mobil, Mitsubishi, and Royal Dutch Shell are good examples. Today, however, we are also witnessing a rapid growth of smaller- and medium-sized enterprises that also conduct business in multiple nations and also have a global presence and reach. Hence, MNCs can be understood as either large or smaller corporate entities that operate on a global scale even though most people think of the MNC as a huge conglomerate with business offices, plants, or facilities worldwide.

MNCs have also undergone great structural changes over the years and they engage in many different and varied kinds of businesses. In addition to the basics of the production, manufacturing, and trading of goods, today MNCs can be found working within a host of business activities that include the delivery of services such as banking or communications both locally and globally, knowledge-based industries, foreign investment and currency exchange, maintaining branch offices or feeder plants in host countries, the extracting of natural resources, the assembly of products in one region (e.g., the maquiladora program in Mexico and elsewhere) for sale in another region, and various forms of technology transfer, among quite a few others. Hence, a picture of the typical MNC is difficult to draw, since there are so many variables and characteristics that can be depicted in the contemporary version of the MNC.

PART II: Corporate Social Responsibility on the Global Stage

THE MNC, BUSINESS ETHICS, AND SOCIETY: INTERNATIONAL CORPORATE RESPONSIBILITY

From the perspective of business ethics and society, the MNC often becomes an object of scrutiny by academic specialists who teach and write about business ethics and business and society issues. There are a number of ethical issues, problems, and dilemmas that have to do with MNC practices, and several classic case studies involving specific MNCs have been analyzed and discussed in the literature of business ethics. As a result of this academic attention, a branch of business ethics has emerged in which the ethics of MNCs and the ethics of international business practices are central. Again, this subdiscipline has been called the international corporate responsibility (ICR).

ICR, taken as a conceptual movement, explores whether MNCs have been cognizant of and have included the rights of stakeholders, and their responsibilities and their obligations to them, in their business strategizing. Questions that an ICR specialist might address include whether international businesses have conscientiously monitored their labor practices, respected the integrity of local cultures and the basic human rights of the individuals within those cultures, carefully measured and reported the environmental impact that they might have, or contributed fairly to the well-being of their "host countries." ICR takes many forms, and those interested in it have much work both in the conceptual clarification of the main ideas of ICR and in continuing empirical studies of how organizational responsibility is or is not fulfilled by MNCs.

Further Readings

Bowie, N. (1988). The moral obligations of multinational corporations. In S. Luper-Foy (Ed.), *Problems of international justice* (pp. 7–113). Boulder, CO: Westview Press.

Broadhurst, A. (2000). Corporations and the ethics of social responsibility: An emerging regime of expansion and compliance. *Business Ethics: A European Review, 9*(2), 86–98.

De George, R. T. (1993). *Competing with integrity in international business.* Oxford, UK: Oxford University Press.

Donaldson, T., & Dunfee, T. W. (1999). *Ties that bind: A social contracts approach to business ethics.* Boston: Harvard Business School Press.

Enderle, G. (Ed.). (1999). *International business ethics: Challenges and approaches.* Notre Dame, IN: University of Notre Dame Press.

Hoffman, W. M., Kamm, J. B., Frederick, R. E., & Petry, E. S. (Eds.). (1994). *Emerging global business ethics.* Westport, CN: Quorum Books.

Hooker, J., Kolk, A., & Madsen, P. (Eds.). (2005). *Perspectives on international corporate responsibility* (Vol. 2). Carnegie Bosch Institute Management Series. Charlottesville, VA: Philosophy Documentation Center.

Kolk, A., & van Tulder, R. (2002). Child labor and multinational conduct: A comparison of international business and stakeholder codes. *Journal of Business Ethics, 36,* 291–301.

Organisation for Economic Co-operation and Development. (2001). *Guidelines for multinational enterprises: Text, commentary and clarifications.* Retrieved from http://www.oecd.org/document/28/0,2340,en_2649_34889_2397532_1_1_1_1, 00.html

Sen, A. (1999). *Development as freedom.* New York: Knopf.

Schiller, H. I. (1989). *Culture, Inc.: The corporate takeover of public expression.* New York: Oxford University Press.

Schiller, H. J. (1976). *Communication and cultural domination.* White Plains, NY: International Arts and Sciences Press.

Tomlinson, J. (1991). *Cultural imperialism: A critical introduction.* London: Pinter Publishers.

United Nations. (1999). *The global compact.* New York: Author. Retrieved from www .unglobalcompact.org

PART III

Corporate Governance, Stakeholders, and Shareholders

CORPORATE GOVERNANCE

In its essence, corporate governance refers to the organization of the relationships between shareholders, board of directors, management, and other stakeholders in a corporation. According to the Cadbury Committee, corporate governance is concerned with the processes by which corporations are directed and controlled. Corporate governance especially deals with exercise of authority over the directions of the company, the supervision of actions of top management, the acceptance of accountability, and the compliance with legal and regulatory frameworks in which the company operates. The term *corporate governance* is not easy to define, as it can be used differently in different contexts. Several academic disciplines that study corporate governance bring their own distinctive meaning of the term. For example, economic theory emphasizes the mechanisms used by financial suppliers of corporations to assure themselves of getting returns on their investment. The study of law examines the power and duties of various corporate governance actors and discusses the legal instruments by which property rights are organized. The authors from the management and business administration focus on internal governance mechanisms that enhance decision making and improve performance.

Definitions of corporate governance have also changed over time to reflect the shift of the purpose and roles of corporations in modern society. In the 1960s, the main purpose of corporate governance was control of business power and authority. Therefore, corporate governance was dominated by investor predisposed definitions supported by agency theory. The corporate discussion was primarily about the control of managerial self-interest and a board of directors' monitoring role. More recent definitions adopt a much broader view, contemplating the whole complexity of corporate life. Margaret M. Blair offers one such definition, according to which corporate governance refers to the whole set of legal, cultural, and institutional arrangements that determine what publicly traded corporations can do, who controls them, how that control is exercised, and how the risks and returns from the activities they undertake are located.

NATIONAL GOVERNANCE SYSTEMS

Although the conceptualization of national differences in corporate governance is often debated, most comparisons categorize countries into three groups: Anglo-American, continental European, and Japanese–East Asian models. The Anglo-American model is characterized in terms of dispersed ownership and corporate financing through equity or short-term debt markets and active markets for corporate control. It is shareholder oriented and perceives the firm as the private property of its owners. This model is prevalent in the United States and the United Kingdom. The continental European model is stylized by concentrated ownership (usually by large blockholders, such as banks and families), long-term debt finance, and underdeveloped market for corporate control. Although it primarily emphasizes the interests of shareholders, it also takes into account the interests of employees. This model is widely adopted in Germany and to a smaller extent in Continental Europe. Japan and East Asian countries follow a model that emphasizes development of long-term relationships among various stakeholders—the main bank, major suppliers, distributors, owners, and employees. In this pluralist framework, employees' interests take priority. Such an inward-oriented and employee-centered environment of strong and long-term internal relationships, which dominates the firm's governance structure, also diminishes most chances for hostile takeover.

Differences in national patterns of corporate governance are shaped by a plethora of historical, political, institutional, economic, and social influences and determinants. A large number of studies have shown how historical conditions and political institutions influence certain features of property rights and financial markets and, consequently, ownership concentration and a company's access to external finance in different countries. Furthermore, some authors argue that one of the main political and social factors relevant to understanding corporate governance is the conflict between owners, managers, and workers. For example, where owners and managers have more power, corporate governance institutions tend to favor shareholders over stakeholders. Property rights, financial systems, and network structures are among the major factors accounting for these national differences.

Property rights define mechanisms through which different groups of shareholders exercise their control and how this control corresponds to managerial discretion. Shareholders rights vary internationally. The outcomes of such a divergence are complex legal and economic arrangements that shape the different mechanisms of corporate control. The Anglo-American system incorporates a liberal market approach. Here, market-oriented mechanisms of control are used to reinforce shareholder rights. Liberal property rights, which postulate relatively high disclosure of company information and establish a one-share–one-vote norm, provide strong protection of minority shareholders. Therefore, this system discourages disproportional control through blocks and favors different dominant interests within corporate governance. The continental European system exemplifies a constitutional model of shareholder control. In this model, shareholders delegate substantial control rights from the general shareholder meeting to a supervisory board. This approach tends to contribute to disproportionate power effects by large blockholders (families, banks, or other corporations). Given the ability of blockholders to secure greater control, they are able to pursue their strategic interests within corporate governance. Empirical research has supported the idea that concentrated ownership increases the external influence over management, whereas in the case of dispersed ownership the shareholders are largely separated from the firm. The Japanese system conforms to a shareholder authority model in which large shareholders hold broad powers. Cross-corporate shareholdings and weak information disclosure predominately protect property rights of majority shareholders and disable minority shareholders from having any influence over the firm.

The second major determinant of governance patterns is the type of financial system on the supply side of the capital market. Financial systems are usually divided into market-based and bank-based systems. The former has greater importance in the United States and the United Kingdom (Anglo-American model). This system promotes equity finance through active capital markets, where suppliers of capital (individuals or institutions) directly or indirectly invest in equity (shares) that is publicly issued by companies. Individual shareholders have little direct influence on management. If dissatisfied with management decisions, shareholders have the ability to sell their equity holdings in the firm. In the United States and the United Kingdom, banks typically do not hold company equity and their representatives do not sit as bank representatives on the board, although bank directors as individuals are represented. The bank-based financial system is found to be a dominant investment pattern in Continental Europe and Japan. Banks are the key financial institutions and are closely involved in ownership of the corporate sector. Banks hold shares either in their own right or collect deposits and invest them into companies for others. Their double role as lenders and important share-holders has often been stressed. It has been a historical tradition for this financial system to mobilize capital to the industry. In doing so, it has contributed to the growth of strong relationships between banks, industrial corporations, and other business partners. Dominance of debt finance, through the bank-based financial system, has caused in Germany, for example, the equity market to be relatively undeveloped when compared with equity markets within the Anglo-American system. The German banks have a mechanism for evaluating companies that is not practiced in the banks of the Anglo-American system. In Japan, the same function is covered by large and powerful planning departments of the *keiretsu's* main bank and trading company. The differences between these two financial systems are evident in several measures—share market capitalization, the distribution of financial assets, and firm debt/equity ratios. Even though a large number of countries occupy a position between the two opposing models, financial systems have significant impact on corporate governance. This grip is based on their ability to provide different sources of finance and via their capacity to influence relationships between different shareholders.

Variations in governance systems are also a consequence of interorganizational arrangements or network structures. A network structure refers to the quality and quantity of direct and indirect relationships between companies. Research on social networks has shown that the company's position within the network determines its access to critical resources, diffusion of practices across the companies, and overall power of the company within the network. Interorganizational arrangements of firms that belong to the Anglo-American system of corporate governance are characterized by loosely coupled connections. Their network structure is usually not based on ownership arrangements. Such weak ownership ties, fostered by financial interests of companies, facilitate market-like behavior in their mutual relations. Corporate networks in countries of the continental European system of corporate governance often involve vertical ownership arrangements with various suppliers and the board, thereby interlocking directorates among critical shareholders and creditors. These interorganizational networks are characterized by a high degree of intercorporate cooperation, which strategically promotes long-term relationships between various stakeholders. Codetermination policies in the German model of corporate governance, for example, see large companies as informal partnerships between labor and capital. At the center of the Japanese corporate grouping is a powerful bank or a financially strong company that can provide the other members of the group with capital at low cost. Reciprocal cross-shareholding in the Japanese system strengthens the commitments of organizations within the corporate network/group and weakens the influence of outside entities. This is why hostile takeovers in Japan are virtually unknown. Companies are acquired by other companies only through mutual consent.

THE SHAREHOLDER WEALTH MAXIMIZATION MODEL OF CORPORATE GOVERNANCE

Given an assumed separation of ownership and control in the modern corporation, the shareholder wealth maximization model regards the firm as a nexus of contracts through which various participants arrange their transactions. This theoretical perspective received the strongest support from the "Chicago School" of law and economics. Relationships between shareholders and managers are seen as classical principal-agent relationships with all the difficulties of enforcement associated with such contractual arrangements. The primary responsibility of management is to maximize the value of shareholders' investment via dividends and market prices of the company's shares. Thus, according to this model, the major concern of good corporate governance is how to control the behavior of top management and get them to run the company in the interest of shareholders.

There are at least four mechanisms by which shareholders can induce management to adopt an orientation toward shareholder value: (1) a relatively large ownership position, (2) compensation linked to shareholder return performance, (3) threat of takeover by another company, and (4) competitive labor markets for corporate executives. It is expected that a management share ownership option will motivate managers to identify more closely with the shareholders' economic interest. Though many top executives own a relatively large percentage of shares in their companies, their perspective on risk may differ from that of shareholders. It can be expected that managers have a lower acceptance of risk than shareholders. Where a company makes risky investments, shareholders can always balance this risk against other risks in their portfolio. Managers, however, can only balance an investment failure against the other activities of the company and are, therefore, more affected by investment risk.

The second mechanism that aligns managers' with shareholders' interests refers to compensation tied to shareholder return performance. This is the most direct means of influencing management behavior. Here, a variable portion of managers' compensation is linked to the shareholders' realized market returns. However, this mechanism is not without limitations. For example, an increase in the price of market share may be the consequence of factors beyond management control, regardless of whether they have worked hard or made good decisions.

The third mechanism is the threat of takeover by another company. Any extensive exploitation of shareholders' or maximization of managers' self-interest should be reflected in low share prices. A lower share price provides a takeover opportunity for another company or investors. The new owners will usually replace existing management. Where such a circumstance is plausible, an active market for corporate control proves to be both an external and ultimate mechanism that has the ability to create a convergence of interests between managers and shareholders.

The fourth and last mechanism of aligning managers' self-interest with those of shareholders is the competitive labor market for corporate executives. Managers compete for positions within and outside the company. Within this market they are evaluated on corporate performance, both in terms of accounting-based and share market-based measures. As a result, executives leading poorly performing companies will be offered fewer top executive positions within and outside the company.

The shareholder value perspective was dominant both in U.S. and U.K. companies in the 1970s and 1980s. An emphasis on sustaining share price and dividend payments at all costs encouraged the use of mergers and takeovers as mechanisms of corporate control to punish managers who were unsuccessful in improving shareholder value. Such an approach created economic instability and insecurity and was widely criticized by various economic and strategic analysts.

Throughout the years proponents of the shareholder value perspective have become more tolerant toward the interests of other stakeholders. Nevertheless, the main principles, which claim the supremacy of the ultimate owner, have remained the same. Consequently, the focus on shareholder value and stakeholder interests has become a foundation of good corporate governance.

THE STAKEHOLDER VALUE PERSPECTIVE
ON CORPORATE GOVERNANCE

The stakeholder view of corporate governance argues that all groups and/or individuals with legitimate interests in the company have the right to participate in the company's activities and gain a share of its economic success. There is no distinct priority of one set of interests and benefits over another. Therefore, a company should be seen as an organizational coalition between numerous and heterogeneous groups who provide their resources (i.e., capital, labor, management, loans, expertise, material, and service) to accomplish multiple, and not always congruent, goals through the company's activities.

Primary stakeholders are considered to be those with a legitimate claim to participate in the company's affairs; that is, those who directly participate in the economic-value-creation process and who are directly affected by the company's policies (e.g., employees, specific customer segments, key suppliers, certain financial institutions, and key governmental agencies). Other interest groups such as local communities, trade associations, and consumer groups, which are indirectly affected by the company's actions, are regarded as the secondary stakeholders.

According to the stakeholder perspective, the major concern of corporate governance is how to balance the interests of different stakeholders. Shareholders' legitimate emphasis on share prices and dividends must be balanced against the legitimate demands of other groups. However, these demands are not only financial. Different groups have different values. For example, employees might highly regard education and training support, suppliers of materials might prefer secure demand, and the local community might appreciate minimal air pollution. The balancing of these interests requires constant negotiation and compromise between inside and outside stakeholders and between directors and managers.

The trend toward the stakeholder perspective of the corporate governance is reflected in existing and emerging regulations of many developed countries. The codetermination laws in Germany, which require employee representation on the supervisory board; harmonization of the rules relating to company law and corporate governance in the European Union, which will take into account interests of employees, creditors, and customers; the Japanese well-known legal and customary model of corporations with its interrelated stakeholders including customers, suppliers, financial institutions, and other business partners; and the campaign toward stakeholder law in the United States all demonstrate demand for formal instruments to democratize the governance of corporations.

BOARD OF DIRECTORS

The board of directors is a governing body elected by shareholders to direct and supervise the management of the company. The board establishes the strategic direction and objectives of the company and sets the policy framework within which the company operates.

Different countries have different governance practices in terms of the board composition and its functioning. However, in general, members of the board of directors can be grouped into two main categories: (1) executive directors, who also have a management function in the company; and (2) nonexecutive (outside) directors, who have no managerial responsibilities. Nevertheless, they can have executive functions in other companies. Nonexecutive directors are selected to ensure that a broad range of skills and experience is available. In addition, a nonexecutive director can be formally classified as "independent." An "independent director" has no direct or indirect, current or previous, professional or personal interest or relationship in the company. It is believed that independent directors will empower the board with their ability to exercise independent judgment and effectively monitor management. Increasingly, the corporate governance practice of some countries has required or encouraged representation of formally independent directors on the board.

Within the tradition of the companies that originate in the Anglo-American system of corporate governance, boards can delegate some of their functions to various committees of the board. The purpose of a committee is to address certain issues in a more detailed manner than is possible at board meetings. The board as a whole, however, retains full responsibility. It is a standard practice for nonexecutive directors to establish the audit committee and remuneration committee. The audit committee oversees compliance with statutory responsibilities, thus ensuring that adequate internal controls are in place, advises the board regarding accounting policies and practices, and reviews the scope and outcome of the external audit. The remuneration committee deals with remuneration packages of the executive and nonexecutive directors and other groups of key executive managers. It may also consider succession issues.

Corporate Governance

Roles of the Board

Board roles can be generally categorized into three groups—control, service, and resource provision roles. The control roles involve the directors' fiduciary duties of monitoring management on behalf of shareholders. Directors' responsibilities in this role include appointing and dismissing the chief executive officer (CEO)/president and other top executives, deciding executive remuneration, and monitoring managers to ensure that shareholders' interests are protected. The services roles consider directors' advisory functions in formulating strategy and providing guidance to the CEO and top managers in other managerial and administrative issues. The resource roles refer to directors' assistance in the acquisition of critical resources for the company.

From a legal perspective, the control role is the primary purpose of the board of directors. Directors owe fiduciary responsibility to the corporation and shareholders. Fiduciary duties include the duty of care and duty of loyalty. Essentially, fiduciary duties call on directors to make every attempt to be well-informed before they make decisions, to act in good faith and the best interest of the shareholders, and to be independent in their decisions. From a financial perspective, directors' control role is primarily grounded in agency theory. That is, directors' source of power is derived from shareholders. Board members are selected by principals (shareholders) to monitor managerial behavior (agents). By actively monitoring management actions and firm performance, the board can reduce agency costs and maximize shareholder value.

One of the most prevalent roles of the board is its service role, that is, provision of advice and support to the CEO. It is argued that this role is most visible in organizations that experience external monitoring mechanisms, such as product and managerial labor markets. The service role is also stressed in the companies with major institutional shareholders, which decrease the need for active board control. Directors' involvement in the determination of corporate strategy is an important aspect of their advisory role. A number of studies have shown that directors engage in various stages of the strategic planning process, from the review of strategic initiatives to active involvement in strategy formulation.

The board is often seen as a key organizational body that could provide critical resources for the company, protect the company from environmental uncertainties, and reduce transaction costs in managing external relationships. Nonexecutive, outside directors, in particular, play an important role in providing (1) specific resources otherwise unavailable to management (e.g., financial funds, information), (2) access to external institutions and influential organizations (e.g., regulatory bodies, consulting firms, and international organizations), and (3) legitimacy. Resource scarcity prompts corporate boards to engage in interorganizational relationships in an attempt to moderate influences of external pressures on their companies. As capital is one of the key resources, companies often use interlocking directorates with financial institutions as a tool to facilitate access to cash. Contextual factors may moderate the importance of the resource role of the board. For example, small and entrepreneurial companies in which access to critical resources is problematic will benefit from the appointment of a reputable and influential director on their board.

Different Board Structures

In the Anglo-American system, boards of directors are usually unified bodies dominated by management. In a great number of large corporations in the United States and the United Kingdom, the CEO is also the chairperson of the board of directors. CEO duality is often criticized as an undesirable feature of this system, as it may limit the board's independent decision making. A typical board has between 9 and 15 members, most of whom are nonexecutive, outside directors. All directors are elected by shareholders in a general annual meeting. It is common for many individual shareholders not to attend these meetings. Most shareholders will vote on the election of directors and important policy proposals by "proxy," that is, by mailing election forms. There is no legal requirement for any specific stakeholder or interest group to be represented on the board. To achieve a greater accountability of directors to shareholders, an attempt is made to restructure the traditional board composition and introduce a majority of nonexecutive directors (i.e., directors not employed by the firm).

The continental European system of corporate governance functions on a two-tier board structure. This model is practiced in Germany, Austria, Holland, France, and Finland. The functions of the board are performed and split between a supervisory board or council and a management or executive board. The supervisory board has three core roles. First, it approves and evaluates the company's strategy and policies proposed by the management board. Second, it monitors the company's performance and accounts. Third, it appoints and dismisses members of the management board and monitors and evaluates the performance of the board itself. All members of the supervisory board are nonexecutives and no common membership is allowed between the boards. The supervisory board is headed by a chairperson, whereas the management board is headed by the CEO. The members of the supervisory council are elected at the general shareholders meeting. The management board is responsible for the day-to-day operations and running of the company. A two-tier board structure may work better where shareholdings are not as diversified as in the Anglo-American system and where there is a strong stakeholder concept, as in Germany.

In the German model, which is the most distinctive in this system, the supervisory council (*Aufsichtsrat*) consists of both employee representatives, appointed through trade unions, and capital representatives, appointed by shareholders. Members of the management board (*Vorstand*) are professional managers. Although all directors in the supervisory council are nonexecutives, they are seldom truly independent of the company. In enterprises with more than 500 employees, employees are represented in the supervisory council. In such cases, the council can have up to one third of employee representatives.

In the Japanese system, the formal corporate structure is that of a unitary board. Japanese boards are usually very large, with sometimes more than 30 members. Some researchers consider the *keiretsu* of cross-shareholdings as an informal governing body. It is a common practice that corporate governance takes place behind the scenes, between the corporate executives and representatives of major institutional shareholders. In general, the board of directors does not have external representatives of shareholders (outside directors). The only external person on the board may be a representative of the main bank. The board is composed of the corporation's own executives and former executives. The majority of directors within Japanese corporations are promoted from within the company and the rest are appointed from parent or affiliated companies. This internal promotion practice is an important component of the lifetime employment policies in Japanese corporations. The advancement to board membership is awarded to employees at the end of their working career for excellent performance during their professional employment. In this way, the boards of Japanese corporations represent the collective interests of the company and its employees rather than its shareholders.

Relations Between the Board and Management

The quality of board-management relationships is an ongoing issue for every board, regardless of the national setting. Both management and the board are responsible for the well-being of a corporation. The main question is how do the board and corporate management strike a balance for sharing these responsibilities?

The CEO is responsible for the day-to-day company operations and is expected to be the best-informed individual and most committed to the company. The directors are usually not involved in the operational affairs of the company and rely on the information provided by the CEO. In general, the directors should give an overall direction to the company, approve strategic decisions, and propose structural changes. It is believed that the separation of the role of the CEO from that of the chairperson enables a greater balance in board functioning, by way of limiting the power of the CEO to dominate the board.

However, many scholars and corporate governance experts also believe that effective functioning of the board depends on the quality of individuals and their ability to interact among themselves, and with the CEO and other managers, rather than only on the structural composition of the board. The fact that shareholders, management, and other stakeholders have changing expectations about the directors' knowledge and contribution to and involvement in the company's strategic affairs have led boards around the world to redesign themselves and their relationships within and outside corporations. Boards are expected to be more proactive in seeking information, in challenging the CEO in a constructive manner, in working together as a team, and in getting a deeper understanding of the company's business.

Some proponents of board redesign emphasize the importance of the dynamic balance between control and collaboration approaches in the board-management relationship. According to this view, a control approach protects a corporation from self-serving behavior and reduces goal conflict, whereas a collaborative approach encourages cooperation between the board and management and fosters trust and goal alignment. Acceptance, understanding, and management of control-collaboration tensions promote learning and improve governance. Other authors stress the role of the CEO and called to attention the evolution of the CEO-board relationship. Following the evolutionary perspective, these authors argue how the advisory role of the board has a relatively higher significance in the early period of CEO tenure while the control-focused approach is emphasized more in the later CEO tenure.

THE CHANGING WORLD OF CORPORATE GOVERNANCE

The emerging research on corporate governance has extensively considered new developments in national corporate governance systems, the increase of institutional shareholders activism, and the changing role of boards in knowledge-based organizations.

Changes in National Governance Systems

The Asian financial crises in the late 1990s and the U.S. corporate scandals at the beginning of this century have fuelled debate concerning the current models of corporate governance. Market failures and corporate collapses have urged the need for radical reforms in corporate governance and regulation. In the last decade, corporate governance transformation has become a major concern of national governments, stock exchanges, international organizations, and corporations themselves. More than 40 countries published corporate governance codes; the OECD has issued the principles and World Bank and IMF released the guidelines. In the United Kingdom, Sir Adrian Cadbury's final report on "The Financial Aspects of Corporate Governance" in 1992 and the final Hampel Report in 1998 were influential in setting in motion corporate governance reforms in the United States and in the United Kingdom. The Cadbury Code became a framework for international standards of governance. The main recommendations related to (1) the clear separation of responsibility at the corporate level, (2) involvement of nonexecutive directors, (3) the role of committees formed by nonexecutive directors, and (4) the formation and functions of audit and remuneration committees.

The most current major initiative to radically improve the corporate governance system in the United States came in the form of the Sarbanes-Oxley Act of 2002. The act was formed in response to a series of corporate collapses, including the Enron, WorldCom, and Tyco International financial scandals. It is designed to protect shareholder value and the general public from corporate wrongdoing. The Sarbanes-Oxley Act dealt with four major issues in corporate governance of public corporations. First, the act created an oversight board to set and enforce auditing standards and discipline public company auditors. Second, the act intended to foster auditor independence. For example, the corporate members with a financial reporting supervision role should not be employed by the external auditor. Third, the act increased corporate responsibility, by requiring that CEOs and CFOs certify all periodic reports containing the company's financial results. Having knowledge of the certification of false statements is subject to criminal liability. Finally, the act enhanced financial disclosure with regard to the off-balance-sheet transactions and obligations with consolidated entities and individuals. These key provisions of the Sarbanes-Oxley Act have significantly strengthened the role of the board of directors and have made managements more accountable.

The cooperative, inward-oriented and employee-centered model of the Japanese corporate governance system was usually portrayed as a source of competitive strength for the Japanese economy. However, since the beginning of the Japanese recession in the 1990s, many studies have shown that some of the reasons for the economic downturn in large Japanese companies originated due to a lack of effective monitoring of managers by shareholders and weak accurate disclosure of companies' financial conditions and business performance. To improve the state of the economy, Japan has embarked on the modernization of the corporate governance system emphasizing better protection of shareholders rights, increased responsibilities of directors, and regular disclosure of information. In 2003, the Corporate Governance Forum in Japan established guidelines and defined best-practice corporate governance principles. The forum proposed the adoption of specific elements of the Anglo-American system. These included appointment of nonexecutive directors on the board, introduction of an executive officer system, and enforcement of auditor power.

The German model of corporate governance has also been pressured to undertake reformative changes. The publication of the official "German Corporate Governance Code" in early 2002 marked a milestone in the development of good governance in Germany. The code addresses all major criticisms, especially from international investors, that point against German corporate governance—namely, inadequate focus on shareholder interests, insufficient independence of supervisory boards, the two-tier board structure, the limited independence of financial statement auditors, and inadequate transparency of the German corporate governance system. The main purpose of the code is to make Germany's corporate governance rules transparent for both national and international investors.

In Europe, the EU Commission's role in corporate governance has increased in recent years but is limited due to major differences in national and company laws. In May 2003, the EU Action Plan was set up to define minimum governance standards for European companies. The idea of the EU Action Plan is not to legislate for all EU member states but to achieve convergence of the many different governance regimes within a well-defined timeframe.

The Rise of Power of Institutional Shareholders

In the 1970s, individual shareholders held almost 80% of the equity in the United States. By the end of the 1990s, however, their holdings had decreased below 45% while institutional shareholding had increased to 53%. In 2002, individual ownership declined further to just over 37% while institutional ownership reached over 55%. Corporate governance is highly affected by changes in power of different categories of shareholders. Controlling shareholders, such as families, individuals, or other corporations, can have significant influence over corporate strategic behavior. Small individual shareholders, on the other hand, do not exercise governance rights as they usually do not have knowledge, power, and incentive to control corporations. However, they are concerned about fair treatment from majority shareholders and management. Institutional shareholders have emerged as a distinctive and demanding voice in corporate governance within the Anglo-American system. Institutional investors, such as large pension and mutual funds, have the power to directly influence managerial decisions in many corporations. Their activism has led to a greater emphasis on shareholder value and directed management to place greater priority on their interests rather than those of stakeholders. The board of directors meets regularly with representatives of institutional and large investor groups to actively communicate corporate developmental strategies. It is expected that such groups have higher knowledge and long-term interest in the company. In this situation, management interests are more likely to be aligned with those of shareholders. Some observers of institutional investor activism assume that this development is bringing the Anglo-American model of corporate governance closer to those of the continental European and Japanese models.

Corporate Governance in Knowledge-Intensive Firms

The context of increasing technological intensity creates additional challenges for corporate governance. A boards' legal and moral authority has always been derived from their representation of shareholders of the firm. This authority, legally translated into accountability for the key strategic assets of the firm, guides deployment of these assets toward the most productive and shareholder-approved uses. However, the nature of strategic assets that needs to be accounted for in a knowledge- or technology-intensive company is significantly different. It is not only that these assets are intangible but also there is difficulty in agreement over who owns them and who is responsible for them. Specific assets, such as human capital, producer's tacit learning, or complex networks of interorganizational interactions, create a governance problem that standard models of control in corporations do not explicitly address. Due to lack of knowledge and inability to evaluate information, a traditional board of directors, for example, may be an ineffective governance mechanism.

The competitive advantage of knowledge-intensive firms comes mainly from nonphysical and nonfinancial assets, which can include employee know-what and know-how, training and development processes, and intellectual property. These companies offer different organizational cultures that thrive on ambiguity and offer an antithesis to control approaches that are more amenable to traditional industries. Such cultures reflect changes in power relations between financial and human capital. In these organizational environments, greater attention is paid to human resource issues because of an increased importance of technical and scientific personnel. As some authors suggest, human capital—the assets that each day go home and which are readily move-able—should be treated with care. Therefore, corporate governors should more explicitly affirm the rights of nonshareholders by allowing them formal involvement in governance processes. This formalization may be initiated through special compensation schemes or other arrangements that align the employees' interests with those of shareholders. Thus, if knowledge is the immanent resource and a critical asset of new companies, are individual employees becoming residual claimants in the changing world of corporate governance?

CONCLUSION

The topic of corporate governance has attracted a lot of attention and has become a subject of enormous debates in the recent years. Corporate scandals and collapses taking place in most countries have prompted regulatory reforms in all national governance systems. The issues of corporate governance are complex and deeply embedded in specific historical conditions and economic and political circumstances. Corporate governance researchers and professionals all agree that there is no one best way to design a governance system. In the modern world, an emerging perspective on corporate governance goes beyond the conventional emphasis on financial aspects of corporate control and takes into account interests, constraints, actions, resources, and influences of all constituencies in the corporate governance system. This entry has attempted to present some of the key building blocks, major perspectives, and the most recent developments and challenges of corporate governance.

—Ljiljana Erakovic

Corporate Governance

Further Readings

Aguilera, R. V., & Jackson, G. (2002). The cross-national diversity of corporate governance: Dimensions and determinants. *Academy of Management Review, 28*(3), 447–465.

Berle, A. A., & Means, G. C. (1932). *The modern corporation and private property.* New York: Macmillan.

Blair, M. M. (1995). *Ownership and control: Rethinking corporate governance for the twenty-first century.* Washington, DC: Brookings Institute.

Cadbury Committee. (1992). *Report of the committee on the financial aspects of corporate governance.* London: GEE.

Carpenter, M. A., & Westphal, J. D. (2001). The strategic context of external network ties: Examining the impact of director appointments on board involvement in strategic decision making. *Academy of Management Journal, 44,* 639–661.

Clarke, T., & Clegg, S. (1998). *Changing paradigms: The transformation of management knowledge for the 21st century.* London: HarperCollins Business.

Demb, A., & Neubauer, F. F. (1992). *The corporate board: Confronting the paradoxes.* New York: Oxford University Press.

Donaldson, T., & Preston, L. E. (1995). The stakeholder theory of the corporation: Concepts, evidence, and implications. *Academy of Management Review, 20*(1), 65–91.

Fama, E., & Jensen, M. C. (1983). Separation of ownership and control. *Journal of Law and Economics, 26,* 301–326.

Fligstein, N., & Choo, J. (2005). Law and corporate governance. *Annual Review of Law and Social Science, 1,* 61–84.

Fligstein, N., & Freeland, R. (1995). Theoretical and comparative perspectives on corporate organization. *Annual Review of Sociology, 21,* 21–43.

Government Commission. (2002, February 26). *German corporate governance code.* Retrieved March 22, 2006, from www.corporate-governance-code.de/eng/kodex

Hampel, R. (1998). *Committee on corporate governance: Final report.* London: GEE.

Hansmann, H. (1996). *The ownership of enterprise.* Cambridge, MA: Belknap.

Hillman, A. J., Cannella, A. A., & Paetzold, R. L. (2000). The resource dependence role of corporate directors: Strategic adaptation of board composition in response to environmental change. *Journal of Management Studies, 37,* 235–255.

Japan Corporate Governance Forum. (2001). *Revised corporate governance principles.* Retrieved March 22, 2006, from www.jcgf.org/en

Johnson, J. L., Daily, C. M., & Ellstrand, A. E. (1996). Boards of directors: A review and research agenda. *Journal of Management, 22,* 409–438.

Keenan, J., & Aggestam, M. (2001). Corporate governance and intellectual capital: Some conceptualizations. *Corporate Governance, 9*(4), 259–275.

Organisation for Economic Co-operation and Development. (2004). *OECD principles of corporate governance.* Paris: Author.

Pfeffer, J., & Salanick, G. R. (1978). *The external control of organizations: A resource dependence perspective.* New York: Harper & Row.

Rappaport, A. (1986). *Creating shareholder value: The new standard for business performance.* New York: Free Press.

Shleifer, A., & Vishny, R. W. (1997). A survey of corporate governance. *Journal of Finance, 52*(2), 737–783.

Sundaramurthy, C., & Lewis, M. (2003). Control and collaboration: Paradoxes of governance. *Academy of Management Review, 28*(3), 397–415.

Yoshimori, M. (1995). Whose company is it? The concept of the corporation in Japan and the West. *Long Range Planning, 28*(4), 33–44.

Zahra, S. A., & Pearce, J. A. (1989). Boards of directors and corporate financial performance: A review and integrative model. *Journal of Management, 15,* 291–334.

Corporate Governance

STAKEHOLDER THEORY

Every company exists in a network of relationships with social actors that affect and are affected by the company's efforts to achieve its objectives. Taken together, these actors are the company's *stakeholders,* implying that they hold a stake in its conduct. Typically, stakeholders of a for-profit company include its customers, employees, stockholders, suppliers, the local community, and many others groups.

Stakeholder theory is the term used to describe broadly the systematic study of these relationships, their origins, and their implications for how companies behave. As used in this context, the word *theory* raises serious problems. Social scientists who study stakeholder relations are interested in many empirical questions, such as why companies and stakeholders behave as they do and why companies succeed or fail. They use the word *theory* to refer to a specific set of cause-and-effect relationships used to answer such questions. The controversy (as explained below) is whether stakeholder theory, as a social science theory, points toward a unique set of causal statements about why organizations behave as they do that no other theory identifies. On the other hand, ethicists use the term *stakeholder theory* to describe a coherent and original answer to the central philosophical question in organizational ethics, How should organizations behave? There is less controversy about whether stakeholder theory is a form of ethical theory, though this does not mean that the theory's content is uncontroversial among ethicists. This entry discusses the development of stakeholder theory in both these contexts (social science and philosophy) and details its answers to both empirical and ethical questions.

HISTORICAL BACKGROUND

The term *stakeholder* is not a new one. It dates back at least as far as the early 18th century, where it sometimes appeared in British legal cases to describe a party holding a stake in a financial transaction. In the narrowest sense, a stakeholder was a neutral party to a transaction or wager who held the money in trust—literally holding the stakes. However, by the early 19th century—as detailed in the *Oxford English Dictionary*—the term had acquired a more expansive definition in two ways. First, its meaning expanded to include all parties to a financial interest, and second, it broadened to describe those parties holding an interest in the broader political system or commonwealth. In some sense, this more expansive use of the term would set the stage for its emergence as a term in the study of business and society.

While the term did not appear explicitly in writing about management for much of the 20th century, the notion that executives must pay attention to the demands of an organization's multiple constituencies has a long history in the early-20th-century precursors to the modern field of organization theory. Mary Parker Follett, an early American management thinker, portrayed the organization as nested in an environment of other actors, each mutually influencing and defining each other. To Follett, the manager's job was to integrate the conflicting interests held by these constituencies, and the success of the company depended, in no small part, on managers recognizing the need to (a) manage all relationships with as much attention as they traditionally paid to personal matters and (b) achieve some degree of creativity in how they dealt with conflicting demands.

Likewise, in his classic book *The Functions of the Executive,* Chester Barnard foreshadowed the eventual emergence of stakeholder thinking. For Barnard, an organization is a cooperative scheme, the result of a conscious effort by many people to work together. As such, an organization's survival depends on its relationship to its environment and its ability to satisfy those individuals interacting with it. The central role, in Barnard's thinking, of executive responsibility—the suppression of personal interest in service of the cooperative scheme—also heralds the eventual exploration of the moral side of stakeholder theory. Barnard introduces notions of balance and touches on questions of whether subordinates should be treated as having intrinsic value (valued for their own sake) or should be treated instrumentally (valued only for what they can do for the executive or the company). These are questions that, today, arise frequently in writing about companies and their stakeholders.

The early works of Follett and Barnard, though often neglected today, played some role in the emergence of the open systems view of organizations in postwar organization theory and, in turn, these authors laid much of the intellectual groundwork for theorizing about stakeholders. Efforts by Peter Blau, W. Richard Scott, William R. Dill, and James Thompson all centered on the nature of the external environment in which organizations existed, paying particular attention to the nature of the *organization set*—the immediate relationships surrounding an organization. In the ensuing decades, the attention of most organization theorists would shift from the study of organization sets to organization fields, a higher level of analysis at which all organizations and their constituents interact to create institutional norms and rules. Yet the initial insight that a company plays multiple roles within a bounded set of actors would lay the groundwork for the advancement of stakeholder theory as a continuing effort to explore the nature of organization set interactions.

The term *stakeholder* emerged in the study of organizations and management in the early 1960s through the work of the Stanford Research Institute, in the work of Albert Humphreys and others. There, efforts to map program management processes and improve long-range planning techniques led to greater attention on the parties to a management process—that is, its stakeholders—and their role in determining the success of a change program. Both Kenneth Andrews and Igor Ansoff, early advocates of the study of corporate strategy, used the term explicitly and suggested that stakeholders might have something to do with the overall strategy formulation process in a company. However, the term did not attract much attention until the early 1980s with the publication of two books, Ian Mitroff's *Stakeholders of the Organizational Mind* of 1983 and R. Edward Freeman's *Strategic Management: A Stakeholder Approach* of 1984. Of the two, Freeman's has made the more lasting contribution to stakeholder theory.

FREEMAN'S SEMINAL CONTRIBUTION

R. Edward Freeman's book *Strategic Management: A Stakeholder Approach* (1984) is widely recognized as the first major work in stakeholder theory, though misunderstandings about its contents abound. It is, therefore, worth devoting some attention to the nature of Freeman's argument and its implications for the subsequent development of stakeholder theory.

The starting point for Freeman's book is to trace those previous schools of thought that lay a groundwork for thinking about a company's strategy in stakeholder terms. There are four primary schools—the corporate planning literature, open systems theory, the study of corporate social responsibility, and organization theory. For each, Freeman discusses the contributions made to the stakeholder concept. Chief among these contributors are the organization set theorists cited above, systems theorists such as Russell Ackoff, corporate strategists such as Ansoff, and business and society scholars such as

Lee Preston and James Post. This section can, in some ways, be read both as a history of the stakeholder concept and as an intellectual genealogy indicative of the various circles in which Freeman was moving at the time that he was conceiving of and developing his approach to stakeholder management.

Freeman's definition of the term *stakeholder* remains the most commonly used (and is the basis for the definition provided above), despite frequent criticisms of its breadth. He writes, "A stakeholder in an organization is (by definition) any group or individual who can affect or is affected by the achievement of an organization's objectives" (p. 46). This definition also lays the groundwork for the visual figure, a hub-and-spoke diagram with the company at the center and stakeholders ranged around in a circle, most commonly associated with stakeholder thinking. Most subsequent writers, however, ignore Freeman's warning that if stakeholder thinking remains at such a generic level—ignoring the specific groups and complex interrelations that characterize actual company-stakeholder interactions—it would have little practical value.

The most obvious and lasting contribution of Freeman's book is the emergence of what has come, more recently, to be called instrumental stakeholder theory—the idea that companies that manage their stakeholder relationships effectively will survive longer and perform better than those companies that do not manage stakeholders well. (This entry will discuss more recent contributions to this stream of research.) In developing this argument, Freeman also offers what remains the most in-depth description of the actual practices and processes by which a company might be said to manage these relationships well. He suggests that stakeholder management "competence" includes a commitment to monitoring stakeholder interests, an ability to formulate strategies for dealing with stakeholders, sophistication in segmenting stakeholder needs, and the alignment of specific business functions (e.g., public affairs, marketing) to dealing with stakeholder needs. In essence, Freeman's book remains one of the most thorough "recipe books" for managers interested in stakeholder management, and far more than its contribution to theory, this remains its greatest strength.

As for Freeman's role in the emergence of an ethical literature on company-stakeholder relations, the genealogy is slightly more complicated. After all, Freeman's book contains little reference to the question of how companies should treat stakeholders, at least insofar as the question goes beyond merely prudential matters of survival or profit. The book contains only one passing reference to ethical and political theory (a stray citation of the writing of the philosopher John Rawls), and it would be a few years before Freeman would acknowledge that, only in later conversations, did he begin to explore seriously the question of stakeholders as moral agents. Yet Freeman's own training as a philosopher and his relationship to the burgeoning scholarly community of business ethicists probably created the conditions by which the 1984 book serves as a foundational work in ethics-based stakeholder theory, despite the fact that it contains little explicitly intended to kindle such discussion.

STAKEHOLDER THEORY IN ORGANIZATIONAL ETHICS

As stated above, stakeholder theory can be looked at as a marriage of two somewhat different theoretical enterprises—ethical and empirical. The first is the search for an ethics-based stakeholder theory. From its onset, in the early 1990s, this project started with several attempts by Freeman and other like-minded philosophers to formulate a so-called normative core from which to deduce the moral obligations of the company in dealing with its stakeholders. Many scholars thus sought to establish a clear philosophical foundation on which to ground statements about how companies *should* treat their stakeholders. Almost every major ethical theory—utilitarianism, property rights, feminist ethics, and Kantian deontology—offered some basis for relevant arguments.

At its heart, the quest for a normative core for stakeholder theory has clear roots in the more long-standing debate over the purpose of the corporation in a capitalist society. Ethicists tend to draw a sharp distinction between stockholder and stakeholder models of capitalism—the central question being "For whose benefit should the corporation be run?" The stockholder model, which received its most ardent defense from Nobel laureate Milton Friedman, holds that the corporation must strive to maximize returns for its shareholders. The property rights of its shareholders, the nature of fiduciary duties, the legal mandates surrounding corporate governance, and public policy considerations all offer some support for the stockholder model.

Set in opposition to this model, however, the stakeholder model holds that a corporation owes obligations to more than just the stockholders. For example, Thomas Donaldson and Lee Preston (in a widely cited article) argue that a more expansive notion of property rights allowed stakeholder groups to make legitimate claims on the value produced by the corporation. Each of the attempts to derive a normative core from some established school of ethical theory arrived at similar conclusions, though often from very different starting points. The object of the corporation, they argue, is to maximize stakeholder wealth—which includes but is not limited to stockholders.

With time, the pursuit of a normative, or ethics-based, stakeholder theory has gone beyond the simple pursuit of a normative core. Today, three major problems occupy ethicists interested in how companies should treat their stakeholders—identification, distribution, and procedure. Each has received attention in existing research but each demands further elaboration.

Identification

The problem of identification seems simple enough: Who should managers of a particular company identify as its stakeholders? Given the potentially vast number of actors claiming a stake in the company's operations, identification involves determining which actors truly have enough moral standing to be considered stakeholders. This is a moral problem rather than merely a question of description. A local business may well pay protection money to a local crime boss, and this person may affect and be affected by a company's actions. However, few ethicists would argue that crime bosses have moral standing vis-à-vis a company. Indeed, companies may well treat any number of social actors as salient (i.e., requiring attention) without considering them to have the moral standing afforded by ethics-based stakeholder theory.

From the earliest days of stakeholder theory, the identification problem has produced a great number of distinctions. Early stakeholder theorists spoke of stakeholders as either primary or secondary, indicating that some groups may have greater or lesser claims to stakeholder status. In a frequently cited article, Mitchell, Agle, and Wood suggest that the characteristics of power, legitimacy, and urgency not only determine who the company is likely to consider salient (an empirical question) but which groups merit this attention (a normative one).

It is, however, Robert Phillips's book *Stakeholder Theory and Organizational Ethics* that offers the most coherent and complete answer to the identification problem. Drawing on a principle of justice as fairness first articulated by John Rawls, Phillips contends that a company should consider as stakeholders all those parties that participate in the cooperative scheme surrounding it. In other words, a company has an obligation to attend to the claims of parties insofar as it willingly receives benefits from them. Based on this notion of fairness, Phillips distinguishes between legitimate stakeholders (i.e., those that possess moral standing based on claims of fairness or reciprocity) and derivative stakeholders (i.e., those parties whose claims on a company are indirect, deriving from their relationship to a legitimate stakeholder). Thus, a company must recognize employees as a legitimate stakeholder because the company willingly accepts benefits from the employees' efforts; however, the company need not consider the labor union acting on behalf of employees a legitimate stakeholder, except insofar as their claims derive from their relationship to employees. In sum, Phillips grounds the debate over identification more firmly in the realm of ethical theory and offers one possible solution.

Distribution

The second and arguably greater ethical question in stakeholder theory is the problem of distribution, "How should a company distribute the value that it creates?" Of course, this is a highly simplified way to express the problem, as businesses tend to generate very different types of value (many of which are incommensurate with each other), operate over long time frames in which seeming trade-offs can worsen or resolve themselves, and generate enormous costs that may well be treated as morally different from the value the company creates. If a company damages the natural environment, for example, it deprives community members of certain intangible goods (peace of mind, quality of life) for which monetary value does not fully compensate. Many of the costs involved manifest over long periods of time, during which the immediate benefits to the company of polluting may place the company in better (or worse) position to remedy the environmental problems that arise. Finally, if the damage leads to deaths in the community, these costs are unlikely to fit naturally into a cost-benefit calculation along with returns to stockholders and employee salaries enjoyed by other stakeholders.

Despite the complexities, stakeholder theorists have continued to wrestle with the distribution problem. To a great degree, solutions to the distribution problem are set in contradistinction to the notion that companies (particularly corporations owned by stockholders) owe all their residual value to their owners. Alexei Marcoux, in an important article in the *Business Ethics Quarterly*, mounts a vigorous defense of this principle. He contends that the notion that a company owes a fiduciary duty to shareholders—a duty to act first and foremost in the interests of shareholders—is the natural moral analog to other situations where fiduciary duties apply. Information asymmetries, the degree of possible harm, and the need for trust all create conditions where the company should acknowledge a fiduciary duty to it stockholders similar to that of doctor to patient or lawyer to client. Of course, this idea—equally present in

Friedman's justification based on the property rights of owners—actually offers only an incomplete response to the distribution problem. After all, we may agree that shareholders, as owners of the company, deserve special consideration and still have few answers about the right way to distribute value and costs. Many of the decisions companies make and the trade-offs they address have only incidental impact on stockholder value.

In most such cases, the causal relationships are so tenuous as to make considerations of fiduciary duty and residual wealth not useful, if not altogether irrelevant, for solving the practical moral problems involved. Consider a simple example of an airline deciding how much airline baggage to allow on the airplane. Insofar as a company (rather than regulators) still gets to make this choice, managers must decide between passenger convenience and the well-being of employees—flight attendants are often injured trying to help passengers with oversized carry-on baggage. To say "the company should do whatever is best for the shareholder" is to say very little indeed. There is no evidence that baggage policies are a major determinant of customer preference and little more evidence that employee morale translates directly into financial returns in this industry. Indeed, fuel costs (a very important driver of profit in the industry) are not affected either way, as the baggage will end up somewhere on the airplane regardless of whether it is checked or carried aboard. The company is still left to decide how to distribute the good among two conflicting stakeholder claims. Though this is a trivial example, it may be more representative of the problems faced by management on a daily basis.

The general principle often attributed to stakeholder theory is that companies should distribute value broadly, that the company should be managed so as to create value for all its stakeholders. In specific terms, Phillips offers the clearest interpretation of this general principle. He argues that a company owes obligations proportional to the relative contribution that the stakeholder makes to the success of the cooperative scheme. Of course, by marking out such a specific position, Phillips exposes himself to critiques that the resulting allocations are still too narrow to be morally justifiable. After all, some groups (e.g., local communities) may offer few tangible benefits to a company, contributing little to the cooperative scheme, but still deserve some consideration if, for example, the company decides to erect a particularly ugly building that will destroy property values for miles around. Still, the distribution question awaits a more persuasive argument.

Stakeholder Theory

Procedure

The problem of procedure concerns the proper role of stakeholders in the formulation of strategies and policies that affect them: Does a company have an obligation to engage with stakeholders and invite their input into policy decisions? Regardless of the moral issues involved, many companies do offer ways for particular stakeholder groups to express their viewpoints. However, given that companies, especially very large corporations, can exercise a great deal of power (often on a par with governmental power) over customers, employees, and local communities, the question of whether managers owe an obligation to provide due process (e.g., via grievance processes, consultations, etc.) remains an important moral question.

Arguments in this vein tend to find their roots in one of two traditions. On the one hand, ethicists may choose to draw on the work of German philosopher Jürgen Habermas. Habermasian, or discourse, ethics hold that morally right decisions in a political context are only possible insofar as they are created through open public discussion and deliberation. The only way to honor man's nature as a reasoning being is to respect reason's role in the act of communication and deliberation. Applying this principle of communicative reason, Jeffrey Smith has argued that a company has an obligation to consult with its stakeholders so that the resulting decisions will not only be better but more ethically legitimate than those created in a vacuum.

A second perspective on the moral problem of procedure is the emerging discussion of multistakeholder dialogue. Though not necessarily rooted in any particular ethical theory, authors such as Jerry Calton and Stephen Payne, drawing on insights from William Isaacs and David Bohm, argue that dialogue is a natural and important facet of all human relationships and that suppressing dialogue in stakeholder relationships is both imprudent and unnatural. It is not clear, of course, what the extent of this dialogue must be—who should be involved, how long it should last—but Calton and Payne seem to suggest that these considerations should flow organically from the dialogue itself rather than according to any external constraints.

STAKEHOLDER THEORY AS SOCIAL SCIENCE

If stakeholder theory is (as suggested above) a marriage between two somewhat different theoretical enterprises—the ethical and social science traditions—the latter has been the more fickle partner. Many social scientists researching these interactions have done so while, more or less, accepting the notion that the normative project remains an essential part of stakeholder research. For these theorists, accepting that stakeholders have intrinsic value is a shared premise for stakeholder theorizing. In other words, the social scientist must accept a fundamental ethical principle and then embark on research that advances understanding either the empirical or the ethical implications of this premise. The ideal outcome, then, is some *convergent stakeholder theory,* a phrase coined by Thomas Jones and Andrew Wicks, in which both efforts combine in a hybrid that includes both a sophisticated morally grounded concept of how companies should treat stakeholders and an empirically robust causal chain linking such moral behavior to desirable outcomes.

A minority of social scientists doing research on stakeholders tend to reject this desire for convergence and see it as a threat to traditional assumptions about how to do proper social science. From this perspective, stakeholder research is merely one domain of scholarly activity that studies how companies and their stakeholders interact, and the relationship between the ethics- and social science–based traditions is, at best, at arm's length. There is, they might argue, no reason to privilege the ethics-based element of stakeholder research (as both ethicists and those seeking convergence have tended to do). Indeed, within this second camp, there is even considerable controversy as to whether there is such a thing as "stakeholder theory," if the term *theory* is interpreted solely in social scientific terms. They ask, Does stakeholder theory refer to some unique set of causal factors that theories of power, resource dependence, networks, and institutions do not encompass?

The interplay between these two camps serves as an intellectual backdrop against which good social scientific investigation of these interactions continues unabated. This section discusses the three main areas of investigation covered to date.

What Are the Effects of Stakeholder Management?

Building on the foundation laid by Freeman's (1984) book, one of the most popular subjects for study in the stakeholder research tradition has been the question of whether it matters (financially) how a company manages its stakeholder relationships. In other words, does stakeholder management actually correlate with widely valued outcomes such as profit or stock price?

In this realm, Jones's influential *Academy of Management Review* article from 1995 on instrumental stakeholder theory remains the central work. Jones argues there that the most important characteristic of a company's behavior toward its stakeholders is its moral quality, the presence or absence of dishonesty and/or opportunism. (It is worth noting, here, that this emphasis on morality as the distinguishing feature of good stakeholder management constitutes a departure from Freeman's original model of stakeholder management as largely concerning the procedures undertaken by the company.) Jones proceeds to argue that opportunism and dishonesty will tend to make stakeholders unhappy and lead to increased contracting costs, whereby stakeholders exact higher costs from the company up-front as a way of safeguarding against future opportunism. These costs translate into lower financial performance for the company. In contrast, companies that are honest and trustworthy in their dealings with stakeholders have more efficient contracting and achieve a competitive advantage. Jones then offers an extended list of specific practices (e.g., disproportionate executive compensation, poison pills, and greenmail) that qualify as opportunism and should, thus, correlate with lower financial performance.

A great deal of empirical research has been done to substantiate, either directly or indirectly, the claims of instrumental stakeholder theory. Much of this research has followed not from the theoretical claims of authors such as Freeman and Jones but from the corporate social responsibility literature that Freeman acknowledged as one of his intellectual antecedents.

Much research, of varying levels of scholarly rigor, has been conducted on the subject of the relationship between corporate social performance and financial performance. They address the rather simplistic question, Does "doing good" lead to "doing well"? Insofar as social responsibility can be taken as a rough proxy for stakeholder management, much research hints at the fact that stakeholder management can have some measurable effect on financial performance.

More persuasive, perhaps, is that genre of empirical research designed to test the specific theoretical propositions advanced by instrumental stakeholder theory. Berman's 1998 study of executive compensation, for example, suggests that companies with abnormally high levels of executive compensation do, indeed, underperform those that do not. Subsequent examinations of similar data also suggest that companies that attend to some important stakeholder issues (e.g., product safety and employee well-being) perform better than those that do not. But there is no evidence to suggest that this relationship occurs because the companies value stakeholders intrinsically; rather, it could occur because of the interaction between business strategy and the treatment of stakeholders.

Of course, it is worth noting that financial performance is not the only outcome variable of interest in stakeholder research. Broader questions of societal welfare may also arise from the ways that companies interact with their immediate stakeholders; however, these remain waters uncharted by stakeholder researchers.

What Are the Sources of Stakeholder Management?

A second interesting area for social science inquiry is the question of why companies adopt certain approaches to stakeholder management. Often branded "descriptive" stakeholder research, this research represents the least promising area of research for those interested in advancing convergent stakeholder theory and the most promising area for those seeking to study company-stakeholder interactions on their own terms. After all, to study how a company manages its stakeholders requires that theorists appeal not to "stakeholder theory" but to more established organization theories to account for a phenomenon (stakeholder management) that is interesting in its own right.

Two contributions to this genre stand out in particular; ironically, both were published in the same issue of the *Academy of Management Review* in 1997. Timothy Rowley's network theory–based account of stakeholder management posits that a company's approach to managing its stakeholders will depend, in no small part, on the company's structural position relative to its stakeholder set. Companies existing in dense networks of stakeholders or who are more central will behave different from those in less dense networks or who have less central positions. Rowley's efforts represent a groundbreaking attempt to conceive of the stakeholder set not as a traditional hub-and-spoke system evoked by simplistic readings of Freeman but rather as a web of interrelated groups tied both to the company and to each other. Yet, as network theoretical accounts of organizational phenomena grow more sophisticated, Rowley's effort seems only a simple first step in what must become a more elaborate model of company behavior.

Ronald Mitchell, Bradley Agle, and Donna Wood's article on stakeholder salience is the second important contribution to the descriptive genre. Mitchell, Agle, and Wood posit that stakeholders possess varying levels of three important characteristics—power, legitimacy, and urgency. Insofar as stakeholders possess more of each characteristic, they will be more salient in managers' thinking, receiving priority in decisions about how to allocate value. This model is a useful integration of important insights from various schools of organization theory (i.e., resource dependence, institutional theory, and social cognitive theories), and the ability to categorize stakeholders using these characteristics is a useful managerial heuristic. However, this account also raises stumbling blocks for those who would seek to build further stakeholder theory based on it. Subsequent researchers have (a) offered various interpretations (and misinterpretations) of the term urgency; (b) overlooked the article's emphasis on managerial perception (it is, after all, not how powerful and legitimate the stakeholder is but how powerful and legitimate managers perceive them to be that determines salience); and (c) ignored the extremely simplistic notion of salience, which serves as a vague proxy for the complexities inherent in classifying approaches to stakeholder management.

Indeed, these two contributions, though exemplary, offer two caveats to those who would understand why companies adopt certain approaches to stakeholder management. First, their appeal to existing schools of organization theory, though well-conceived, exposes the stakeholder research domain to the popular critique that stakeholder research has no theory of its own. Second, their emphasis on the causal factors involved (networks, stakeholder characteristics) rather than on the outcome (stakeholder management) does little to remedy the confusion (which must, by now, be apparent to the reader) surrounding how we conceive of stakeholder management. The practices cited by Freeman, the moral qualities of Jones, and the general orientations envisioned by Rowley, Mitchell, Agle, and Wood are all elements of a many-headed beast, and we have little reason to prefer one to the other, scattering the continued efforts of stakeholder researchers.

Why Do Stakeholder Groups Behave as They Do?

From a practical standpoint, a more interesting question for the manager is the issue of how to predict stakeholder behavior. This question forms the basis of the third and, at present, the most rapidly growing stream of stakeholder literature, asking "Why do stakeholder groups behave as they do?" Marshalling theories of collective action, resource dependence, game theory, and social identity, stakeholder researchers have explored this question in several steps, starting first with the question of why stakeholder groups mobilize and then advancing to the question of why, when they do mobilize, they choose the influence strategies that they do. A final step, as yet relatively unexplored, is what conditions determine whether or not these influence strategies actually succeed.

The question of stakeholder mobilization would, at first glance, seem simple enough. Stakeholders act when their interests are threatened. For many years, students of business and society argued some variant of this thesis, contending that stakeholder action resulted from some violation (real or perceived) of the stakeholder group's expectations. When they did not receive what they expected, they tended to strike, boycott, protest, or otherwise mobilize against the company. This was both an intuitive and, in many cases, entirely adequate explanation, but in many important cases, stakeholders mobilized around relatively small violations of their interests, and in many more instances, groups with clear interest did not mobilize or, at least, did not manage to do so in sufficient numbers to have much impact.

Efforts by Timothy Rowley and Mihnea Moldoveanu represent one attempt, premised on an identity-based account, to explain these phenomena. They argue that interests do play an important role in mobilization; so, too, does the collective identity of stakeholder group members. Groups (e.g., certain activist groups) that see protest as a fundamental piece of their group identity are more likely to mobilize. Moreover, structural conditions can strengthen or undermine a common sense of identity. People who are, for example, both parents and churchgoers may be much more likely to mobilize against television violence than those who occupy only one of those groups. Likewise, some groups will possess more or less of the resources necessary to overcome the considerable barriers to collective action for stakeholder groups. Here, again, previous experience with protest and overlapping identities play an important role. In sum, companies must attend to the constellation of interests and identity that surround them, lest they inaccurately assess the likelihood of stakeholder group mobilization.

A second important step in this stream of literature involves the study of why stakeholder groups, once mobilized, choose the strategies that they do to influence the company. Here, the work of Jeff Frooman, extending resource dependence theory to a stakeholder context, sheds some insight. Frooman maintains that a stakeholder's choice of influence strategy depends on just how dependent the stakeholder group is on the focal company for resources and on how dependent the company is on the stakeholder. Depending on how these conditions combine, stakeholders will choose to act either directly or indirectly and will choose either to coerce or compromise with the company. Subsequent empirical research on the subject suggests that there is much to these insights, though other institutional factors may be at play as well.

The final step in this area remains relatively unexplored: When do these influence strategies succeed or fail to change company policy? Here, as Rowley has argued in his earlier piece, a link can be forged back to the question of antecedents of stakeholder management, yet much work remains to make this connection explicit.

CONCLUSION

Stakeholder theory remains a high growth field of research in the study of business and society, with numerous articles and books being published each year. With students of business strategy and organization theory now showing renewed interest in studying this subject, this is likely to continue. This entry has only hinted at the complexities of this literature, yet it is hoped that it has shown important steps in our evolving understanding of the empirical and normative dimensions of company-stakeholder interaction.

—Michael E. Johnson-Cramer

STAKEHOLDER RESPONSIBILITY

The primary focus of stakeholder theory has been the proposition that firms have a moral responsibility to take into account the interests of stakeholders other than just stockholders. Given the focus on the corporation within organization studies, this emphasis in theorizing is understandable. The emphasis on corporate responsibility to stakeholders has not to date been balanced by a complementary focus on the responsibilities of stakeholders. Though some models within the stakeholder literature portray a two-way relationship between the firm and the stakeholder, writers predominantly argue that firms are responsible for taking into account stakeholder interests, without noting the reciprocal moral responsibility of stakeholders to consider the interests of the firm in their actions and policies. A focus on stakeholder responsibility compels theorists, corporations, and stakeholders to direct greater attention to the importance of the responsibilities stakeholders have to firms and to other stakeholders who are part of the collective enterprise.

CORPORATE RESPONSIBILITY AND STAKEHOLDER THEORY

With the emergence of stakeholder theory in the mid-1980s and its rapid growth up to the present time, numerous writers questioned the primacy of corporate responsibility to shareholders. Writers building the foundation of stakeholder theory argued for expanding the domain of corporate responsibility beyond shareholders to include a number of critical stakeholder groups.

Over time, the legitimacy of the stakeholder perspective has grown and has influenced the direction of work in business ethics, organization theory, and the strategic management literature. Stakeholder theorists have argued for managers to acknowledge the moral "stake" of stakeholders by paying attention to stakeholders and their interests for both prudential reasons (i.e., it is good for the firm and its profitability to listen to stakeholders) and normative reasons (i.e., they argue that there are compelling moral arguments for considering stakeholder interests).

CORPORATE AND STAKEHOLDER RESPONSIBILITY

As noted earlier, there has been a lack of attention to the fundamental question of whether stakeholders have moral responsibilities to firms. This is not to say that the topic of stakeholder responsibility has been completely ignored by business ethics writers. A series of articles and books were published in 2002 to 2003 that attempted to establish a conceptual foundation for stakeholder responsibility. This work emphasized the importance of stakeholders assuming responsibility for negative outcomes associated with actions directed to firms and other stakeholders and reinforced contemporary notions of responsibility in terms of accountability and responsiveness.

There are other ways of understanding responsibility in relation to stakeholders. Tracing the term back to its Latin roots (*respondere*), responsibility literally means to *pledge back*. In contrast to notions of responsibility that focus on an externally imposed obligation, this form emphasizes the idea of people and organizations choosing to pledge things to each other to foster cooperation and a better life for all. This definition of responsibility extends what it means to be a stakeholder beyond the traditional definition of stakeholders as individuals, groups, or organizations potentially affected by the actions and policies of an organization. Stakeholders are not only the recipients of organizational actions but actors as well with reciprocal responsibility for the implications of their actions in relation to firms and other stakeholders.

The idea of stakeholder responsibility draws its legitimacy from fundamental philosophical arguments. There are consequentialist arguments for both corporate and stakeholder responsibility that focus on whether a person, firm, or stakeholder can produce benefits or harms that are of importance to others. Writers have devoted primary attention to corporate responsibility particularly in light of their size and power and the potential significance of harms and benefits associated with corporate actions. From a stakeholder responsibility perspective, attention shifts to stakeholders, who are responsible for reciprocating benefits from firms and other stakeholders and addressing intended and unintended harms, particularly deriving from the role responsibilities of stakeholders and their ability to inflict harm on (or create benefit for) the firm and other key stakeholders. In the same way that responsible corporations must consider how specific actions and policies might harm stakeholders, especially those who are in highly dependent and potentially vulnerable positions, stakeholders bear reciprocal responsibilities as well for taking into account potential harms to firms and other stakeholders.

Beyond an emphasis on consequences, specifically responsibility for negative consequences, there are arguments for stakeholder responsibilities that rely on a deontological or rule-based approach to ethics, particularly those connected to justice and the ethics of interdependence. Notions of reciprocity and responsibility—for benefits and harms—are central to the literature on justice and fairness. The notion of reciprocity is a fundamental element of justice and fairness, and contemporary business ethics scholars have developed a "principle of fairness" to determine whether firms have responsibilities to stakeholders (Does the firm receive benefits from the stakeholder?) and to which stakeholders firms should give primary attention (How significant are the benefits received from a particular stakeholder?).

This literature provides a rich foundation for thinking about firm responsibility to stakeholders and can be extended to consider how firms benefit from their interactions with stakeholders. Employees, customers, suppliers, investors, and other stakeholders benefit in a variety of ways from their relationships with firms and each other. Employees gain in tangible (e.g., wages) and intangible ways (e.g., commitments) from their relationships with firms. Customers may come to appreciate the high-quality products a firm offers and value as well the service employees provide in purchasing these products. The receipt of these benefits from firms may generate responsibilities on the part of employees and customers to these firms (and other stakeholders). In drawing attention to the benefits stakeholders gain from specific relationships with firms and other stakeholders, considerations of fairness and reciprocity encourage stakeholders to recognize reciprocal responsibilities for helping others achieve these goals and interests.

In like manner, as agents of the firm, stakeholders have a responsibility to create benefits for the firm that further the firm's and stakeholders' mutual interests. There are strong signs that many firms understand and depend on such responsibility in their operations. For example, firms presuppose and depend on employees taking ownership of customer service and acting responsibly toward them. Many firms take steps to put into place supplier codes of conduct that establish responsibilities critical for suppliers to fulfill for these firms to achieve important goals and commitments to other stakeholders.

As more attention is directed to stakeholder responsibility, there will be opportunities to enrich the business ethics literature and create an understanding of business ethics that emphasizes both corporate and stakeholder responsibility.

—Jerry Goodstein and Andrew C. Wicks

Further Readings

Andriof, J., Waddock, S., Husted, B., & Rahman, S. (2002). *Unfolding stakeholder thinking* (Vol. 1). Sheffield, UK: Greenleaf.

Andriof, J., Waddock, S., Husted, B., & Rahman, S. (2003). *Unfolding stakeholder thinking* (Vol. 2). Sheffield, UK: Greenleaf.

Bowie, N. (1991). New directions in corporate social responsibility. *Business Horizons, July-August,* 56–65.

Jones, T. M., Wicks, A. C., & Freeman, R. E. (2002). Stakeholder theory: The state of the art. In N. E. Bowie (Ed.), *Blackwell guide to business ethics* (pp. 19–37). Malden, MA: Blackwell.

Phillips, R. A. (1997). Stakeholder theory and a principle of fairness. *Business Ethics Quarterly, 7*(1), 51–66.

PART III: Corporate Governance, Stakeholders, and Shareholders

SHAREHOLDER WEALTH MAXIMIZATION

The principle of shareholder wealth maximization (SWM) holds that a maximum return to shareholders is and ought to be the objective of all corporate activity. From a financial management perspective, this means maximizing the price of a firm's common stock. In pursuing this objective, managers consider the risk and timing associated with expected earnings per share to maximize the price of the firm's common stock. When this is properly executed, management will also have maximized the future stream of dividends and capital gains that accrue to its shareholders. The most defensible form of SWM looks to long-term rather than short-term maximization.

The maximization of shareholder wealth is described as the "monotonic" view of the purpose of the corporation and, therefore, of the responsibilities of its managers. It is monotonic because it focuses on the interests of a single group, the shareholders, to the exclusion of other groups that may be affected by the activities of the firm or that could benefit from the activities of the firm. It is for this reason that the principle of SWM is controversial. Economic, legal, and moral considerations have been used both to defend and criticize the view that the firm should be managed so as to maximize the interests of a single group, namely the shareholders.

THE JUSTIFICATION OF SWM

Historically, from a legal perspective, the corporation was regarded during the 19th century as an instrument of public policy with a social responsibility. These social concerns gave way to the idea of managing the firm for the shareholders' profits. Legal theorists began to regard stock ownership as no different from other forms of private property. The corporation was viewed as owned by its shareholders. This legal model is entirely consistent with SWM. The directors' role is to manage the property of the owners, that is, the shareholders. As stewards of the shareholders' interests, their sole responsibility must be to the shareholders, and promoting the interests of other groups would be a misuse of the property entrusted to them. Insofar as private property plays such a powerful role in the American ethos, the argument for SWM, based on the value ascribed to private ownership, has had profound appeal.

At the same time, property rights are viewed as the foundation of a capital-driven economic system, and the principle of SWM also makes sense from the perspective of economic efficiency. The shareholders, as the owners of the corporation, purchase stock because they are looking for financial return. In most cases, shareholders elect directors who then hire managers to run the company on a day-to-day basis. Since managers are supposed to be working in the interests of shareholders, it follows that they should follow policies that enhance shareholder value. Property rights are deemed essential to the workings of the system, and the resulting outcomes are at the same time beneficial to society. Profits are indicative of the fact that an organization has transformed a set of inputs into a productive output of goods or services that have a higher value than the original inputs. Thus, when SWM is properly pursued, the financial benefits are alleged to include the following: efficient, low-cost businesses that produce high-quality goods and services at the lowest possible prices; products and goods that consumers need and want, such as new technologies, new products, and new jobs; courteous service; adequate stocks of merchandise; and well-located establishments.

But one could underline that corporations often have a diversified class of investors with financial claims not only from shareholders but also bondholders and other debtholders. Why is it not more economically efficient to focus on this diversity of financial claimants? It is claimed that SWM remains a more economically efficient *modus operandi* because the maximization of shareholder value requires the initial satisfaction of the financial claims of other investors and interests to secure a profitable return. SWM is, therefore, not inconsistent with the satisfaction of the claims of other investors.

Moreover, defenders of the principle of SWM or shareholder primacy hold that it is not merely consistent with but that it also promotes the interests of all nonshareholders who have financial interests in the firm, such as bondholders and other secured and unsecured creditors. Shareholders are less risk averse than nonshareholders, whereas managing the firm on behalf of interests other than shareholders can lead to greater risk aversion. This will occur if the firm is managed in the interests of its fixed claimants. Fixed claimants, such as bondholders, refer to those financial interests to whom the firm has pledged a fixed rate of return or sum that cannot be varied regardless of the firm's financial success. In contrast, residual claimants are only guaranteed a return after all fixed financial claims have been satisfied, and the amount of the return, if any, will vary according to the financial success of the company. In this situation, bondholders, for example, base decisions on the bankruptcy risk on a firm's cash flows, not the firm's value-maximizing potential from free cash flows. The result may well be that the company fails to invest in new opportunities for growth, innovative products, and new technologies or markets, which in the long run may undermine the capacity to remain competitive. It is argued that shareholders have a greater incentive to induce firms to engage in activities that other claimants such as bondholders may regard as excessively risky. Shareholders, thus, push the managers of the corporation to operate at levels beyond those sufficient to satisfy the interests of fixed claimants. However, it is also true that it is the shareholders who bear the greater loss from excessive risk taking if the firm does badly because, in any case, other claimants have a guaranteed fixed rate of return. At the same time, it is argued that in maximizing shareholder wealth, managers seek to increase market share (insofar as this is compatible with long-term profits), which will increase the size of the pie that is available to all participants in the corporate enterprise. In this way, the success of the company will offer greater security for fixed claimants by ensuring that the firm is in a better position to cover possible future losses and thereby maintain its commitments to its fixed claimants.

Defenders of SWM also argue that attempting to maximize in more than one dimension at the same time may well be impossible unless the multiplicity of objectives can be reduced to an overall monotonic purpose. The resulting loss of direction from pursuing multiple objectives can mean an equally fatal loss of competitiveness. Moreover, managing the firm for a variety of interests including fixed and residual claimants means a diversity of goals in which overall performance cannot be accurately assessed. In contrast, the principle of shareholder value offers an unambiguous standard, which is measurable and observable.

THE CONTRACTARIAN LEGAL MODEL AND SWM

The earlier legal view of the corporation as a form of property that is subject to ownership rights has given way to a contractarian model, which sees the corporation as a nexus of contracts. This alternative model envisions the corporation as offering an umbrella that allows private parties to contract with one another more efficiently than they could in a market by limiting the transaction costs. This view avoids the ontological issues that result when one regards the corporation as a thing that could possibly be owned. In any case, regarding the corporation and its assets as being owned by the shareholders is highly misleading insofar as shareholders usually have no right to manage these assets or unlimited access to information and records relating to these assets. The corporation is, therefore, more accurately viewed as a device that operates as a nexus for all contracts that various individuals have voluntarily entered into for mutual benefit. Although, theoretically, the activities of the corporation could be carried out by individuals through individual contract in a market outside the corporate structure, the costs associated with enlisting cooperation would be significant. As R. H. Coase argued in 1937, the law in effect offers a standardized form of contract or a set of default rules that facilitate private ordering. This legal entity, which is actually a legal fiction, allows those with money and resources to contract with those who have managerial skills but little money to forge a mutually advantageous cooperative enterprise. Moreover, those with labor to sell but lacking monetary resources or managerial skills can negotiate with the managers acting as agents of the corporation to form employment contracts.

However, according to contractarians, interpreting the corporation as a nexus of contracts rather than a form of property that is owned does not invalidate the principle of SWM. The contractarian perspective describes the corporation as being composed of explicit and implicit contracts held by shareholders and nonshareholders. The interests of nonshareholders, such as employees, suppliers, bondholders, communities, and customers, are protected by contract, law, and regulation. Shareholders are said to be entitled to the firm's residual cash flow. However, the management's obligation to realize and promote this residual cash flow is open-ended because there are no sets of specified actions that can be enforced to realize this objective. In other words, management has a legal obligation to create a healthy residual cash flow, but there are no terms that specify particular actions for achieving this goal. But to give greater definition to the relationship that embodies this particular understanding, the legal system creates a fiduciary duty to maximize shareholder wealth. This fiduciary duty fills the gaps that arise in terms of management's unspecified or imperfect obligations to maximize shareholder wealth.

Moreover, agency theory supplements the contractarian position and adds weight to the view that the purpose of the firm is the maximization of shareholder wealth. Agency problems arise because contracts are not "costlessly" written and enforced. Agency costs include the costs of structuring, monitoring, and bonding a set of contracts among agents with conflicting interests, plus the residual loss incurred when the cost of full enforcement of contracts exceeds the benefits. It is argued that the necessity of a corporate structure in which ownership and control are separated entails that only the residual claimants can provide appropriate monitoring. It follows that the agency costs inherent in a team organization, such as the firm, are controlled, and maximization of output occurs when control rights are assigned to the residual claimants.

We have considered the economic and legal rationales that justify SWM. We will now proceed to consider a normative critique of SWM.

ETHICAL AND LEGAL IMPLICATIONS OF CONTRACTARIAN AND COMMUNITARIAN THEORY

The nexus of contracts view of the corporation also has an underlying ideological basis that embodies a particular moral perspective. We have discussed the view of the corporation as an economic and financial arrangement with an objective of SWM. However, we have not considered whether this particular governance relationship is and ought to be a product of individual choice. Those who advocate SWM argue that we should leave it up to the various participants in corporate activity to specify respective rights and obligations through contract, rather than legally imposing relationships. According to this view, shareholders bargain and secure from management a commitment to a fiduciary duty to direct the corporations so as to maximize shareholder wealth. This is an open-ended responsibility because it is not realistically possible to specify in detail what exactly is to be done to fulfill this fiduciary duty. On the other hand, other participants in the corporate enterprise contract with the agents of the corporation for more specific rights in return for the particular services provided. Accordingly, nonshareholders are free to protect themselves through contracts by bargaining for whatever protections they deem necessary to protect interests that may be threatened by the pursuit of SWM. For example, workers could bargain for protections against a policy of employment at will or seek other legal protections.

The communitarian view stands in contrast to this contractarian position. While contractarians advocate that the law should play a minimal role in structuring relationships, communitarians argue that the law must intervene to prevent harmful externalities that may result from the single-minded promotion of SWM. For example, factories may be closed down and workers laid off to protect profits, but at the same time, this may significantly damage the local community, which depends on this income and indeed may have invested in infrastructure that supports the corporate enterprise. Communities may find it difficult to foresee such events and contract to protect their interests from uncompensated losses. At the same time, public goods that are often essential to the communities in which corporations operate are difficult to secure through the market.

An important difference between the communitarian and contractarian positions is their focus. Communitarians tend to highlight the undeniable social effects of corporate activity, seeing corporations as institutions that have a profound effect on those who are outside the corporation. Accordingly, it is appropriate that the state intervene to enhance the social environment and minimize the deleterious effects of market activity. On the other hand, contractarians focus on the internal relationships. They see the corporation as an organization constituted by private contracts that have been voluntarily entered into. This difference in emphasis sheds light on the important ideological differences that also manifest contrasting and opposing moral values.

Contractarians see society as constituted by autonomous citizens who ought to be free to make the choices that shape their destiny without intervention from outside authority, so long as they are not actively harming other individuals. Governments should not dictate matters involving the type of agreements we make, our individual economic behavior, or the redistribution of wealth. Contractual arrangements are a way in which we express this autonomy and freedom. The latter, they claim, form an important foundational value for our social existence. Communitarians, in contrast, emphasize social interdependence and the fact that individual persons and corporate persons derive many benefits from life in society that have no contractual basis. On this rationale, it is appropriate that the state intervenes to structure relationships that reflect this interdependence and protects constituencies such as workers and the local community from the deleterious effects of unregulated SWM. Although contractarians claim that nonshareholders can always enter into contractual relations to protect their interests from harmful externalities, communitarians point out that unequal distribution of wealth produces inequality of bargaining power. In many cases, nonshareholders lack the resources to bargain and negotiate effectively to protect their interests. In reality, nonshareholder protection from the externalities of SWM depends on people's capability and willingness to pay for contractual guarantees. Communitarians argue that it is unrealistic to believe that unskilled workers have the resources to buy layoff protection from the shareholders or their agents. Ultimately, the existence of contractual relations alone does not ensure that arrangements are fair to all parties or even reflect the individual contributions that are made to the greater social body.

STAKEHOLDER THEORY

Many who see a moral dimension to business activities that extends beyond mere contractual obligations and the single-minded pursuit of making money for shareholders propose a stakeholder approach to business activities. Stakeholder theory emphasizes that managers are also moral agents who are responsible to a wide array of groups for their actions. Much of the groundbreaking work is associated with R. Edward Freeman. A stakeholder is broadly defined as any individual or group who can affect or is affected by the achievement of the organization's objectives. If one fails to recognize these responsibilities to other groups, it becomes easy to rationalize a questionable practice that potentially harms nonshareholder stakeholders, such as workers or suppliers, to whom managers supposedly have no moral obligation, in order to realize increased profitability.

The stakeholder theory of corporate responsibility is a developing response to the view that a firm should be run in such a way as to maximize the wealth of the shareholders.

The stakeholder approach argues that it is not only those with a financial claim on the institution who are worthy of consideration, but that there is a multiplicity of groups with a stake in the operations of the firm, all of whom merit consideration in managerial decision making. The word "stakeholder" first appeared in usage in 1963 in an internal memorandum of the Stanford Research Institute and has since become a prominent concept in corporate and academic communities. The theory, which is clearly designed to extend the ethical responsibility of the firm, is an alternative to the monotonic fiduciary model offered by the property rights and contractual approaches. According to stakeholder theory, a person who holds a stake in the activities of an organization, a "stakeholder," is entitled to consideration in some ways similar to shareholders.

Stakeholder theory has also apparently been reflected in changes to the law, especially in the United States. In the 1990s, many jurisdictions in the United States passed so-called "other constituencies legislation" and determined that the directors should consider not only the profit margin in their decisions but also the interests of the employees and the general public. These statutes have been enacted by at least 25 U.S. states. The typical nonshareholder constituency statute authorizes (but does not require) a director of a corporation, in considering its best interests, to consider the interests of persons (often referred to as stakeholders) other than shareholders and frequently also consider generalized factors such as local and national economies, societal factors, and any other factors deemed by the directors to be pertinent. The various nonshareholder constituencies may be seen to include employees, customers, creditors, suppliers, and communities in whom the corporation has facilities. However, whereas some have hailed "other constituencies legislation" as rejecting shareholder primacy, many are far more cautious. It has been pointed out that there is little meaningful case law relating to these statutes and so they still stand in need of interpretation. The American Bar Association's Committee on Corporate Law recommends that constituency statutes be interpreted according to the relatively recent Delaware precedent. This precedent states that courts should not allow consideration of nonshareholder interests without relating such considerations in an appropriate fashion to shareholder welfare. Moreover, constituency statutes apply only to a narrow range of decisions, which essentially involve change of control, that is, takeovers. This means that the range of situations in which boards have the right to consider other constituencies is rather limited. It can therefore be argued that these statutes are really not proshareholder but in fact are designed to entrench management.

Again, many of the arguments used to support SWM can be used to reject the stakeholder model of corporate responsibility. As we pointed out earlier, defenders of SWM would argue that adopting strategies in accordance with the stakeholder view, which means acknowledging the interests of multiple constituencies in addition to fixed and residual financial claimants, may well result in increased indecision and confusion. Satisfying a diversity of interests may well be impossible unless the multiplicity of objectives can be reduced to an overall monotonic purpose. Loss of competitiveness may well follow. As said before, it is not easy to manage on behalf of multiple constituencies when their goals come into conflict, and it may not be socially desirable to give managers unlimited liberty to make choices between competing interests. In contrast, the principle of shareholder value offers an unambiguous standard, which is measurable and observable.

Finally, if the law intervenes and seeks to enforce the stakeholder model, for example, by requiring that investors take on increased liabilities with respect to employees, forgoing employment at will or giving the employees the right to buy the business at less than market value, any benefit to employees might well be short-lived. Investors cannot be compelled to supply capital to the corporation. Shareholders may demand a higher price for capital and thus increase the firms' cost of capital with damaging financial consequences for nonshareholder constituencies. On the other hand, investors may simply look to other forms of investment if the monotonic principle is abandoned and shareholder interests are compromised, resulting in insufficient monetary returns. Alternatively, potential shareholders could invest in real estate, gold, Treasury bonds, or shares in overseas Japanese corporations, to mention a few examples.

Those who disagree with these points and promote the stakeholder model argue that emphasizing the principle of SWM fails to appreciate entrepreneurial risk in the wider, richer context of joint stakeholder relationships. In addition, emphasizing a single responsibility to make money for shareholders fosters a myopic worldview in which managers fail to see themselves as moral agents who are responsible to a wide variety of groups for their actions. In the long run, this monotonic approach may well work to the disadvantage of the shareholder's interests. However, defenders of shareholder value maximization argue that their position does not encompass the exploitation or alienation of the firm's other constituencies. Strategies that do not take into account the morally acceptable relationships with other stakeholders, including effects on the local community, are incompatible with long-term shareholder value creation. In this manner, SWM can be interpreted as an inclusive principle that does not deny that these other interests exist and must be acknowledged in the decision-making process. Ultimately, both those who advocate shareholder value and those who advocate the multifiduciary stakeholder approach can make reasonable claims that their preferred approach enhances the interests of all related constituencies. One concludes that the monotonic and pluralistic approaches only become clearly distinguishable in those cases in which managers of a firm, following ethical principles, decide to benefit a particular nonshareholder group in circumstances that negatively affect both short-term and long-term shareholder wealth creation.

—David Riordon Lea

Further Readings

Alchian, A. A., & Demsetz, H. (1972). Production, information costs, and economic organization. *American Economic Review, 62,* 777–795.

Ambler, T., & Wilson, A. (1995). Problems of stakeholder theory. *Business Ethics: A European Review, 4*(1), 30–35.

Berle, A. A., & Means, G. C. (1932). *The modern corporation and private property.* New York: Macmillan.

Coase, R. H. (1937). The nature of the firm. *Economica, 4,* 386–405.

Donaldson, T., & Dunfee, T. W. (1999). *Ties that bind: A social contracts approach to business ethics.* Cambridge, MA: Harvard Business School Press.

Evan, W. M., & Freeman, R. E. (1993). A stakeholder theory of the modern corporation: Kantian capitalism. In T. Beauchamp & N. Bowie (Eds.), *Ethical theory and business* (4th ed.). Englewood Cliffs, NJ: Prentice Hall.

Freeman, R. E. (1984). *Strategic management: A stakeholder approach.* Boston: Pitman.

Freeman, R. E., Wicks, A. C., & Parmar, B. (2004). Stakeholder theory and the corporate objective revisited. *Organization Science, 15*(3), 364–369.

Friedman, M. (1970, September 13). The social responsibility of business is to increase its profits. *New York Times Magazine,* p. 32.

Fama, E. F., & Jensen, M. C. (1983). Agency problems and residual claims. *Journal of Law and Economics, 26*(2), 327–349.

Jensen, M. C., & Meckling, W. H. (1976). Theory of the firm: Managerial behaviour, agency costs and ownership structure. *Journal of Financial Economics, 3,* 303–360.

Lea, D. R. (2004). The imperfect nature of corporate responsibilities to stakeholders. *Business Ethics Quarterly, 14*(2), 201–218.

Maitland, I. (2001). Distributive justice in firms: Do the rules of corporate governance matter? *Business Ethics Quarterly, 11*(1), 129–145.

Millon, D. (1993). Communitarians, contractarians and the crisis in corporate law. *Washington and Lee Law Review, 50*(4), 1373–1380.

Millon, D. (1995). Communitarianism in corporate law: Foundations and law reform strategies. In L. E. Mitchell (Ed.), *Progressive corporate law.* Boulder, CO: Westview Press.

Nesteruk, J. (1995). Law and the virtues: A review article. *Business Ethics Quarterly, 5*(2), 361–369.

Smith, G. D. (1998). The shareholder primacy norm. *Journal of Corporate Law, 23,* 277–283.

Smith, T. A. (1999). The efficient norm of corporate law: A neotraditional interpretation of fiduciary duty. *Michigan Law Review, 98*(1), 214–268.

Sundaram, A. K., & Inkpen, A. C. (2004). The corporate objective revisited. *Organization Science, 15*(3), 350–363.

BERLE-DODD DEBATE

The Berle-Dodd debate of the early 1930s, between specialists in corporation law, was the opening exchange in the still-raging controversy about shareholder versus stakeholder views of the firm. This controversy concerns the primary purpose of the publicly owned corporation. Adolf A. Berle Jr. proposed that public policy should define a strict fiduciary duty for management. E. M. Dodd Jr. replied in favor of public policy safeguarding multiconstituency and community responsibilities. Dodd may be regarded as a forerunner of stakeholder and corporate social responsibility theories. The debate itself had an important impact on the U.S. securities acts of 1933 and 1934.

THE DEBATE

The debate originated in the perceived problem of separation of investor ownership and management control. Adolph Berle and Gardiner C. Means, then an economics doctoral student at Columbia University, where Berle taught, argued this thesis in *The Modern Corporation and Private Property*. Separation effectively destroyed the traditional property rights basis for shareholder control of business decisions. The shareholder had become purely a "rentier." Berle's proposed solution was for public policy to define a strictly fiduciary duty for management. Berle's article drew on the established legal doctrine of trusts to argue that the manager should be strictly a trustee for assets owned by investors.

Dodd replied that the business corporation had in addition a vital social service function. Dodd made three points. He drew a distinction between the equity (i.e., money) capital of investors and the "capital" of other constituencies defined in terms of their cares and concerns invested in the firm. Dodd argued that the common law had earlier treated business as a public profession; this view had subsequently been limited to businesses deemed to have some public interest. The 19th century was a judicial reversal of the previous common-law tradition. Dodd argued a case for public policy explicitly strengthening customers' and employees' rights. Dodd basically agreed with

145

Berle that managers could not be trusted with discretion concerning multiple responsibilities.

Berle responded in a rejoinder that Dodd's position was an expression of theoretical rather than practical principles. Berle's concern was that weakening of a strict fiduciary duty for managers would prove dangerous in practice. Berle conceded that Dodd had won the debate (at least temporarily) in the sense that social fact and judicial decisions had over time come to support Dodd's general viewpoint against strict fiduciary duty.

HISTORICAL BACKGROUND OF THE DEBATE

This debate between two legal experts had roots in the development of corporation law. In the United States, a corporation exists artificially and only in contemplation of the law, according to Chief Justice John Marshall in the 1819 U.S. Supreme Court case *The Trustees of Dartmouth College v. Woodward.* The Michigan Supreme Court addressed the basic elements of the Berle-Dodd debate in 1919 in the case of *Dodge v. Ford Motor Co.* Henry Ford had paid a double dividend for some years (i.e., a regular dividend and a special dividend). He announced his intention not to continue the special dividend in order to reduce prices to customers and increase wages to employees. The Dodge brothers filed suit in state court for continuation of the special dividend. The Michigan Supreme Court ruled that the primary purpose of the investor corporation was investor wealth and supported continuation of the special dividend. The opinion also articulated the business judgment rule, holding that managers and directors are not expected to have perfect judgment but only to exercise business acumen reasonably for the goal of profit seeking. Ford did not use a line of defense that arguably might have proven successful. He could have argued that reducing prices and increasing compensation was a reasonable strategy under the business judgment rule for increasing sales and labor productivity.

In the 1883 case of *Hutton v. West Cork Railway Co.,* Lord Justice Bowen considered whether a company could properly provide gratuities to employees. He concluded that liberal dealing with employees could ease friction and thus benefit the company. This opinion accords with Dodd's view that, in the long run, management consideration of employee welfare would increase shareholder profits.

EFFECT ON SECURITIES LEGISLATION

The Berle-Dodd debate had important impacts on the content of the U.S. securities acts of 1933 and 1934. Berle had significant influence on the drafting of the legislation. Because shareholders did not control management, control must rest on full disclosure of information. Disclosure follows from either Berle's view of the separation of ownership and control or Dodd's view of constituency and social responsibilities. Such disclosure and transparency remain the fundamental philosophy of the securities acts.

MODERN CONCERN WITH THE DEBATE

The modern version of Berle's thesis was famously stated by the Nobel Prize–winning economist Milton Friedman. He explicitly characterized discretionary corporate social responsibility by managers as theft from the primary stakeholders (customers, employees, and investors alike). In addition to invoking a primitive stakeholder model of the firm, Friedman also noted an irreducible role for customary ethics as well as for public policy. He admitted that companies might need to engage in prudential altruism to forestall even more burdensome public policy developments. In contrast to Friedman, subsequent authors have tended to omit ethics and reduce limitation on managerial conduct strictly to law. The formal version of this line of reasoning is principal-agent theory. Any managerial behavior other than maximizing shareholders' wealth, up to the limits imposed by law, arguably reduces social wealth due to increased agency costs.

The debate continues to this day. Justice Bowen's line of reasoning was rejected decades later in the 1962 case *Parke v. Daily News Ltd* on the basis that enlightened industrial relations do not meet the standard of short-term profit calculation. This opinion accords with Berle's and Friedman's concerns that it is not practical or wise to deviate from strict fiduciary duty. The two U.K. decisions noted above simply place business strategy and company law in plain conflict. There may be no strong empirical evidence of any definite relationship among corporate social responsibility, stakeholder management, and profitability.

U.S. corporate governance law, enacted at the state rather than the federal level, is bifurcated. Some 29 states have adopted corporate constituency statutes that permit or require director attention to the interests of one or more stakeholders other than investors. Available evidence suggests that these statutes

Berle-Dodd Debate

effectively do nothing to increase stakeholder influence or interests; rather, they simply increase managerial discretion at the expense of shareholder control for no tangible gain by other stakeholders. The evidence tends to support Berle's contention. It has been argued that managers can handle only one objective at a time, so that objectives must be ordered hierarchically—meaning wealth seeking primacy (within the law) and stakeholder considerations being secondary. A strategic view suggests, however, that managers would be well advised to practice enlightened stakeholder management: Since employee sentiments can affect employee morale and hence productivity, consideration must be given to those sentiments.

The general case for constituency or stakeholder attention rests on the experiences of European and Japanese industrial relations in contrast to the U.K.-U.S. legal doctrine. German industrial democracy, in effect since 1920, includes dual boards (a supervisory board including employee representatives appoints the management board) and works councils at establishments. Japanese business operated after World War II on the basis of management–labor cooperation. Both Germany and Japan, as examples of employee-oriented industrial relations (they may or may not be beneficial to consumers in the long run), reflect a scheme of industrial conflict management. It is difficult to see that these approaches are truly multiple-constituency models—everything depends on whether one believes that the approaches are in the long run in the public interest. European unemployment is structurally much higher than U.S. unemployment (reflecting more flexible labor markets and higher economic growth rates), and while Japanese unemployment is considerably lower, there is some evidence that it has risen and that lifetime employment practices are deteriorating. Evidence suggests that stakeholder management practices in Europe are measurably costly.

During the 1980s and 1990s, U.S. corporations—following the lead of General Electric (Jack Welch, CEO), for example—pioneered in shareholder value maximization (or wealth seeking) practices. The long success story (until tarnished by the dot.com bubble burst and recent corporate scandals) seemed to indict stakeholder or multiple-constituency theory. The Dey Report from Toronto in 1994, the Hampel Report from London in 1998, and the Peters Report from Amsterdam in 1997, issued by stock exchanges, all attempted to increase the weight of shareholder orientation without reducing the existing weight of stakeholder orientation.

Critics of stakeholder theory have returned to Berle as a touchstone—arguing why Dodd was wrong despite Berle's tentative concession. The general lines of argument run as follows: (1) investors have property rights that should not be reduced; (2) U.K.-U.S. corporate governance law should emphasize shareholder primacy; and (3) efficient, competitive markets generate social wealth without the need for governmental regulation or discretionary corporate social responsibility.

This reasoning tends to ignore the Berle and Means separation thesis. Principal-agency theory suggests imperfect control by investors and substantial discretion for managers. It is more likely that directors and executives emphasize corporate wealth, defined as corporate assets under discretionary managerial control rather than shareholder primacy. The latter remains a legal and economic ideal, if not a fiction, rather than the functioning reality.

BIOGRAPHICAL INFORMATION ON BERLE AND DODD

Both Berle and Dodd were Harvard graduates, lawyers, and ultimately university professors. Dodd spent most of his career at Harvard, while Berle went into government service and returned to Columbia after World War II. Both Berle and Dodd practiced and taught in the field of corporation law.

Adolf Augustus Berle Jr. (1895–1971), born in Massachusetts, graduated from Harvard College and then Harvard Law School. His parents were active in the Social Gospel approach to progressive reform and politically connected. He first worked in the Boston law firm of liberal Justice Louis D. Brandeis. Later, he provided legal services for the Henry Street Settlement House on Manhattan's Lower East Side. He formed his own law and Wall Street firms with specialization in corporation law. He commuted from New York to teach at the Harvard Business School. Resigning from the American delegation to the Paris Peace Conference in protest against the terms of the Versailles Treaty, Berle returned to practice law in New York City and, in 1927, began teaching "law of corporation finance" at Columbia, where he met Means. Berle became a member of Franklin D. Roosevelt's (FDR's) New Deal "brain trust" and an adviser to New York City Mayor Fiorella La Guardia. As assistant secretary of state for Latin American affairs (1938–1944), Berle was spokesman for FDR's Good Neighbor Policy. During World War II, he was the head of State Department intelligence activities. After serving (1945–1946) as ambassador to Brazil, when the Vargas dictatorship was toppled, he resumed his professorship at Columbia and was a founder and chairman (1952–1955) of the Liberal party. In 1951, he became chairman of the board of trustees of the Twentieth Century Fund. During the Kennedy administration, Berle chaired a task force on Latin America that originated the Alliance for Progress.

Berle-Dodd Debate

Edwin Merrick Dodd Jr. (1888–1951), born in Rhode Island, also graduated from Harvard College and then Harvard Law School, several years ahead of Berle. He practiced law in Boston and then joined the Washington and Lee School of Law for 1 year, resigning to join the War Industries Board. After World War I, Dodd returned to legal practice in Boston and then in 1922, to teaching and scholarship on the law faculties successively of Nebraska, Chicago, and from 1928, Harvard. He died untimely in an automobile accident.

—Duane Windsor

Further Readings

Berle, A. A., Jr. (1931). Corporate powers as powers in trust. *Harvard Law Review, 44,* 1049–1074.

Berle, A. A., Jr. (1932). For whom corporate managers are trustees: A note. *Harvard Law Review, 45,* 1365–1372.

Berle, A. A., Jr. (1960). Foreword. In E. Mason (Ed.), *The corporation in modern society.* Cambridge, MA: Harvard University Press.

Berle, A. A., & Means, G. C. (1932). *The modern corporation and private property.* Chicago: Commerce Clearing House.

Dodd, E. M. (1932). For whom are corporate managers trustees? *Harvard Law Review, 45,* 1145–1163.

Dodd, E. M. (1935). Is effective enforcement of the fiduciary duties of corporate managers practicable? *University of Chicago Law Review, 2,* 194–207.

Macintosh, J. C. C. (1999). The issues, effects and consequences of the Berle-Dodd debate, 1931–1932. *Accounting, Organizations and Society, 24,* 139–153.

Nunan, R. (1988). The libertarian conception of corporate property: A critique of Milton Friedman's views on the social responsibility of business. *Journal of Business Ethics, 7,* 891–906.

Reynolds, A. (2001). Do ESOPs strengthen employee stakeholder interests? *Bond Law Review, 13,* 95–108.

Schwarz, J. A. (2000, February). Berle, Adolf Augustus. *American National Biography Online.* Retrieved from www.anb.org/articles/07/07–00357.html

Sommer, A. A., Jr. (1991). Whom should the corporation serve? The Berle-Dodd debate revisited sixty years later. *Delaware Journal of Corporate Law, 16,* 33–56.

Washington and Lee University School of Law. (n.d.). *Edwin Merrick Dodd (1888–1951).* Retrieved from http://law.wlu.edu/faculty/history/dodd-em.asp

Weiner, J. L. (1964). The Berle-Dodd dialogue on the concept of the corporation. *Columbia Law Review, 64,* 1458–1467.

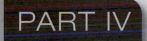

PART IV

Corporate Social Responsiveness: Public Affairs and Public Relations, Politics, and Philanthropy

CORPORATE SOCIAL RESPONSIVENESS

Corporate social responsiveness refers to how business organizations and their agents actively interact with and manage their environments. In contrast, corporate social responsibility accentuates the moral obligations that business has to society. Responsiveness and responsibility can be viewed on a means-end continuum in that responsiveness can be shaped or triggered by public expectations of business responsibilities. Generally speaking, these responsibilities are implied by the terms of the social contract, which legitimizes business as an institution with the expectation that it serve the greater good by generating commerce while adhering to society's laws and ethical norms. From this perspective, corporations are in a dynamic relationship with society of which responsiveness is key.

Corporations actively interact with and manage their environments through various programs, policies, and procedures, which are formulated by top managers and carried out by other employees. Ideally, these processes of responsiveness are informed by long-term strategic planning, which starts with an assessment of the firm's external environment from which information about its constituents or stakeholders can be gleaned. To illustrate, this kind of assessment might reveal a trend that society has increased expectations that firms will enhance the quality of life in communities. A more fine-tuned analysis would identify the stakeholders who hold this expectation and the issues of importance to them. This information might prompt a bank to make a commitment to invest in community development projects aligned with the goals of local residents and aimed at generating goodwill befitting public expectations of corporate citizenship. In terms of strategic management, these projects would necessarily reflect the bank's formal policy toward community development carried out by employees in departmental programs guided by specific procedures, such as the criteria for approving loan applications. In this way, an awareness of environmental factors can prompt concrete changes in corporate responsiveness or the ways firms interact with and manage their social relationships.

While responsiveness ideally results from long-term strategic planning, it can also take the form of a more immediate reaction to a crisis. Whether a crisis results from an oil spill, product tampering, or another unexpected event, the conventional wisdom is that corporations should develop the capacity to anticipate emergencies and respond swiftly to the needs of adversely affected stakeholders. The case of the Johnson & Johnson Tylenol poisonings has become a classic study of swift crisis responsiveness. In 1982, seven people died after cyanide was added to Tylenol capsules while they were on store shelves, prompting Johnson & Johnson, the maker of the product, to incur hefty expenses by voluntarily recalling and destroying remaining capsules. During this process, James Burke, the chief executive officer, made aggressive use of the media to apprise consumers of the steps that were being taken to address the crises. Shortly thereafter, Johnson & Johnson introduced tamper-resistant packaging as a preventative measure, demonstrating that crisis management involves not only swift responses and effective communication with stakeholders but also organizational learning.

Corporate social responsiveness is defined not only by a firm's policies, programs, and procedures but also by a firm's overall stance toward the environment. A constructive attitude is evident when corporate agents try proactively to anticipate stakeholder concerns and accommodate them whenever possible. That is, corporate managers can direct their firms to learn about the environment in which they operate and be attuned to it. In contrast, firms may exhibit a reactive or defensive posture toward stakeholders or may even neglect social issues altogether. Such attitude is apt to invite unwelcome criticism, unfavorable media coverage, stakeholder pressure tactics such as protests and consumer boycotts, and government intervention and oversight. In the first case, firms seeking to be attuned to stakeholder interests are fulfilling the spirit of the contract between business and society. In the second case of corporate neglect, this implicit contract is violated.

It can be seen that corporate responsiveness is not value neutral, especially since corporate actions impact society in beneficial and harmful ways. For example, benefits to society can accrue when corporations respond to the need for innovative products with research and development that leads to an enhanced quality of life for consumers. On the other hand, harmful impacts can result when corporations neglect their responsibilities, as when they fail to clean up the pollution traceable to their production facilities. The extent to which society encourages benefits and tolerates harms is reflected in the standards embodied in the law, public policy, and government regulation. In this context, business managers and public policy makers can assess or audit the impacts of corporate activity and attempt to direct firms to respond affirmatively to public expectations of responsibility. A cautionary note is that businesses are increasingly exerting influence on the government by political advocacy, which includes lobbying policy makers and contributing financially to their election campaigns. As a result, the link between responsiveness and responsibility is compromised to the extent that this influence results in legislation that favors business interests at the expense of the greater good. Under the terms of the social contract, corporate social responsiveness does not equate to corporations responding to their own rules.

Corporate social responsiveness, corporate social responsibility, and corporate social impacts are encapsulated in the phrase *corporate social performance*. Of these three concepts, responsiveness is the most forward looking, action-oriented, and malleable, since it is based on the precept that corporations have the capacity to anticipate and adapt to environmental factors. The potential is that corporate managers can learn to prevent or minimize the kind of unwelcome surprises that necessitate crisis management and government intervention while responding proactively to public expectations of how business can serve the greater good.

—Diane L. Swanson

Further Readings

Carroll, A. B. (1979). A three-dimensional model of corporate social performance. *Academy of Management Review, 4*, 497–505.

Frederick, W. C. (1987). Theories of corporate social performance. In S. P. Sethi & C. Falbe (Eds.), *Business and society: Dimensions of conflict and cooperation* (pp. 142–161). New York: Lexington Books.

Swanson, D. L. (1995). Addressing a theoretical problem by reorienting the corporate social performance model. *Academy of Management Review, 20*, 43–64.

Swanson, D. L. (1999). Toward an integrative theory of business and society: A research strategy for corporate social performance. *Academy of Management Review, 24*, 506–521.

Wartick, S. L., & Cochran, P. L. (1985). The evolution of the corporate social performance model. *Academy of Management Review, 10*, 758–769.

Wood, D. J. (1991). Corporate social performance revisited. *Academy of Management Review, 16*, 691–718.

CORPORATE PUBLIC AFFAIRS

Corporate public affairs is that arm of the organization that deals with interactions of the organization in the nonmarketplace arena of action. The external environment in which organizations operate today is becoming increasingly intrusive and active in attempts to influence and shape organizational actions and decisions. Public affairs is the center of the organization's actions to anticipate, plan, and respond in a thoughtful and articulated manner to issues, problems, and situations. These problems/situations can arise as a result of corporate and industry action or inaction, regulatory proposals, legislative actions, media and special interest actions, and so on. This can involve then dealing with regulatory agencies at all levels, with governmental bodies of all kinds and types, with the media, with the general public, and with nongovernmental entities either individually or simultaneously. This nonmarketplace arena is often referred to as the marketplace of ideas (as opposed to the marketplace for goods and services). Both for-profit and not-for-profit organizations have public affairs departments. The existence of these departments recognizes the critical role the marketplace of ideas plays in setting the rules and regulations under which competition is conducted and the costs that actions in this arena can impose on organizations. In addition, organizations have now recognized that their legitimacy as a societal actor is related to how they are perceived by society and government.

THE DEVELOPMENT OF PUBLIC AFFAIRS

Modern-day public affairs activities and organization can trace its roots back to three streams of development starting in the 1920s. These three areas—corporate philanthropy, urban and community affairs, and public relations—each contained elements of what was to emerge as today's public affairs department. Corporate philanthropy (financial contributions to not-for-profit and other socially oriented organizations) arose out of stormy relationships between and among businesses, governments, and society. In many ways the interest in philanthropy arose out of prior corporate excesses and this was the response to those poor behaviors. Although this was meant to demonstrate "corporate" charity, it too has become embroiled in controversy (most notably in charges by shareholders that this is not what they want done with their monies and by external groups who today see this as a skeptical and cynical approach to influence external actors to the corporation).

As urbanization occurred worldwide, with ever more numerous cities of ever larger size, unique problems arose (racial strife and tensions, slums, education, etc.), and the focus of organizations shifted to what was termed urban affairs. Although this could also be considered philanthropy, it was not focused solely on giving of funds for broad general purposes but the giving of funds, talents, and organizing skills to improve urban life. It should be noted that both corporate philanthropy and urban affairs activities were often pursued for self-interest motives by the organizations involved.

The final "root" of public affairs lies in public relations as corporate philanthropy and urban affairs were not sufficiently broad enough in focus for the organization and the increasingly complex environment it found itself embedded in. Originally, public relations were focused on struggles the organization had with regulatory agencies, politicians, and leaders of organized labor. Although this was a more thoughtful advance on the organization's relationship with the larger environment, it was limited in its role and impact. Many viewed public relations as the organization's attempt to spin an issue or problem after the fact. That is, public relations was *not* about preparedness and foresight but instead was focused on damage control once an issue, problem, or situation achieved visibility. It was recognized that public relations, corporate philanthropy, and urban affairs were simply not enough for the modern-day organization in dealing with a growing variety and sophistication of external actors all demanding that the organization respond to them and their issues and concerns.

But how do organizations respond to such concerns? They responded with the development of public affairs departments to deal with the breadth and depth of external issues and actors. Despite the documented growth in public affairs, corporations still use different names for this function. The most popular names are governmental affairs/relations, public affairs, corporate relations/affairs, corporate communications, and external affairs/relations. The key point is that whatever the name of the department, its focus has to be broad, on the interpretation and monitoring of the marketplace of ideas and on the prioritization of those external concerns, developing policy to reply to those concerns, and then advocacy for the corporation's position with external actors and agencies. Finally, the activities and focus of public affairs should be carefully aligned with the strategy and strategic plan of the corporation as a whole.

TOOLS AND TECHNIQUES OF PUBLIC AFFAIRS

To be effective and to aid the organization in pursuit of its objectives, public affairs have developed a set of activities, tools, and techniques for dealing with these external groups and pressures. A modern-day public affairs department can encapsulate the following types of activities: lobbying (at all levels), political action committees, issues management, stakeholder management, trade association involvement, coalition building (both within the industry and with diverse external groups), grassroots activities, philanthropy, community relations, crisis management, regulatory affairs, media relations, environmental affairs, institutional investor relations, stockholder relations, educational relations, corporate social responsibility, employee communications, and nongovernmental organization relationships.

This is an impressive list, but what fundamentally defines a public affairs department is not the list of activities it engages in but the orientation to serving as a window into the organization for non-market-based challenges and organizations (e.g., nongovernmental organizations) and as a window out for the organization to those external players. The core of activities in public affairs are oriented to assessing the future risks to the organization of issues (in any forum—legislative, judicial, regulatory, general public), trends, situations, and stakeholders that challenge or limit the legitimacy of the organization or its ability to operate in a discretionary fashion.

Although the activities noted above are lengthy, they can be organized into larger categories of tools and techniques. One useful organizing tool is to consider short- and long-term time frames. In the area of strategy one thinks of a strategic plan as the organization's long-term response to its environment and tactics as the plan to achieve the short time frame operational choices to achieve the long-term goals. In a similar fashion, we can look at issues management and stakeholder management as reflective of long- and short-term considerations.

Issues Management

Organizations looking toward the future attempt to assess which issues (differences in facts, values, or policies) are likely to gain traction in the marketplace of ideas and which issues have an impact on the organization and therefore require planning and action. This action can range from attempts to block the emergence of an issue in a given arena (e.g., prevent global warming becoming a legislative or regulatory issue) to altering the definition of an issue after it has appeared and is being actively discussed (e.g., a discussion of immigration could be in the context of opening a country's borders to the oppressed or it could be couched in terms of blocking terrorism). Such definitional manipulation can impact on how stakeholders become energized to act or not and also impact on the arena where the issue might be resolved (e.g., in a regulatory hearing as opposed to legislative action). Issues management, therefore, is the tool of public affairs that allows the organization to think about the longer-term horizon of issues, problems, and/or situation that might arise; have an impact on the organization; and demand some sort of planned response.

Tools and techniques within issues management can include media relations, lobbying, grassroots campaigns, coalition building (within an industry, with other industries, and with outside actors), political action committees (organized fund-raising for politicians and their election efforts), web activism, employee communications, and community relations. The goals are straightforward, to prevent the issue from arising and if that fails to amend, alter, and shape the issue in ways favorable to the organization and/or to place the issue in a specific area of resolution (legislative, judicial, regulatory) where the organization believes it has an advantage over other stakeholders on this issue.

Stakeholder Management

Issues management is simply not specific enough for an organization to act on in any meaningful manner. Although issues management can focus the organization's attention on a specific topic—global warming as an example—the next logical question is what do we do with this issue. This requires an exploration of who the likely "stakeholders" are with regard to this issue. Stakeholders, as might be easily surmised, are those individuals, groups, and organizations who have a "stake" in an issue and how it is resolved. Usually, this stake or level of interest and involvement is significant; otherwise, the organization will see no reason to become engaged in the issue. In global warming, for example, oil and energy companies have a stake in how that issue is discussed, debated, and ultimately resolved. The resolution of this issue might impose additional costs, threaten the legitimacy and survival of the firm, and/or limit the ability of the organization to make discretionary choices. Other stakeholders in this issue can include environmental and regulatory organizations, alternative fuel manufactures (e.g., nuclear power), and other related industries and individuals. The specific constellation of stakeholders will have major impacts on how an issue is resolved and where it is resolved.

It should be very clear that lobbying; coalition building; community, regulatory, and external affairs; and other techniques and tools noted earlier can be brought to focus when dealing with stakeholders. To be very clear, public affairs is about positioning the organization in such a way that it can deal with external pressures, groups, and situations in a thoughtful manner that meets organizational objectives. Although not widely considered, public affairs is also about advising the organization on issues and situations where it cannot "win" and that fighting the specific issue or situation at hand is unlikely to yield positive responses and is more likely to cost the organization (both in terms of finances and image/reputation/credibility/legitimacy).

INTERNATIONAL PUBLIC AFFAIRS

The growth of the Internet and other forms of communications, along with global trade, poses new problems for corporate public affairs. In years past, geographical distances, cultural differences, and language meant that issues, problems, and situations would not easily migrate across geographic borders. This meant that a problem in China might not become a concern in Europe until years after it arose in China. This afforded organizations the "luxury" of following these new problems and how they arose and were treated. The organization could learn from this problem and be better prepared to treat it when it arose in a different area. It also allowed the organization to experiment with approaches to the problem, with the crafting of specific messages in predetermined arenas, and in interactions with stakeholders.

The luxury of time and geographical space no longer exists; an issue or problem (such as global warming) can arise simultaneously in multiple areas of the world, with different stakeholders involved, who define and conceptualize the problem or issue differently. Further, these problems can be defined and conceptualized differently, with the problems having highly different impacts on various societies, and might be addressed in different forums (e.g., legislative, judicial, regulatory).

In essence, the organization is compelled to fight a "multifront" situation, with all the attendant complexities such a multifront battle entails. One aspect that should not be underestimated is the impact of different cultural milieus on the identification, shaping, evaluation, and response of external national groups to an organization's actions.

Now an organization's response to a situation can become known worldwide in moments to a much larger audience and the response can be analyzed by external actors in different locales that can then shape their subsequent actions. As a result, there has been, over the last decade, an increase in outsourcing of public affairs activities. Clearly, the outsourcing of activities in international venues makes great practical and strategic sense.

ASSESSMENT OF PUBLIC AFFAIRS

No discussion of public affairs would be complete without addressing assessment. As in any area of organizational activity, the age-old question of value received in relationship to resources expended can and must be asked with regard to public affairs. In asking any such question, however, it must be remembered that using traditional corporate measures (profitability, costs, return on investments, etc.) may have little relevance to public affairs.

Consider the marketplace of ideas in which public affairs operates—a highly fluid and dynamic environment where losing a specific battle may be the best strategic and tactical choice available to the firm. The suggestion here is that the measurement and assessment of public affairs is difficult and is clearly both quantitative and qualitative in nature. Adding to the complexity of measurement is that a public affairs campaign on a specific issue with multiple stakeholders in different geographical locales might take years before a resolution is achieved—yet the time delay in the resolution of the problem might in itself provide advantages to the organization.

In addition, the public affairs department is constrained in being too public (either internally or externally) about its successes. A frequent "success" story for public affairs is that it successfully manages an issue in the legislative or regulatory arena that prevents the imposition of additional costs on the firm or preserves discretion for the firm to act. It might be unwise for the department or for the firm to tout its successes here.

However, there are broad areas in which public affairs can be assessed. Such areas would deal with the following: (1) Do public affairs actions preserve markets for the organization? (2) Do public affairs actions control and/or reduce risk for the organization? (3) Do public affairs actions afford the organization access to key decision makers on issues of import to the firm? (4) Do public affairs successfully prioritize and inform key organizational leadership of changes and issues arising in the marketplace of ideas with sufficient time to take action? (5) Do public affairs actions advance the organization's image and reputation with key stakeholders? (6) Do public affairs activities reduce the instances of crises for the organization and/or help the organization manage a crisis successfully?

The Foundation for Public Affairs in Washington, DC, recently surveyed corporations on their assessment of public affairs. They found that performance assessment of public affairs was improving—with more than 50% of their respondents noting that they had a highly developed performance measurement capacity (only 42% answered this way in the previous survey). Fifty-six percent of the firms have a formalized process for measuring and evaluating public affairs performance. It is clear that measurement of public affairs performance is becoming increasingly sophisticated and formalized. In their survey, the tools and techniques for the assessment of performance fell into two major areas—outcomes and processes. In the category of outcomes, they found that corporations use three tools/techniques most often—objectives achieved, legislative wins/losses, and costs reduced/avoided. In the category of processes, the most used measure was internal customer satisfaction, followed by external customer perception/attitude. Notice the balance here between external-focused activities and internal-focused activities (the window in, window out phenomena) and the use of both quantitative and qualitative assessments.

No matter what the approach, there is agreement that measurement and assessment of public affairs leads to improved public affairs performance. Since a key aspect of the public affairs department is to maintain relationships outside the boundaries of the corporation, a key assessment approach to use is focus groups with external entities. In this manner the organization can set up a baseline comparator to use in unfolding assessments. Although objectives achieved is a primary measurement tool, one must be careful in its application.

Although organizational objectives can be easily specified, the marketplace of ideas in which the organization operates must be assessed. Reasoned objectives might be unachievable in a given ideas marketplace. The reasons for being unachievable might range from the timing of an issue (the marketplace is not ready to deal with this issue at this time) to the organization's poor reputation on this issue that precludes them from achieving success on the issue. Simply put, the tools of assessment for public affairs departments must be constructed not only with normal corporate procedures and objectives but also in light of the larger external marketplace of ideas.

The external environment in which organizations operate today continues to grow in complexity. Time is no longer an ally for an organization in decision making. Corporations are facing an increasing number of well-financed and organized nongovernmental organizations around the world. Public affairs management is and will continue to be a major organizational capability to represent the firm in the marketplace of ideas.

—John F. Mahon

Further Readings

Cobb, R. W., & Ross, M. H. (Eds.). (1997). *Cultural strategies of agenda denial: Avoidance, attack, and redefinition.* Lawrence: University Press of Kansas.

Fleisher, C. S. (1993). Public affairs management performance: An empirical analysis of evaluation and management. In J. E. Post (Ed.), *Research in corporate social performance and policy* (pp. 139–167). Greenwich, CT: JAI Press.

Foundation for Public Affairs. (2005). *The state of corporate public affairs.* Washington, DC: Author.

Harris, P. H., & Fleisher, C. S. (Eds.). (2005). *The handbook of public affairs.* Thousand Oaks, CA: Sage.

Mahon, J. F. (2006). Public affairs and game theory. In M. J. H. Epstein & K. O. Hanson (Eds.), *The accountable corporation, Vol. 4: Business-government relations* (pp. 183–205). New York: Praeger Perspectives.

Mitnick, B. M. (Ed.). (1993). *Corporate political agency: The construction of competition in public affairs.* Thousand Oaks, CA: Sage.

Post, J. E., Murray, E. A., Dickie, R. B., & Mahon, J. F. (1982). The public affairs function in American corporations: Development and relations with corporate planning. *Journal of Long Range Planning, 15*(2), 12–21.

Post, J. E., Murray, E. A., Dickie, R. B., Mahon, J. F., & Jones, M. (1981). Public affairs officers and their functions: Highlights of a national survey. *Public Affairs Review*, 1981, 88–99.

PUBLIC RELATIONS

Public relations is a business function that can have any number of names—namely, corporate communications, corporate affairs, public affairs, or external affairs. The senior public relations officer usually reports to the chief executive officer, although sometimes the function reports to a second-level senior officer (e.g., chief administrative officer or, occasionally, the general counsel).

No matter what the name, the function will have a core mission of ensuring good relations with important constituencies, particularly the media. In many instances, the function will include a government relations component, manage corporate charitable contributions, handle relationships with the local community (and sometimes plant communities), and maintain relationships with important activist and interest groups involved with issues affecting the company's business. The same function is also likely to manage internal communications with employees and may have an important role in communications to the financial community—for example, it may produce annual reports and organize annual meetings.

EVOLUTION OF THE FUNCTION: THE FIRST DECADES

Public relations has grown and evolved as a business function from its earliest days at the beginning of the 20th century. Ivy Lee is often credited with being the "founder" of the field when he began to advise John D. Rockefeller about ways to improve his public image, through philanthropy, policies toward workers, selection of plant sites, and so on.

While the press agency aspect of public relations was—and remains—a core activity, Ivy Lee's determination to go beyond simply issuing press releases laid the groundwork for a much broader business function that would provide input to basic business decisions. Rockefeller at first resisted the advice but eventually gave in to the notion that public reaction had to be a factor in his business decisions.

Later, when Edward Bernays, another "founder" of the public relations profession, wrote the first book on the profession, *Crystallizing Public Opinion,* he too went beyond press relations. A student of Freud, he discussed the critical roles that events, third-party opinions, and social trends played in forming public opinion. He argued that public relations professionals had to be able to manipulate these elements if they were to be truly successful.

The early founders of the public relations function focused on image making. Given the historical period in which they were operating, which included the influence of F. W. Taylor's scientific management and the development of sophisticated mass marketing, Bernays and others worked to develop a scientific patina for public relations that ultimately came close to being a glorification of propaganda. Indeed, Bernays's second book was titled *Propaganda.* In it, he argued that in a complex democratic society, propaganda provided the means through which consensus could be reached, and he posited that those who knew how to manipulate public opinion were, in essence, the true ruling power in society.

While public relations professionals learned to shy away from promoting themselves in such terms during the 1930s, 1940s, and 1950s, the focus remained on image making. The corporate public relations function was grounded in press relations activity—sending out press releases, maintaining good contacts with reporters, holding press conferences—but also included speech writing and the development of corporate brochures and films and, occasionally, systematic "speaker's bureaus" that would send out representatives to make speeches and presentations to schools and community groups. Ronald Reagan, for example, spent many years doing the speech circuit for General Electric.

Companies such as AT&T (then a national telephone monopoly), DuPont ("Better Things for Better Living Through Chemistry"), and General Motors were practitioners of very sophisticated image efforts, as were many smaller companies and some industries. Several also worked with the emerging field of public opinion research to develop public opinion tracking surveys to monitor their image and report back to management on how they were doing.

EVOLUTION OF THE FUNCTION: INTO THE MAELSTROM

Rachel Carson's *Silent Spring* and Ralph Nader's *Unsafe at Any Speed* ushered in a new era for public relations. Suddenly, the companies and industries that had felt confident about their image-making abilities found their reputations collapsing under a barrage of new questions about corporate behavior—environmental impacts, workplace discrimination, safety, operations in South Africa, and so on. The age of issue management had begun.

The term *issue management* is credited to Howard Chase, who coined it in 1976, describing a process of how issues emerge through a mixture of events, media, and activist groups: how issues grow and how they eventually lead to regulation—as they did in the early 1970s, in a panoply of new federal regulatory agencies, including the Occupational Safety and Health Administration, the Environmental Protection Agency, the Consumer Product Safety Commission, the Equal Employment Opportunity Commission, and so on. Like Bernays and Lee, Chase argued that smart business management disciplines could be applied to the world of public opinion if a company or industry acted quickly during the early stages of issue development to reduce the underlying problem, to show that the perceived problem was not really a problem, or to offer other solutions besides regulation.

The public relations function—both within companies and in the agency world—expanded exponentially to deal with the new issue-laden environment, becoming more focused on public affairs activities. New lobbying offices were opened, not just in Washington but also in state capitals and in many European nations (and ultimately in Brussels). Public affairs experts emerged to offer new services, such as ally development (i.e., finding or creating third parties to communicate points of view), constituency mobilizations (e.g., letter-writing campaigns), and issue advertising (a technique pioneered by Mobil Oil during the energy crisis of the 1970s because of what it viewed as biased media coverage of energy issues).

Drawing on the evolving techniques used in political campaigns, public relations practitioners began to target their audiences through psychographic profiling, becoming more sophisticated at identifying and then mobilizing political forces. No longer was public relations concerned about a generalized public opinion; now the question was who were the opinion leaders on particular issues and who were the mobilizable publics who needed to be reached through direct mail, telemarketing, or targeted media campaigns.

The field of marketing offered other new possibilities, such as focus group message testing to determine the right mobilizing messages. One of the most visible and successful issue-driven campaigns was probably that launched by insurance companies, pharmaceutical companies, and others to stymie

President Bill Clinton's health care reform in the early 1990s. The message was crafted around protecting the right of health care consumers to choose their own providers. Through television and print advertising, targeted mobilization of letter writing, ally development, and other techniques, the Clinton plan was stopped in its tracks.

Parallel to these developments was the emergence of television as the dominant medium both in the United States and elsewhere. Until the 1960s, the public relations function had been mostly focused on print media—the leading local newspapers, the wire services that fed them, and major national magazines. Following the Kennedy assassination, television stations and the three nationally dominant networks (NBC, CBS, and ABC) vastly expanded news coverage and created new programs that covered issues of the day (e.g., *60 Minutes,* the morning news and talk shows). Then came CNN, followed in later decades by CNBC, MSNBC, Fox News, and so on.

Television became—as it continues to be—the most powerful force in defining and prioritizing public concerns. And it changed the timetable of the news cycle, which used to define the day in terms of the deadlines for going to press or the nightly news shows. Now there was no cycle—only endless news coverage.

Public relations professionals developed new skills and techniques to respond, taking advantage of the technological changes. An early innovation was media training for executives appearing on television, a medium where physicality is often as important as the words spoken and where message delivery strategies can differ depending on whether an interview is live or on tape.

In the 1980s, public relations agencies invented the video news release (VNR) and Radio Actualities, which were electronic versions of the traditional press release. They also developed "B-roll," which is a collection of video snippets with or without audio components that TV producers can use in developing a news segment. They learned how to create press conference environments that played first and foremost to television and only secondarily to the print media.

As satellite technology developed, both VNRs and B-roll could be distributed electronically and instantaneously. Equally important, companies and agencies discovered that they could have their own broadcast studios on the premises, offering a business executive live for an interview with a TV news host thousands of miles away. By the 1990s, "satellite media tours" allowed a spokesperson to sit in a small studio for a few hours and make sequential appearances on multiple local TV shows, answering local reporters. Then, with the advent of the Internet, "sound bite" sequences could be stored centrally for any reporter to pull down on demand.

These technological innovations became particularly useful for crisis communications, yet another emerging specialty in public relations. Starting with the nuclear accident at Three Mile Island in 1979, the Tylenol cyanide poisonings in 1982, and the chemical plant disaster in Bhopal, India, in 1984, companies began to realize that rapid and appropriate communications were critical in a fast-moving crisis environment. Various crisis communications experts began to outline procedures for managing communications in a crisis, and companies developed crisis communications manuals. Crisis preparedness planning became part of normal business practice. Companies in industries susceptible to large accidents (oil, chemicals, airlines) established technology-laden crisis communications centers on their premises, and many companies began to engage in crisis simulation exercises, in which press inquiries and press management were critical factors.

Another new field that developed was litigation communications. More and more companies under legal fire began to realize that battles were fought in the court of public opinion long before they were engaged in the court of law. With the investment community concerned about the potential costs of litigation, and customers and employees worried about corporate or product reputation, no company could afford to be silent while plaintiff lawyers leaked documents and information to television and print reporters. So more experts emerged in the public relations profession—many of them trained as lawyers—to develop communications strategies that would precede courtroom activity and then carry the company through a trial and/or to a settlement.

PUBLIC RELATIONS TODAY

The globalization of the media and the development of the web have offered even more challenges and opportunities. Public relations functions are now the owners and operators of the company's website and, often, the company's web communications strategy. Public relations professionals design and proactively manage large corporate websites containing massive amounts of information that once had to be printed in brochures and sent out in press kits. Reporters—once only reachable by phone, mail, or fax—now became available by e-mail, and conversely, reporters can now have quick access to in-depth and constantly updated information, statements, visuals, and video snippets any time of the day or night.

Today, the field of public relations involves activities, techniques, and subspecialties that parallel the social and technological complexities of the age. But the focus remains constant. Now it is called "reputation management," a reformulated statement of "image making." And while companies are more successful at managing political issues, the reputation of business in general and of most companies remains at an all-time low—as it was even before a series of corporate scandals (Enron, Tyco, WorldCom) raised new questions about corporate ethics and integrity.

Ironically, approaching its 100th year of existence, the public relations field also retains its own image problem. Phrases such as "flack" hang over the field, left over from movies and novels (e.g., *The Sweet Smell of Success* of 1957) in which the press agent is portrayed as amoral and scheming. There are more ominous phrases, such as "spin doctor," not unrelated to the profession's once lauded relationship to propaganda. Even the acronym *PR* continues to carry negative connotations, the reason why so many corporate departments now bear names such as Corporate Communications, Corporate Affairs, or External Relations. Countless professional confabulations have discussed the dilemma of the bad image of the public relations profession, but the experts in image making cannot seem to solve their own image problem.

BEYOND MESSAGE DELIVERY TO DIALOGUE

During the 1990s, the newly emerging ideology and methodology of corporate responsibility (sometimes corporate social responsibility) offered a new approach to the field of public relations. The underlying assumption of corporate responsibility—once articulated by Ivy Lee to John D. Rockefeller—is that a business cannot survive and be sustainable in the long term without the support of key constituencies. Those constituencies are not limited to those with economic ties (investors, employees, customers, suppliers) but include other critical social groups (the media, the government, communities, and what is now termed "civil society" and was once called interest groups).

The theory of corporate responsibility does not focus on the image of the company with these groups, however. It focuses on the concept of stakeholder engagement and the need to carefully listen to constituency groups as part of the decision-making process, attempting to address concerns as part of business development. It is a model where the company becomes a more transparent and open-minded entity, discussing issues and even business ideas with others so that social groups become involved actors in what is decided, while not, in any way, controlling the decision. The goal is not image or reputation but rather decision making that is compatible with the social and ethical concerns of communities that could be affected by it.

While the "managing reputation/image" model of public relations has always included the notion of "listening," this activity has been largely left to opinion research and to the intuition and accumulated experience of the public relations professional. More important, listening has been merely a step in the process of developing the message that then gets delivered by the most effective voices and techniques to get the particular perceptual outcome—for example, an issue belief, favorability for the company, and so on.

Now, according to the theory of corporate responsibility, listening has to be redefined as a serious kind of dialogue—a two-way conversation—where views are shared, common ground defined, and disagreements respected. The quality of the relationship is paramount, not the perception of the company.

This approach creates new challenges for the public relations field, which as of 2005, only some companies and industries have embraced—and only in some narrow issue areas. It changes the job of the public relations function to not just carry messages to the outside but also bring the outside in. In this way, business management is more likely to make decisions that are compatible with societal expectations and values.

This redefinition of the function requires that public relations professionals become more adept at give-and-take exchanges and at finding common ground, not in a context of a negotiation but in a context of dialogue and respectful sharing. This is a different skill set from that which has generally guided the profession—namely, the ability to develop influential messages (in print and in visual and aural forms) and deliver them creatively to intended audiences.

BECOMING MORE BUSINESSLIKE

While public relations functions learn to operate within the new corporate responsibility paradigms, it is unlikely that they will stop doing what they have long existed to do. Companies will continue to need core public relations activities—media relations, internal communications, website management, corporate identity and positioning, financial communications, issue monitoring and management, government affairs, contributions, and community relations—all being performed at the leading edge of technology and of communications theory and practice.

These public relations activities are increasingly managed in ways that parallel other core business functions. Long-term and short-term plans are developed as part of the business-planning process. Desired outcomes are agreed on and often expressed in perceptual terms—that is, a particular audience will hold a particular belief—or in terms of an action that an audience will take as a result of a belief: for example, purchase shares in the company. As in any business plan, the situation analysis is laid out, and strategies are outlined along with tactics (messages, messengers, and media).

Measurement can occur at several levels. *Output* is a measurement of the activity of the function: issuing press releases, making contacts with government officials, writing speeches, or improving the website.

Impact is a measurement of target audience exposure to the messages. This measurement parallels the field of advertising where reach, frequency, and gross rating points can be used as readings of how often an intended audience target is exposed to the message. Impact in public relations can be measured in terms of both message accuracy (described through word counts and subjective analyses of whether media coverage accurately delivered the desired message) and the number of people exposed to the media that carried the information.

The most elusive measurement is *outcome*—that is, whether all the public relations activity (the output) reached the audience the right way (the impact) to actually create or sustain the desired belief. Opinion research can be used to measure outcome (e.g., Did the percentage of believers increase?), but often public relations professionals are not eager to have their work judged on their ability to move public opinion. This reluctance then raises the question of whether the public relations profession will allow itself to be measured on its core mission, which is to influence opinion.

The movement of public relations into more of the business mainstream, including the use of business tools such as planning, objective setting, strategy articulation, and measurement, has not yet closed the gap that most public relations professionals—all the way back to Ivy Lee—would like to have closed. That is the gap that keeps them somewhat to the side in critical decision making. Public relations professionals yearn to have a "seat at the table" earlier in the decision-making process. They know that the adage "Actions speak louder than words" is valid, and that no "spin doctor" or "message delivery strategy" can turn a bad corporate behavior into an acceptable one. In the end, good public relations can help a company, but it can never replace—or cover up—bad decisions.

—Jim Lindheim

Further Readings

Argenti, P. (1994). *Corporate communication*. Boston: Irwin.

Breakenridge, D., & Deloughry, T. J. (2003). *The new PR tool kit: Strategies for successful media relations*. Upper Saddle River, NJ: Financial Times Prentice Hall.

Caywood, C. L. (1997). *The handbook of strategic public relations & integrated communications*. New York: McGraw-Hill.

Marconi, J. (2004). *Public relations: The complete guide*. Mason, OH: South-Western Education.

Shafer, P. (1994). *Adding value to the public affairs function*. Washington, DC: Public Affairs Council.

White, J., & Mazur, L. (1994). *Strategic communications management*. Cambridge, UK: Addison-Wesley.

Public Relations

CORPORATE POLITICAL ADVOCACY

Corporate political advocacy addresses a firm's participation in the formulation of public policy at various levels of government. As the regulatory environment has become more intense and complex and as other changes have taken place in society, firms have had little choice but to become more politically active. Attempts by firms to influence government are a major and accepted part of the public policy process in the United States. The U.S. political system is driven by the fervent participation of interest groups striving to achieve their own objectives. The business sector is, therefore, behaving in a normal and expected fashion when it assumes an advocacy role for its interests. As decisions about the current and future shape of society and the role of the private sector shift from the marketplace to the political arena, firms, like all interest groups, find it imperative to increase their level of political advocacy.

Historically, firms engaged in vigorous debates in Washington, DC, only on an issue-by-issue basis and with no overall sense of a purpose, goal, or strategy. Also, firms tended to be reactive; that is, they dealt with issues only after the issues had become threats. Today, success in Washington is just as important as success in the marketplace. Just as business has learned that it must develop competitive strategies if it is to succeed, it has learned that political strategies are essential as well. The firm engages in this activity by using techniques such as having a political strategy, lobbying, political action committees, and coalition building through organizations to influence rules, regulations, and laws enacted by government that affects its environment. One of the things that the firm has to manage in its environment is the government's actions and its effect on the market. The U.S. government abides by a stringent privatization model for the business market. The government frowns on owning and operating businesses in the United States. Instead, it monitors the firm's activities in the market to ensure that on balance efficiency and fairness are practiced throughout. The government, through its complex rule-making process, attempts to ensure that the market is fair, a firm does not have an unfair advantage, and the resources in the environment are not abused. At any point in time, the government can veer the market's direction by using controls that impact the business and consumers. Over the past 100 years, firms have been very successful in acquiring a coveted status in the market similar to that of a person. Today, firms are beheld as a legal "fictitious person" and are afforded the same rights, privileges, and protections as individuals. Thus, firms are able to use constitutional safeguards identical to what individuals exercise when their rights are abridged. More specifically, numerous clauses in the constitution including the First, Fourth, Fifth, and Fourteenth Amendments grant enormous rights to firms against government actions. With the advent of these new rights, firms have taken the liberty of using its influence to affect the actions implemented by government.

Under Articles 1, 2, and 3, the government may delegate some of its duties for rule making, enforcing rules, and interpreting the laws to the legislative, executive, and judicial branches. Accordingly, the legislative branch has established federal agencies to monitor the activities taking place in the market. Some of these agencies report directly to the executive branch while others are independent from both the legislative and executive branches. Some examples of executive branch agencies are the Department of Commerce, the Department of Agriculture, and the Department of Transportation. These agencies report directly to the president of the United States. Conversely, independent administrative agencies operate on an autonomous basis from the president. Examples of these agencies include the Federal Trade Commission, the Federal Communications Commission, and the Securities and Exchange Commission. Executive branch agencies function under a concerted policy orchestrated by the president of the United States. These branches venture to provide a certain type of structured environment for firms to operate in. Each branch has a specific role in the process of establishing policy for the government.

The legislative and executive branches of government are easier for firms to influence. There are specific parts of the rule-making process that afford firms the ability to intercede and influence the policy before it is developed. Conversely, it is more arduous for the firm to influence the judicial process because most federal judges are appointed for life, although some federal judges, who are appointed by the president, serve for a limited term in office. Federal judges who are appointed to preside on the tax court, bankruptcy court, or international trade commission serve for limited terms. However, they can be subsequently reappointed to successive terms. So the vast majority of a firm's resources are headed for the political advocacy arena and used to influence the legislative and executive rule-making process.

Special interest politics have become a way in which most legislation is passed in the United States. Subsequently, most firms have come to recognize that to endure it one must be an active and effective player in the process. One telling example of not being involved in the process demonstrates what can happen to firms that take an isolationist policy toward the rule-making process. Microsoft used a superficial presence in Washington, DC, prior to the Justice Department bringing an antitrust case against it for monopolistic competition. Before the suit was brought, Microsoft used one lobbyist and its office was in the Microsoft federal sales office. The lobbyist had no secretary and no relevant lobbying experience in Washington. Microsoft had no real savvy in understanding how the lobbying system worked in Washington. Microsoft transposed its isolationist strategy for political advocacy as a result of being sued by the Justice Department. Microsoft began to increase its level of political giving to both parties. It retained an impressive cadre of well-connected lobbyists and public relations officials to adduce its case to legislators and the public. The in-house staff swelled from one person to 14, and it used a multitude of high-powered help on retainer.

Microsoft contributed millions to both political parties in the 2000 presidential election, hired both Bush and Gore advisers as lobbyists, and became the ninth largest "soft money" corporate donor in the United States. Microsoft ran a national ad campaign featuring a "warm and fuzzy" Bill Gates, while simultaneously touting the multimillion-dollar charity campaign contributions it made to various organizations. Think tanks that supported Microsoft interests received major donations; those that espoused views contrary to it were abdicated. Microsoft even hired almost entirely all the law firms in Washington, DC, so that nearly all the lawyers in town would be unable to work for its competition. In 2004, after years of struggling with antitrust cases, both domestic and abroad, Microsoft situated one of its best lawyers to chair the American Bar Association's antitrust section, a group that has significant influence over the expatiation of antitrust policy and law.

POLITICAL STRATEGY

As illustrated from the example concerned with Microsoft, it is fatuous for a firm to engage in the political activism process without a sound strategy. The firm should have a goal of what it wants to accomplish and specific objectives for how it is going to get there. Befittingly, the impetus for developing a comprehensive strategy for engaging in the political process is to alter legislation. As firms devise and execute political strategies, it is useful to see their initiatives as factors in their development of stakeholder management capabilities. Unlike actual persons, corporations antithetic to actual persons cannot be imprisoned or suffer "capital punishment" by being forced out of business by the judicial system.

The firm has a multitude of objectives that it wants to pursue in developing a political strategy. First, it will attempt to limit the issue from taking a prominent position on the policy stage. Second, if the firm can't limit the initiative from moving into the limelight, it will attempt to define the public issue. Third, if the firm can't shape the issue, it will find a coalition to limit the impact on the industry. So the firm has to proceed in a manner that will yield the greatest results. The firm has to develop an approach to this process that allows it to engage the decision makers in a manner that focuses on outcomes. So the firm must determine how best to advocate its concern either for or against a proposed rule. The firm can influence the process at different stages and affect the ultimate policy that is created. Given the extreme nature of our competitive environment today, most firms find themselves working with other firms to develop a national agenda with a focus on a more progressive role in the public policy process. With so much pressure coming from foreign markets, firms are forced to band together to find workable solutions that benefit its industries. This mode does not require a recusant departure from traditional goals and strategies but is more biddable and adaptive to a changing political environment and structure.

LOBBYING

The business community engages in lobbying at several different organizational levels. At the broadest level are umbrella organizations, which represent the collective business interests of the United States. The best examples of umbrella organizations are the Chamber of Commerce of the United States, the National Association of Manufacturers, State Chambers of Commerce, and City Chambers of Commerce. Out of these groups have grown organizations that represent some subset of business in general, such as the Business Roundtable, which was organized to represent the largest firms in America, and the National Federation of Independent Businesses, which represents smaller firms.

At the next level are trade associations, which are composed of many firms in a given industry or line of business. Examples include the National Automobile Dealers Association, the National Association of Home Builders, the National Association of Realtors, and the National Association of Medical Equipment Suppliers. Firms that are actively involved with an association do so by preference. They usually pay some type of member fee to be affiliated with the association. Also, they are in league with other firms that they compete directly against on a day-to-day basis.

Another tier of coalitions constructed to confront political issues are international associations. Examples of these organizations include the World Trade Organization, the International Chamber of Commerce, the International Fair Trade Association, and the United States Council on International Business (this is a U.S. group dealing with international business). These organizations work to provide a basis for firms to influence the foreign government's policy-making process.

Finally, there are the individual company's lobbying efforts. Here, firms such as IBM, BellSouth, Time Warner, Viacom, and Chase Manhattan Bank lobby on their own behalf. Typically, companies use their own personnel, establish lobbying offices for the sole purpose of lobbying, or hire professional lobbying firms or consultants located in Washington or a state capital. The business lobbyist plays a significant role in assisting firms in achieving their political strategy. The business lobbyist engages in the following activities for its clients including getting access to key legislators, monitoring legislation, establishing communication channels with regulatory bodies, protecting firms against surprise legislation, drafting legislation, communicating sentiments of association or company on key issues, influencing the outcome of legislation, assisting companies in coalition building around issues that various groups may have in common, helping members of Congress get reelected, and organizing grassroots efforts. Lobbyists also play the important role of showing busy legislators the virtues and pitfalls of complex legislation.

POLITICAL ACTION COMMITTEES

Political action committees (PACs) have been around for years, but their influence has been most profoundly felt in the past two decades. This is perhaps because the bottom line in politics, as well as in business, is often measured in terms of money—who has it, how much they have, and how much power they are able to bring to bear as a result. Business PACs appeared on the scene in the early 1970s as a direct result of the 1974 amendments to the Federal Election Campaign Act. Under this law, organizations of like-minded individuals formed together and created a PAC for the purpose of raising money and donating it to candidates for public office. Under the law, PACs may contribute $5,000 per candidate per election including primary, runoff, general, or special. There are no aggregate limits on how much a PAC may contribute to numerous candidates. The $5,000 limit is less restricting than that placed on individuals, who are limited to donating $2,500 per federal candidate per election.

At the start of 2004, 3,868 PACs were officially registered with the Federal Election Commission. This represents a decline from more than 4,000 PACs that were registered in 2001. Corporate PACs were the largest subgroup with 1,538 committees. In the 2000 elections, PAC contributions to the House and Senate totaled $200 million, with another $200 million going to national parties as well as candidates for local and state offices.

In addition, firms have used a loophole in the PAC legislation to donate what is called soft money directly to political parties instead of political candidates. The Bipartisan Campaign Reform Act (BCRA) of 2002 attempted to limit the use of soft money and curtail the use of certain political ads. BCRA bans national parties from raising and spending soft money. In addition, BCRA prohibits federal officeholders and candidates from raising soft money for political parties at the federal, state, and local levels and, likewise, from soliciting or raising soft money in connection with federal or nonfederal elections. Shortly after passage, certain special interest groups challenged the law's constitutionality in court. In May 2003, a federal court held the soft money ban to be unconstitutional and allowed political parties to raise soft money again while setting restrictions on the airing of issue ads. This was immediately appealed to the U.S. Supreme Court. On September 8, 2003, the Supreme Court upheld the soft money and issue ad restriction of the BCRA in a five to four ruling. This legislation did not stop firms from finding other mechanisms to pour soft money into political campaigns. Despite all efforts to limit the amount of soft money contributions, other strategies are being deployed to continue raising significant sums of capital for political campaigns. For instance, nonprofit organizations, known as 527s, are allowed to raise and spend soft money on campaigns. Some are concerned that these groups will be less accountable than the political parties were prior to the law's inception. In the 2004 elections, Democrats made particularly strong use of 527s to create a shadow Democratic Party that could circumvent campaign financing restrictions.

Yet another means by which firms are able to get around campaign financing reform is the act of bundling. Bundling is the collection of individual donations, with a limit of $2,000, that are then delivered in bulk to the candidate. Typically, a senior executive will host a fund-raising event and invite high-level employees to attend and donate up to the $2,500 threshold. Clearly, one unintended consequence of campaign financing reform has been to shift the burden for political contributions from firms to their employees. Furthermore, firms can abuse this legislation by discretely pressuring employees to support one particular political party or candidate and not another. These tactics undermine the integrity of the legislation and work to deteriorate the objective nature of the political process.

COALITION BUILDING

Another technique that seems to be growing in popularity is the use of coalitions to influence the government process. A coalition is formed when distinct groups or parties realize they have something in common that might warrant joining forces to combat a specific issue. More often than not, an issue that various groups share similar views about something creates the opportunity for a coalition. In recent years, coalition formation has become a common practice for firms interested in achieving political goals or influencing public policy. The isolationist approach to confronting the political system is not as effective in today's business climate. If a firm or an association wants to pass or defeat specific legislation, it needs to mobilize the support of any firm that shares the same position on the issue. The greatest benefit to the firm in using coalitions is that they diversify the exposure and impact on the firm. Clearly, the petition resonates louder if many firms object or applaud the virtues of the legislation. Coalitions allow firms to spread limited resources in a more efficient manner. Firms can avoid overextending resources while trying to represent their interest. This allows them to fight or support the legislation on many different fronts. Coalitions allow the firms to be zealous about representing their interest while taking a lesser lead position in the process. Coalitions provide a very effective way for firms to gather support for their issues and protect the interest of the market at the same time. Coalitions allow firms to be involved without necessarily having their name attached to the issue. One high-profile example of coalition building around a specific issue is the Coalition for Economic Growth and American Jobs. Backers of this coalition included the U.S. Chamber of Commerce, the Business Roundtable, the American Bankers Association, the National Association of Manufacturers, and scores of other trade groups and individual companies. Recognizing that the issue of business outsourcing was evolving into a hot button for the 2004 election, they joined to fight the growing number of state and federal initiatives aimed at keeping jobs at home and restraining globalization.

CONCLUSION

Corporate political advocacy is an essential part of our system in the United States. Thus, lobbying, corporate political contributions, and coalition building will likely remain a permanent part of the political landscape in the United States. Unlike what firms considered involvement to be in the past, for the most part they are required to take an active role in the political process today. So firms should have a good idea of what their interests are and how certain activities occurring in the environment will affect those interests. As new regulations evolve and the environment changes, firms must be poised to modify their strategies for implementing new innovative programs that offer meaningful benefits to the firm. Ultimately, firms negotiate with political officials for the best arrangement that in some way promotes their interests. Similarly, firms have to advocate their positions and pursue a structured strategy to achieve that end through the political process. Firms can develop a proactive approach to managing this process without appearing to be hostile toward the government. In most instances, firms that have developed constructive relationships with government institutions are better suited to be in a position to address proposed changes that potentially could affect the environment. In this regard, it is necessary for firms to have a flexible plan of action in place that anticipates the actions of governmental institutions.

—Sylvester E. Williams, IV

Corporate Political Advocacy

Further Readings

Hillman, A. J., Keim, G. D., & Schuler, D. (2004). Corporate political activity: A review and research agenda. *Journal of Management, 30*(6), 837–857.

Hoover, H. D. (1997). *Corporate advocacy: Rhetoric in the information age.* Westport, CT: Quorum Books.

McAdams, T. (with J. Freeman & L. P. Hartman). (2002). *Law, business, and society* (6th ed.). New York: McGraw-Hill.

Schuler, D. A., Schnietz, K. E., & Bagget, L. S. (2002). Determinants of foreign trade mission participation: An analysis of corporate political and trade activities. *Business & Society, 41*(2), 6–35.

Steiner, G. A., & Steiner, J. F. (2006). *Business, government, and society* (11th ed.). New York: McGraw-Hill.

PART IV: Corporate Social Responsiveness

CORPORATE PHILANTHROPY

Corporate philanthropy is the practice by companies of giving charitable donations to a wide range of societal institutions, especially nonprofit or nongovernmental organizations (NGOs), including social service agencies, environmental groups, housing and poverty agencies, schools and universities, hospitals, and other organizations, whose goals are to benefit society in some way. Sometimes termed corporate social investment, corporate philanthropy can be considered part of companies' overall approach to corporate community relations and to the somewhat broader concept of corporate social responsibility (CSR). CSR is defined as the direct attempt by companies to contribute to the betterment of society. CSR with its elements of philanthropy is part of the larger picture of companies' corporate citizenship, which is defined as the ways in which a company's strategies and practices, that is, the business model, affect its stakeholders, society, and the natural environment.

Corporate philanthropy takes a number of forms including direct monetary donations and grants to not-for-profit organizations; in-kind donations, such as product and service donations; employee volunteer programs; technical support; and the deployment of skilled managers into social enterprises on a volunteer or advisory basis, including sometimes as members of boards of directors of nonprofit organizations. In the most progressive firms, managers and sometimes employees are evaluated partially on their contribution to the community, which is seen as an important element of a company's philanthropic endeavors. In addition, multisector or public-private collaborations are frequently considered to be part of a company's philanthropic program or CSR. These types of contribution will be discussed in more detail below.

Companies in the United States are estimated by associations such as the Conference Board and the American Association of Fundraising Counsel to give between 0.7% and 1.3% of pretax profits in philanthropic contributions, according to Business for Social Responsibility. The American Association of Fund Raising Counsel estimates that about 5% or about $13.5 billion of the total amount of charitable gifts of nearly $251 billion in the United States in 2000 was donated by corporations. The use of corporate philanthropy is most prevalent

181

in the United States, where the practice began, though multinational corporations from other nations are increasingly developing giving programs as well. Some NGOs are skeptical of strategic philanthropy programs because they believe that there should be an intrinsic value to philanthropy that is diminished when the company benefits and because only those interests that benefit the corporation will receive philanthropy; however, there is also evidence that strategic philanthropy approaches are becoming increasingly popular.

RATIONALES FOR CORPORATE PHILANTHROPY

There are numerous reasons why companies engage in philanthropy. Some of them have to do with improving their relationships with important stakeholders such as employees and customers. In surveys, many employees claim that they will make decisions about employment partially on the basis of a company's reputation for CSR. Similarly, some customers claim that, assuming quality and price are comparable, they will take a company's reputation for corporate responsibility, of which philanthropy and community relations is an important aspect, into account in their purchasing decision.

A survey by the Center for Corporate Citizenship at Boston College and the Points of Light Foundation found in 2003 that 52% of companies incorporate a commitment to their local communities into their mission statements. Thus, in some respects corporate philanthropy serves as a public relations vehicle for improving a company's image and, more important, its reputation with important stakeholders, though other uses are more strategic. Companies, of course, also hope that their philanthropy will engender greater loyalty from stakeholders, leading to reduced employee turnover and greater retention and repeat purchases on the part of customers.

In the early days of corporate philanthropy, much of the giving centered on societal issues and organizations that drew the attention and interest of the chief executive officer. By the early 2000s, most large companies had moved beyond giving donations simply on the basis of the chief executive's and other top managers' interests toward more structured programs of giving, some of which can be characterized as strategic philanthropy, in which donations are directly linked to business goals. Of course, one important reason for corporate philanthropy's existence is that of altruism, a desire on the part of company executives to do explicit good for society, which can be characterized as a normative or ethics-based rationale. The second major rationale for philanthropy is called enlightened self-interest and argues that there is a business case to be made for companies giving away money in ways intended to do social good. While there is a trend toward more strategic giving, which will be discussed below in more detail, usually both motives are embedded in philanthropy programs.

Companies that attempt to use philanthropy simply as a public relations activity rather than actually improving on their actual stakeholder-related practices subject themselves to criticism. Such companies are attempting to create a good public image for the firm just by giving corporate donations. The criticism focuses on the fact that philanthropy alone cannot make up for bad practices elsewhere in the firm. Still others, particularly people coming from the perspective of neoclassical economics, criticize corporate philanthropy as giving away shareholders money and suggest that only individuals should be allowed to give money away. The courts, however, have agreed with the philanthropists that companies can engage in corporate philanthropy as part of their practice of good corporate citizenship.

METHODS OF CORPORATE PHILANTHROPY

Companies direct their giving efforts in a number of ways. These methods include direct grants, gifts, and donations; cause-related marketing; in-kind donations; community investment and economic development activities; and volunteerism, which are discussed in the sections below.

Grants, Gifts, and Donations

Many companies have direct giving programs to which charitable organizations or NGOs can apply directly for grants, which can range from very small to quite substantial amounts of money. Most of these grants go to the nearly 800,000 nonprofit organizations estimated to be in the United States, as well as to other socially beneficial programs around the world. The U.S.-based Foundation Center estimates that corporate foundation giving decreased by about 2% in 2003, following a significant gain in 2002, which was partially attributable to giving related to the terrorist attack on New York's World Trade Centers in 2001. Some of the decline is attributable to declines in the stock market. The overall amount of corporate cash donations is generally relatively stable though was decreasing somewhat during the early 2000s, with other kinds of corporate philanthropy assuming a bigger proportion of giving.

Processes for nongovernmental or nonprofit organizations receiving grants from companies or their foundations range from quite informal, for example, the submission of a letter explaining the purposes to which the grant will be put, to formalized application processes with extensive internal review and monitoring of outcomes and results.

Cause-Related Marketing

Cause-related marketing, which falls between philanthropy and marketing, occurs when a company links the level of sales or use of its products or services to donations to specific charities, often those whose interests are aligned with those of the company. Pioneered by American Express in the 1980s, when use of the company's credit card was tied to charitable donations, cause-related or cause marketing has become quite common. Types of cause marketing include corporate sponsorships of events, partnerships with NGOs for specific fund-raising purposes for the NGO, and campaigns aimed at developing new business for the company while the NGO receives funding.

In-Kind Donations

Many companies provide in-kind donations, that is, donations of their particular products or services, to NGOs as part of their philanthropy programs. Such donations are termed noncash donations by the U.S.-based Conference Board and can include products manufactured by the firm; the donation of services for which customers usually pay; technical support that can be offered as a result of a company's expertise; and sometimes recycling and reuse of outdated equipment, which is given to NGOs. Loaned executives or other employees who use their skills to help NGOs by working for them part of the time—for instance, helping with strategic planning or day-to-day operations; making organizational changes; or improving operations, marketing, accounting, finance, or other functions—can also be considered as performing a type of in-kind giving. In-kind donations are estimated by the Conference Board to be on the order of 25% of total contributions, as measured through tax valuation or fair market value. Because companies draw resources from society, many people in society expect that the company will be involved in helping communities and society more generally to thrive, hence the growth in in-kind and charitable contributions.

Community Investment and Economic Development Activities

Some companies' managers believe that it is important to help the communities in which they have operations to thrive for a number of important reasons and do so through their community relations programs using community investment strategies. One reason is to build local communities that are healthy, have good amenities such as arts and culture, and good educational programs so that employees will want to live in those communities. Many companies donate to local schools and youth organizations because they recognize that having a well-educated workforce in the future will be critical to their long-term success. In addition, local communities provide much of the infrastructure, including telecommunications, sewers, roads, and public services of all sorts, on which companies' facilities rely, and establishing good relationships with local community officials, often done through the charitable donations to local service agencies and NGOs, helps ensure their success. Corporate philanthropy is directed at a number of types of causes, including local arts and cultural organizations, schools and universities, community development and housing programs, mentoring and job training programs for youth, children's organizations, environmental organizations, sports leagues and events, local economic development including both inner city and rural.

Community investment is an important form of philanthropy for many companies, although it can generate free rider problems when one company contributes and others simply benefit from the community improvements derived from those contributions. Typically run through the community relations program, community investment focuses on assuring the sustainability of local communities where a company has operations and is frequently most focused on the locale where the company is headquartered. A number of the donation strategies listed above are used to implement community investment locally. In addition, when some company leaders become actively involved in local civic and political life, the community relations program can invest in local businesses or create local investment opportunities and source at least some supplies locally to support the community. Sometimes corporate facilities are used for local events. Managers and other employees can sometimes get release time—paid time away from work—to volunteer in community-based organizations, participate in civic events and policy dialogues, and otherwise engage in activities that support a thriving community.

Volunteerism

Another aspect of corporate philanthropy is company support of employee volunteerism. Again, as with other forms of philanthropy, volunteering is more popular in the United States than in the other parts of the world, though it is increasing globally. Some companies encourage their employees to volunteer and some even provide paid leave for volunteer activities in the recognition that local communities will benefit directly from employee volunteer time and the company itself may well benefit indirectly. Some companies recognize employees who volunteer on their own time through awards ceremonies and publicity about their activities; others provide matching grants for volunteer services.

Some companies' leaders believe that there are direct and indirect benefits to the firm when employees volunteer. For example, when employee volunteers work in teams at a nonprofit organization, they can gain useful team-based skills that translate back to their work situations. In addition, employee volunteers make local connections with community and civic organizations and their leaders, providing better links between the company and its community-based stakeholders. Occasionally, companies find that good business data, new contacts, and even new markets can evolve from information and new insights brought back by employees from volunteer experiences. Thus, some of the benefits to the company and employees from volunteering can be enhanced skills, leadership opportunities that might not happen within the work setting, and better teamwork, particularly when teams of employees volunteer together. Business for Social Responsibility suggests that other benefits may also inspire volunteer programs, for example, the ability to develop a local labor pool, improve the company's reputation with the community, create connections that help communities when there is a crisis or problem, and leverage other philanthropic resources better. Companies that have volunteer programs, in turn, may find it easier to recruit employees because they find the company to be a better employer, easier to create satisfying relationships with local officials in the community, and easier to work with public officials when the company needs new infrastructure or community support for a new facility.

Multisector Collaboration/Social Partnerships

In addition to giving away money, products and services, and employee time, some companies find that their corporate philanthropy involves establishing ongoing partnerships or collaborations with NGOs, including schools, local social service and health agencies, and sometimes governmental organizations. Partnerships and collaborations can involve monetary donations, but they are more interactive, in that they also require ongoing involvement in whatever the focal activity of the partnership is. For example, many companies become involved in partnerships to improve local schools in communities where they have facilities because they recognize the importance, on a long-term basis, of a well-educated and highly skilled workforce. Other companies become involved in collaborative efforts to improve the community through community development activities that can include improved housing, better community policing and safety standards, and the creation of economic opportunity through improving access to local jobs and higher education for all.

STRATEGIC PHILANTHROPY

Companies increasingly view their philanthropy activities through a strategic lens, in what has come to be called strategic philanthropy, although some observers are skeptical about how strategic such philanthropy actually is. In strategic philanthropy, the company attempts to link its own mission, or particular products and services, with the charitable activities it funds, so that the society, through the social mission of the NGO, and the business benefit simultaneously.

In developing a strategic philanthropy program, a company takes into account its own strategic objectives, the interests of its stakeholders, the issue area in which it wants to make contributions, and what the company and the NGO with whom it will link do best—that is, what are both organizations' core competencies. When there is alignment between the missions of the two organizations, then philanthropic activities can be considered strategic in nature. For example, a sports equipment or gear manufacturer might associate some of its philanthropy with sporting events, perhaps aimed at youth, the disadvantaged, or people with disabilities, so that the company generates goodwill with a specific target market potentially interested in the use of its products. These events carry the company's name and have the potential to enhance its image and reputation with a group of actual or potential customers.

Harvard Business School economist Michael Porter suggests that corporate philanthropy can actually be strategic when it is somehow used to improve the competitive context—that is, the quality of the business environment where businesses operate. By improving local education, providing individuals with

Corporate Philanthropy

training in skills that the company needs, or improving the community in significant ways, the company can actually reap long-term benefits. Porter identifies four elements of the competitive context that can be enhanced by strategic philanthropy. One element is the availability of high-quality, specialized inputs, such as human and capital resources, physical and administrative infrastructure, scientific and technological infrastructure, and natural resources. A second aspect of the competitive context is the status of local policies and incentives that either help or hinder businesses and vigorous local competition. A third element is the presence of sophisticated and demanding customers, who create specialized local demand that also reaches far beyond the community. The fourth aspect is strong local suppliers and related companies clustered within a given region or community. Porter advises investment in strengthening these aspects of the environment through strategic donations to key organizations within the community that can help strengthen these elements.

CORPORATE PHILANTHROPY PROGRAMS

Philanthropy programs in companies can take three general forms, although numerous variations of these are possible. The least formalized programs simply allocate some money for donations, often based on the charitable interests of the chief executive officer. Most large U.S. companies today, however, have gone beyond such informal programs and established formally structured giving programs. Within the corporation, these programs are typically housed within the corporate community relations department, the public affairs unit, or in a similar function within the company. Alternatively, they are sometimes set up as separate corporate foundations, which receive money from the corporation or its founder but are managed independently of the firm.

Corporate philanthropy is more prevalent in the United States than in other parts of the world, because there is a long history of individual philanthropy in the United States that has translated to corporations. Most large corporations have some sort of giving program established; however, the tendency seems to be to allocate most of the giving domestically with smaller proportions going to international divisions. Among the major targets of overall philanthropy at about $251 billion in 2003, according to the Giving USA Foundation, are educational organizations (about 13% of total giving); religious institutions (about 36%); foundations (about 9%); international affairs (about 2%); environment and animals (about 3%); public-society benefits (about 5%); arts, culture, and humanities (about 5%); human services (about 8%); and health (about 9%), with the rest unallocated.

In 2003, *BusinessWeek* published its first annual ranking of the most philanthropic companies in the United States, citing retail giant Wal-Mart stores as the most philanthropic company in its study for donating $156 million in cash, although the company did not make the top 10 in terms of contributions compared with total sales. The company topping the list in terms of both cash and in-kind gifts compared with total sales was Freeport-McMoRan Copper & Gold at 0.879% of sales, followed by Corning at 0.787%, and Computer Associates at 0.640% of sales. Critics sometimes charge that companies give away money to burnish their images through what is called greenwashing; that is, trying to look environmentally or socially friendly when they actually are not. Others, however, believe that there are both sound business reasons and altruism for companies working directly to improve society. Despite the conflicts, what is clear is that many companies do give substantial amounts of money, products and services, employee time, management assistance through collaborations of various sorts, and other forms of giving.

—Sandra Waddock

Further Readings

Conlin, M., Hempel, J., Tanzer, J., & Polek, D. (2003, December 1). The corporate donors. *BusinessWeek,* No. 3860, pp. 92–95.

The Foundation Center [website]. Retrieved March 2, 2005, from http://fdncenter.org

Porter, M. E., & Kramer, M. R. (2002). The competitive advantage of corporate philanthropy. *Harvard Business Review,* December, 57–68.

Saiia, D. H., Carroll, A. B., & Buchholz, A. K. (2003). Philanthropy as strategy: When corporate charity "begins at home." *Business & Society*, *42*(2), 169–201.

Smith, C. N. (1994). The new corporate philanthropy. *Harvard Business Review*, *73*(3), 105–124.

Smith, C. N. (2003). Corporate social responsibility: Whether or how? California *Management Review*, *45*(4), 52–76.

Corporate Philanthropy

PART V

Measuring Corporate Social Responsibility and Implications for Financial Performance

Corporate Social Performance (CSP)

Social Accountability (SA)

Social Audits

Triple Bottom Line

Corporate Social Financial Performance

Corporate Social Responsibility as Profit Maximization

CORPORATE SOCIAL PERFORMANCE (CSP)

As suggested earlier, the concept of corporate social performance (CSP) is an extension of the CSR concept that places more of an emphasis on *results achieved*. The development of the CSP concept has occurred somewhat in parallel with the CSR concept, but with a slightly different emphasis. The *performance* focus in CSP is intended to suggest that what really matters is what companies are able to accomplish; that is, the results or outcomes of their CSR initiatives and the adoption of a responsiveness strategy or posture. Many of the writers on CSR would argue that results were implied in their concepts and discussions of CSR, but the literature added a branch in the 1970s when writers began emphasizing the "performance" aspect rather than the "responsibility" aspect. Obviously, the two go hand in hand.

Actually, many of the earlier discussions of CSR transitioned to an emphasis on corporate social *responsiveness* before the performance focus became common. Brief mention should be made of this in the discussion on CSP. William Frederick is often credited with best describing the difference between responsibility and responsiveness when he dubbed them CSR_1 and CSR_2. With CSR_1, he was referring to the concept of CSR that we discussed in the previous section. The emphasis there is on accountability. CSR_2, in contrast, was intended to reflect the emphasis on responsiveness, or action. In the responsiveness focus, attention turned to the mechanisms, procedures, arrangements, and patterns by which business actually responds to social expectations and pressures in society. The responsiveness focus, therefore, turned the attention from responsibility (business taking on accountability) to responsiveness (business actually responding to social expectations).

In many respects, the emphasis on performance in CSP continues to carry this line of thought forward. That is, the term implies the field has transitioned from *accountability* to *responding* to *results* achieved.

The concept of CSP began appearing in the literature in the mid-1970s. Writers such as Lee Preston, S. Prakash Sethi, and Archie Carroll were among the early authors to speak of the importance of CSP. As mentioned earlier,

Carroll presented a conceptual "model" of CSP that motivated a series of improvements and refinements to the concept. Steven Wartick and Philip Cochran took Carroll's three dimensions and broadened them into more encompassing concepts. Wartick and Cochran proposed that the social issues dimension had matured into a new management field known as social issues in management. They extended the model further by proposing that the three dimensions be viewed as depicting *principles* (corporate social responsibilities, reflecting a *philosophical* orientation), *processes* (corporate social responsiveness, reflecting an *institutional* orientation), and *policies* (social issues management, reflecting an *organizational* dimension). In short, Wartick and Cochran updated and extended the three dimensions of the model.

The CSP model was further developed by Donna Wood in her reformulation of the model. Wood expanded and elaborated on Carroll's model as well as Wartick and Cochran's extensions and set forth a reformulated model that went into further detail emphasizing the *outcomes* aspect of the model. Wood argued that CSP was a business organization's configuration of principles of SR; processes of social responsiveness; and policies, programs, and other observable outcomes related to the firm's relationship with society. More than previous conceptualizations, she emphasized the importance of the *outcomes* of corporate efforts.

Diane Swanson extended Wood's model by elaborating on the *dynamic nature* of the principles, processes, and outcomes reformulated by Wood. Relying on research from corporate culture, Swanson's reoriented model linked CSP to the personally held values and ethics of executive managers and other employees. She proposed that the executive's sense of morality highly influences such policies and programs of environmental assessment, stakeholder management, and issues management carried out by employees. One of Swanson's major contributions, therefore, was to integrate business ethics into the implementation of the CSP focus.

Other concepts have developed in recent years that have embraced a concern for CSR and CSP. They are mentioned here but not developed because they get somewhat outside the traditional boundaries of these concepts. *Corporate citizenship* is a concept that must be mentioned because in the minds of many it is synonymous with CSR/CSP. The entire *business ethics movement* of the past 20 years has significantly overlapped these topics. The *stakeholder concept* has fully embraced and expanded on these concepts. The concept of the "triple bottom line," a concern for economic, social, and environmental performance, has embraced the CSR/CSP literature. The concept of "sustainability" has also embraced CSR/CSP thinking. Corporate sustainability is the goal of the triple-bottom-line and CSR/CSP initiatives—to create long-term shareholder value by taking advantage of opportunities and managing risks related to economic, social, and environmental developments.

BUSINESS'S INTEREST IN CSR AND CSP

To this point, we have been discussing primarily the contributions of academics to the development of the concepts of CSR and CSR. To be sure, the business community has had a parallel development of its interest in the concepts as well. The business community, however, has been less interested in academic refinements of the concept and more interested in what all this means for them, in practice. Prominent business organizations have developed specialized awards for firms' social performance. One example of this would be *Fortune* magazine's "most admired" and "least admired" categories of performance. Among *Fortune*'s eight attributes of reputation, one will find the category of performance titled "social responsibility." The Conference Board is another organization that has developed an award for corporate leadership in the CSR realm. The Conference Board annually gives an award titled the "Ron Brown Award for Corporate Leadership" that recognizes companies for outstanding achievements in community and employee relations. Among the core principles for this award are that the company be committed to corporate citizenship, express corporate citizenship as a shared value visible at all levels, and it must be integrated into the company's corporate strategy.

For several years now, *Business Ethics* magazine has published its list of Annual Business Ethics and Corporate Citizenship Awards. In these awards, the magazine has highlighted companies that have made stellar achievements in CSR/CSP. One of the important criterion used by the magazine in making this award is that the company have programs or initiatives in SR that demonstrate sincerity and ongoing vibrancy that reaches deep into the company. The award criteria also stipulate that the company honored must be a standout in at least one area of SR, though the recipients need not be exemplary in all areas.

Though one will always find individual businesspeople who might reject or fight the idea of CSR/CSP, for the most part today, large companies have accepted the idea and internalized it. One of the best examples of this acceptance was the creation in 1992 of the association Business for Social Responsibility (BSR). BSR is a national business association that helps companies seeking to implement policies and practices that contribute to the companies' sustainability and responsible success. In its statement of purpose, BSR claims to be a global organization that helps its member companies achieve success in ways that respect ethical values, people, communities, and the environment. A goal of BSR is to make CSR an integral part of business operations and strategies. An illustrative list of BSR's more than 1,000 members includes such well-known companies as ABB Inc., AstraZeneca PLC., Coca-Cola, Johnson & Johnson, Nike, Inc., Office Max, GE, GM, UPS, Procter & Gamble, Sony, Staples, Inc., and Wal-Mart.

THE BUSINESS CASE FOR CSR AND CSP

After considering the pros and cons of CSR/CSP, most businesses today embrace the idea. In recent years, the "business case" for CSR/CSP has been unfolding. Before buying in to the idea of CSR, many business executives have wanted the "business case" for it further developed. The business case is simply the arguments or rationales as to why businesspeople believe these concepts bring distinct benefits or advantages to companies, specifically, and the business community, generally. Even the astute business guru Michael Porter, who for a long time has extolled the virtues of competitive advantage, has embraced the concept that corporate and social initiatives are intertwined. Porter has argued that companies today ought to invest in CSR as part of their business strategy to become more competitive. Of course, prior to Porter, many CSR academics had been presenting this same argument.

Simon Zadek, a European, has presented four different business rationales for being a civil corporation. These reasons form a composite justification for businesses adopting a CSR/CSP strategy. The first is the defensive approach. This approach is designed to alleviate pain. That is, companies should pursue CSR to avoid the pressures that create costs for them. The second is the cost-benefit approach. This traditional approach holds that firms will undertake those activities that yield a greater benefit than cost. The third is the strategic approach. In this approach, firms will recognize the changing environment and engage in CSR as a part of a deliberate corporate strategy. Finally, the innovation and learning approach is suggested. Here, an active engagement with CSR provides new opportunities to understand the marketplace and enhance organizational learning, which leads to competitive advantage. Most of these rationales have been around for years, but Zadek has presented them as an excellent set of business reasons for pursuing CSR.

Putting forth the business case for CSR requires a careful and comprehensive elucidation of the reasons why companies are seeing that CSR is in their best interests to pursue. Two particular studies have contributed toward building this case. One study by PricewaterhouseCoopers, presented in their 2002 Sustainability Survey Report, identifies the following top 10 reasons why companies are deciding to be more socially responsible:

1. Enhanced reputation

2. Competitive advantage

3. Cost savings

4. Industry trends

5. CEO/board commitment

6. Customer demand

7. SRI demand

8. Top-line growth

9. Shareholder demand

10. Access to capital

A survey conducted by the Aspen Institute, in their Business and Society Program, queried MBA students about attitudes regarding the question of how companies will benefit from fulfilling their social responsibilities. Their responses, in sequence of importance, included the following:

- A better public image/reputation
- Greater customer loyalty
- A more satisfied/productive workforce
- Fewer regulatory or legal problems
- Long-term viability in the marketplace
- A stronger/healthier community
- Increased revenues
- Lower cost of capital
- Easier access to foreign markets

Between these two lists, a comprehensive case for business interest in CSR/CSP is documented. It can be seen how CSR/CSP not only benefits society and stakeholders but also how it provides specific, business-related benefits for business.

SOCIAL ACCOUNTABILITY (SA)

Social Accountability (SA) is the process of assessing and reporting a business's performance on fulfilling the economic, legal, ethical, and philanthropic social responsibilities expected of it by its stakeholders. While corporations have long been held responsible to investors and stockholders, many firms and stakeholders now advocate an expanded view of this accountability, which includes reporting on the role of business within broader society. SA is part of a movement known as SEAAR, the acronym for social and ethical accounting, auditing, and reporting.

VERIFYING SOCIAL COMMITMENT

Social audits, SA reports, and corporate citizenship audits are common names for tools that companies employ to identify and measure their successes and ongoing challenges with social responsibility. Regardless of the name, these reports are important for demonstrating a firm's commitment to ensuring the continuous improvement of its social responsibility efforts. Thus, SA has to be treated similarly to any other corporate initiative in terms of budget, assessment, and executive commitment. Without reliable measurements of the achievement of social responsibility objectives, a company has no concrete way to verify their importance, link them to organizational performance, justify expenditures, or effectively address stakeholder concerns.

Therefore, a key issue with SA is the way in which companies measure, represent, and report on their social responsibility activities and stakeholder relationships. SA reports are currently voluntary, as no law or regulation requires a specific reporting method or verification of the report's claims. Thus, SA is not subject to internal auditing standards and external assurance practices that accompany financial statements and related reports. However, some firms seek independent verification of the SA report. Major accounting firms and other consultants conduct assessments and attestations as to the accuracy and completeness of such reports.

Since this type of verification is rare, critics worry that some SA reports are merely public relations efforts that contain disinformation and distortions. Critics also question the extent to which companies may use these reports to enhance their reputations rather than as tools for sincerely improving stakeholder relationships.

SA8000 CERTIFICATION

To remedy these concerns and to create a best practices approach, there are several organizations devoted to ensuring SA within the global marketplace. Social Accountability International, formerly known as the Council on Economic Priorities Accreditation Agency, seeks to create and refine consensus-based ethical workplace standards, accredits qualified organizations to verify compliance with these standards, and promotes the understanding and implementation of social performance standards worldwide. SAI developed and supports SA8000 certification for assuring humane workplaces. SA8000 covers eight primary elements: (1) child labor, (2) forced labor, (3) health and safety, (4) freedom of association and right to collectively bargain, (5) discrimination, (6) disciplinary practices, (7) working hours, and (8) remuneration.

Each of the areas includes a number of specific criteria that must be met for a facility to be certified. For example, in the case of disciplinary practices, a facility must demonstrate that it neither engages in nor supports corporal punishment, physical or mental coercion, and/or verbal abuse of employees. The remuneration category requires a facility to compensate employees fairly and legally, communicate clearly about wages and benefits, and ensure wages are sufficient to meet the basic needs and some discretionary choices of its personnel.

In mid-2005, there were nearly 800 facilities certified as SA8000 compliant. These facilities are found in 47 countries, represent 54 industries, and employ more than 450,000 employees. India, Italy, China, and Brazil have the largest number of certified facilities. The industries most prevalent include apparel, textiles, chemicals, and transportation.

AA1000 PROCESS FRAMEWORK

AccountAbility is another organization dedicated to advancing the area of SA. This group, which was formally known as the Institute of Social and Ethical

AccountAbility, performs research to find best practices in corporate accountability, promotes the development of accountability competencies in various professions, works with public policy makers, and promotes effective accountability tools and standards. The AA1000 framework is designed to improve corporate accountability and performance by learning through stakeholder engagement. In this framework, accountability includes transparency, responsiveness, and compliance.

Much like quality control initiatives, AA1000 is focused on processes and principles rather than substantive issues. Thus, AA1000 does not prescribe performance on ethical issues (i.e., child labor) like the SA8000, Coalition for Environmentally Responsible Economies (CERES), Caux Principles, and other issues-based standards. The key process elements of AA1000 include planning, accounting, auditing and reporting, embedding, and stakeholder management. AccountAbility has published a number of other helpful tools, including an assurance standard for assessing materiality, completeness, and responsiveness of an organization's social report and the processes that inform its reporting.

GAP INC.'S SOCIAL RESPONSIBILITY REPORT

A number of well-known corporations have published SA reports. Gap Inc. is an international retailer offering clothing and other items under the Banana Republic, Old Navy, and Gap brand names. Along with the traditional corporate annual report, Gap Inc. also published a separate social responsibility report that reflected its activities between February 2004 and January 2005. The 60-page report included a short financial overview and focused on four major social responsibility issues: (1) labor conditions and certification issues within its supply chain and manufacturing sites; (2) core values and ethics training for employees; (3) community involvement and philanthropy through the Gap Foundation; and (4) environmental, health, and safety standards in the firm's manufacturing and retailing operations. To provide assurance for the accuracy of its report, the Gap incorporated specific examples, photographs, the results of stakeholder outreach sessions, and comments from external consultants.

Beyond SAI and AccountAbility, other nonprofit organizations, membership groups, consumer advocates, and companies are devoting efforts to increasing SA. Stakeholders are demanding increased transparency and are taking a more active role in gaining information from companies. Corporations are communicating about their social responsibility via published reports and website material. Government regulators are calling on companies to increase the quantity and quality of information disclosed. All these efforts are aimed at increasing companies' SA as well as access to accountability information.

—Debbie M. Thorne

Further Readings

Gap, Inc. (2004). Facing challenges. Finding opportunities: 2004 social responsibility report. Retrieved from www.gapinc.com/public/documents/CSR_Report_04.pdf

Moerman, L., & van der Laan, S. (2005). Social reporting in the tobacco industry: All smoke and mirrors? *Accounting, Auditing, and Accountability Journal, 18,* 374–389.

Social Accountability International [website]. Retrieved from www.sa-intl.org

Thorne McAlister, D., Ferrell, O. C., & Ferrell, L. (2005). *Business and society: A strategic approach to social responsibility* (2nd ed.). Boston: Houghton Mifflin.

SOCIAL AUDITS

Social auditing refers to the process of identifying, analyzing, measuring, evaluating, and monitoring the impact of an organization's operations on different stakeholder groups. The auditing process is carried out in five steps.

First, an exhaustive enumeration of the organization's social activities is compiled into a social data bank. Since compiling such a data set may prove to be a daunting task, due to the wide range of social activities that the organization performs, a lengthy and well-planned study may be required.

Second, the compiled data are analyzed such that the meaning and cost-benefit ratios of the social activities may be inferred. Analysis is conducted by using sophisticated statistical analysis tools and expert judgment.

Third, the impacts of the organization's activities on different stakeholder groups are measured. Since measures of social effects are not as well-developed as economic measures, proxies such as opinion and attitude measures are usually used.

Fourth, social performance is evaluated. The effectiveness of the organization's social activities is assessed by comparing actual performance to standards developed using norms and goals. The more clear and specific the norms and goals are, the more accurate the evaluation is. Fifth, continuous monitoring of social effects is maintained.

The success of the social audit depends on the accuracy of the steps discussed above. In addition, three recommendations need to be met. First, the social audit needs to strictly adhere to the selected norms and goals used as standards in the evaluation step. Second, the results of the social audit need to be integrated into the decision-making process of the corporation in the form of feedback as an integral part of the management of the company's social activities. Third, the social audit has to be carried out by competent and skilled professionals who are knowledgeable of the relevant social issues and problems.

THE EVOLUTION OF SOCIAL AUDITING

As different stakeholder groups, especially interest groups, increased their pressure on business organizations to pursue more socially responsible goals, and as the notion of corporate social responsibility gained more acceptance, business organizations started responding to their stakeholders' demands. Businesses' responses materialized in efforts such as natural environment awareness programs and equal employment opportunity initiatives. However, a suspicious public demanded measures to assess businesses' social impact, similar to the economic measures that assess a corporation's economic impact. Corporate social performance had to be accounted for. Simply portraying a socially responsible image through a corporate public relations office was not enough any more. The need for a rigorous process that accurately assesses corporate social performance and holds corporations accountable for their practices was clear. Time has come for social auditing.

TYPES OF SOCIAL AUDITS

Research and practice produced several types of social audits. There are six major types of social audits: (1) the social balance sheet and income statement, (2) the social performance audit, (3) the macro-micro social indicator audit, (4) the constituency group attitudes audit, (5) the government-mandated audits, and (6) the social process/program management audit. These six types of audits vary with respect to the intent for which they are conducted, the methods used, the scope covered, and the audit report form. In addition, the group conducting the audit varies among the several types. Following is a brief summary of the six major types of social audits.

The Social Balance Sheet and Income Statement

Similar to a financial balance sheet and income statement, the social balance sheet and income statement represent the social costs and benefits in dollar terms. This type of social audit attempts to parallel the methods of financial accounting. However, the lack of generally accepted standards and guidelines represent a major weakness of this type. In addition, in the absence of generally accepted standards and guidelines, assessment of the audit is at best subjective, if at all possible.

Two versions of this audit have been proposed, the first by Clark Abt, of Abt Associates, and the second by David Linowes, a certified public accountant. Two main differences between the two versions are with respect to audit scope and the group conducting the audit. First, the scope of the Clark Abt version of the audit is the whole company. In contrast, the scope of the Linowes version is the company's voluntary activities. Second, the group conducting the audit, for the Abt version, is composed of an external expert team. The Linowes version, on the other hand, is carried out by a team internal to the organization.

The Social Performance Audit

The social performance audit is carried out through a study of select companies in given industries. The audit results in a critical evaluation of the companies' social performance aimed at influencing investment decisions. Social issues such as environmental pollution and minority personnel policies are usually targeted. External critics conduct the audit. The Council on Economic Priorities and the Interfaith Center on Corporate Responsibility are the main two organizations that support and use this type of audit.

The Macro-Micro Social Indicator Audit

The micro-macro social indicator audit is a quantitative audit that uses both social indicators and indicators of the social performance of companies. The macro social indicators reflect the actual and desired general well-being of a community in general. Areas such as health and safety, education, and housing are usually covered. The micro social indicators, on the other hand, assess a single company's performance in any of the areas covered by the macro social indicators. Using these measures, two types of comparisons may be conducted. The first aims at assessing a single company's progress. To achieve this aim, the social performance of the company in a given year is compared with its performance in previous years. The second contrasts a company's performance to the performance of other companies or the industry as a whole. External or internal experts may carry out the audit. The major strength of this type of social audit is the use of quantitative measures that enables the public to systematically evaluate a company's social performance.

The Constituency Group Attitudes Audit

Most suitable for corporations that interact with different stakeholder groups, also called corporate constituency, the constituency group attitude audit identifies and measures the stakeholder attitudes. The information gathered about stakeholder attitudes and preferences is then used to help corporations better manage social pressures from the different stakeholder groups. An external team of experts carries out this audit. The audit may cover the activities of the whole company or activities of areas of concern.

The Government-Mandated Audits

The government-mandated audits, as suggested by its name, are a type of audit that is required by different agencies of the federal government or by local and state governments. The most notable agencies of the federal government that have required this type of audit are the Environmental Protection Agency, the Equal Employment Opportunity Commission, and the safety and health administration.

This type of audit focuses on corporate performance in specific areas such as environmental pollution, minority personnel practices, and workplace safety. Corporate performance is expressed in numerical and statistical terms. The scope is either the whole company or a division. An internal team conducts the audit on behalf of the overseeing government agency.

The Social Process/Program Management Audit

This type of audit aims at assessing the effectiveness of select organizational programs that are considered to have a significant social impact. The social process audit, also called the program management audit, unlike other types of audits that focus on program outcomes, takes a holistic approach to assessing program effectiveness. First, antecedents and program development processes are evaluated. At this step, the factors that led to the development of the program are the subject of evaluation. Such factors usually are in the form of organizational and environmental forces that affect corporate decision making. Second, program goals are evaluated. Similar to the first step, the effects of organizational and environmental forces are considered. Third, the transformation process where inputs to the program are transformed into outputs is evaluated. Finally, the program evaluation process itself is assessed.

The standard against which the effectiveness of the program is compared is the set goals. In other words, the actual outcome of the program is compared against the set goals. The evaluation process uses both quantitative and qualitative measures. Quantitative measures such as cost-benefit analysis are used. Qualitative measures, on the other hand, are concerned with the description and analysis of program activities. The two main organizations that are responsible for this type of audit are the Social Audit Research Group at the Graduate School of Business at the University of Pittsburgh and Bank of America.

CORPORATE SOCIAL ACCOUNTING, AUDITING, AND REPORTING

Concerned with corporate social responsibility and performance, David Hess argues that further steps need to be taken beyond the current state of social auditing. He proposes the Social Accounting, Auditing, and Reporting (SAAR) system. Under SAAR, the corporation will not only be required to disclose select aspects of corporate social performance but will also be required to put in place a systematic process for evaluating corporate performance. SAAR has four general requirements or characteristics. First, it must be stakeholder oriented. Stakeholder orientation is manifested through (1) taking into account the views of all stakeholder groups, (2) developing a dialogue between the corporation and its stakeholders, and (3) handling the competing views of the different stakeholder groups. Second, the SAAR system must encompass a set of established procedures and policies that ensure effectiveness. Third, the report and the findings of the audit must be verified by independent auditors. Fourth, the report must be disclosed to corporate constituencies in an intelligible and accessible manner. Preferably, the report should be published annually, thus allowing for utilization of the feedback in the next auditing cycle.

CHALLENGES OF CONDUCTING A SOCIAL AUDIT

Various factors may interfere with the auditing process and, accordingly, affect its success. These factors may be classified into four main categories—attitudinal, organizational, political, and technological challenges. First, attitudinal challenges are posed by individuals within the organization. Their attitudes toward and acceptance of the audit would influence the process and its outcomes. Personnel attitudes may affect the decision of which programs are to be audited, getting permission to audit, gaining access to the data, and determining how the audit results are to be used. Positive attitudes toward and acceptance of the audit normally would facilitate the process and enhance its effectiveness. Second, the organizational challenges that face the audit refer to those organizational forces that would influence the direction and effectiveness of the audit. Third, the political challenges posed by different interest groups might push the audit away from its rational path. Fourth, the technological challenges are mostly measurement problems: What should be measured, how should it be measured, and which standards should be used?

CRITICS OF THE SOCIAL AUDIT

Given the above-stated challenges that face social auditing, some critics argue that due to the lack of standards and generally accepted rules and regulations, the social audit is merely a tool that some corporations use to portray a positive image of social responsibility. The legitimacy, accuracy, reliability, and validity of the audit are questionable at best.

ADVOCATES AND SUPPORTS OF THE SOCIAL AUDIT

In spite of the challenges and criticisms directed at the social audit, some companies remain committed to this practice. One of the most widely known social audits is that of Ben & Jerry's, an ice-cream company well known for its social responsibility and philanthropic activities. Ben & Jerry's has published its social audits since 1999 on the Internet. Also, the company's website clearly reveals its commitment to corporate social responsibility.

—Kareem M. Shabana

Further Readings

Ben & Jerry's [webpage]. Retrieved from www.benjerry.com/our_company/about_us/social_mission/social_audits/index.cfm

Blake, D. H., Frederick, W. C., & Myers, M. S. (1976). *Social auditing: Evaluating the impact of corporate programs.* New York: Praeger.

Hess, D. (2001). Regulating corporate social performance: A new look at social accounting, auditing, and reporting. *Business Ethics Quarterly, 11*(2), 307–330.

Morimoto, R., Ash, J., & Hope, C. (2005). Corporate social responsibility audit: From theory to practice. *Journal of Business Ethics, 62,* 315–325.

TRIPLE BOTTOM LINE

The "triple bottom line" captures the three ways in which a company's performance can be conceptualized and measured. John Elkington refers to these three domains as economic prosperity, environmental quality, and social justice. The concept of the triple bottom line implies that a company's effectiveness cannot be judged by financial performance alone. To become more sustainable, a company needs to meet the requirements and expectations of most, if not all, of its stakeholder groups, which include shareholders, employees, customers, suppliers, the local community, and the natural environment. Performance with respect to all these stakeholder domains is reported, for example, in Global Reporting Initiative (GRI) measures, on which an increasing number of companies rely. However, some observers argue that even future generations must be considered in such stakeholder measures since the UN's Brundtland Report defined *sustainable development* as "development that meets the needs of the present world without compromising the ability of future generations to meet their own needs." The concept of the triple bottom line pays tribute to the interdependence of the aforementioned three broad areas, in the sense that there is no social progress without economic development and there is no economic or social prosperity without ecological sustainability. Furthermore, the concept acknowledges the interrelationships between these three areas, which are in constant flux due to social, political, economic, and environmental influences.

ECONOMIC PROSPERITY

This element of the triple bottom line represents, to some extent, a company's conventional financial bottom line. Usually, profitability is used as a proxy of the financial strength and value of a company's physical and financial assets. As per standard accounting practice, profit figures are expressed as earnings per share (EPS) or return on assets (ROA). However, under the triple-bottom-line nomenclature, economic prosperity is a broader concept than financial performance because it takes into account a company's direct and indirect economic impact on various stakeholders (e.g., in the form of investments, dividends, or wages). For example, to achieve economic prosperity, companies use and deploy human capital or knowledge-based assets. To achieve economic prosperity, companies must constantly evaluate their employees' skills, experiences, and knowledge. These elements are often dubbed *intellectual capital,* which companies must maintain, develop, and enhance to achieve economic prosperity.

Hence, the concept of the triple bottom line requires that companies think more broadly about economic prosperity than just ROA. Particularly the sustainability agenda pushes toward long-term business planning. For example, Porter and van der Linde argued that, especially in the long run, there is no trade-off between environmental protection and economic competitiveness. Furthermore, a psychometric meta-analysis by Orlitzky, Schmidt, and Rynes showed that the empirical links between the economic, social, and environmental dimensions of corporate performance are, on average, positive and strong or moderately strong. In contrast, conceptualizing social and ecological improvements as in "natural" opposition to business success may only hinder the implementation of the triple bottom line. Therefore, in line with the empirical evidence, corporate executives must be persuaded that this broader thinking about company performance (as explained by three complementary, or synergistic, rather than contradictory forces) will, in the final analysis, pay off for the companies that they lead.

ENVIRONMENTAL QUALITY

Environmental quality addresses the ecological bottom line. It focuses on a company's impact on the natural environment. Environmental resources consist of renewable resources (e.g., wood, fish, corn) and nonrenewable resources (e.g., soil quality, fossil fuel). The natural environment also provides so-called ecosystem services, such as climate stabilization and water purification. Many of these services are presently invaluable, that is, either no known substitutes exist or there is one available only at a prohibitive price. To achieve environmental quality, companies should consume natural resources at a rate below either their natural reproduction or the development of substitutes. They should not emit pollution that is greater than that which can be absorbed by natural systems.

This argument running opposite to conventional economics is that not all types of natural resources and ecosystem services have substitutes in the form of economic capital or technological innovations. In the short run at least, many resources and ecosystems are irreplaceable. Complex combinations of various natural resources in an ecosystem restrain their substitutability. Forest ecosystems, for example, offer raw material for paper (which is substitutable), but forests also absorb carbon dioxide (CO_2), regulate the flow of rainwater, and provide protection for native plants and animal species. Hence, in many ways, environmental quality and economic prosperity are complementary. Companies have to improve or maintain the quality of natural resources to provide for their long-term economic prosperity. This improvement or maintenance represents the aforementioned investment in *natural capital,* which is likely to explain the performance of future, sustainable organizations.

One of the foremost goals in achieving environmental quality is eco-efficiency. According to the World Business Council for Sustainable Development (WBCSD), *eco-efficiency* is achieved by the delivery of competitively priced goods and services that satisfy human needs and bring quality to life, while progressively reducing ecological impacts and resource intensity throughout the life cycle, to a level at least in line with the Earth's estimated carrying capacity. More specifically, eco-efficiency can be achieved through (a) dematerialization, which involves the substitution of knowledge flows for material flows or product customization; (b) production loop closure, which returns every output to natural systems as a nutrient or as an input to future manufacturing; (c) service extension, in which customers lease rather than buy goods, especially durable goods (such as interior furnishings); and (d) functional extension, which enhances the functionality of products, often in the form of additional service delivery.

SOCIAL JUSTICE

Social justice refers to the company's human and social bottom line. This element of the triple bottom line is often called "corporate social responsibility" (even though many scholars would consider social responsibility to include environmental responsibilities as well). Social justice concerns a company's impact on knowledge, skills, motivation, and loyalty of employees and business partners. Proxies for this impact might be turnover, training opportunities, and occupational health and safety within the company. More broadly, social justice also refers to how a company may influence social aspects in its relationships with various external stakeholders, such as involvement in community projects, entrepreneurial culture, and encouragement of innovative suggestions furthering social progress.

To accomplish social justice, companies need to add social value to the communities within which they operate. They can do this by effectively communicating with their stakeholder groups, involving their stakeholders in learning and development opportunities, increasing the number of choices available to customers, and respecting property rights.

A problem with such an aim is that a company typically cannot satisfy all stakeholders simultaneously. Some decisions in favor of certain stakeholders may require trade-offs (e.g., capital invested in state-of-the-art recycling technology will prevent this money from being invested in workers' training and development), which makes these types of business decisions inherently distributive. However, an acknowledgment of this balancing act does not necessarily imply an inevitable erosion of *social capital,* which is a capability that arises from the prevalence of trust in a society (or in certain sectors of society). Because the level of trust between a company and its external stakeholders is a key determinant of long-term survival, a company must clearly identify the status of certain stakeholder claims and, more often than not, engage in a variety of stakeholder dialogues and partnerships.

Like natural resources, social resources are not always substitutable. Companies can introduce economic incentives (e.g., lower prices of products or higher salaries) to substitute for dissatisfaction of their stakeholders. However, economic substitutes have their limits in a social context. Certain social resources such as community spirit, innovative culture, or reputation have no traditional economic substitutes. Hence, in many ways, social justice or social responsibility can be seen as a precondition for a company's economic prosperity and environmental sustainability.

The triple bottom line emphasizes the need for integration of these three dimensions of economic prosperity, environmental quality, and social justice. The concrete measurement of these dimensions aids in this integration in practice.

TRIPLE-BOTTOM-LINE REPORTING

The metaphor of the triple bottom line highlights the importance of measurement and reporting in all three domains of company activities and impact. In line with the increasing popularity of the triple bottom line, many corporations shifted from reactive, accounting-based reporting to proactive, value-added, and comprehensive reporting of a company's performance. Triple-bottom-line reporting is supposed to address both primary stakeholders (e.g., employees, investors, business partners, customers) and secondary stakeholders (e.g., governments, social activists, communities, the media) and provide these stakeholder groups with valid, comprehensive, and reliable data about a company's economic, environmental, and social performance. Apart from financial indicators, a company's triple-bottom-line report typically includes narrative statements (such as an explanation of equal employment opportunity policies and programs) and environmental impact measures (such as amount of waste by type and destination).

Although there is at present no universally accepted reporting model, the GRI is a comprehensively developed framework that is widely used. Established in 1997, the GRI sought to bring together business executives, accountants, social and environmental activists, labor organizations, the United Nations Environmental Programme (UNEP), and governments to enhance the comparability and legitimacy of triple-bottom-line reporting standards worldwide. The GRI elements are (a) CEO statement; (b) key indicators; (c) profile and financial performance; (d) policies, organization, and management systems; (e) stakeholder relations; (f) management performance; (g) operational performance; (h) product performance; and (i) sustainability statement. However, so far, integration of these different domains of the triple bottom line has proven elusive. Triple-bottom-line principles similar to the GRI have been promoted by the Caux Roundtable (a coalition of European, U.S., and Japanese business leaders) and the Clarkson Centre for Business Ethics & Board Effectiveness, as well as a number of private organizations, such as SustainAbility, Trillium Asset Management, and KLD Research & Analytics, Inc.

Reporting about the traditional bottom line (i.e., the company's financial performance) is a well-established practice grounded in standard methodology and common systems. Yet, as mentioned before, under the triple-bottom-line approach, economic performance is more broadly defined. Therefore, a step toward more comprehensive reporting on companies' economic prosperity has been made by replacing the conventional financial performance indicators, such as ROA or return on earnings (ROE), with economic value added (EVA), an indicator promoted by several U.S. investors. Application of EVA shows whether a company is adding or destroying value. Within this reporting approach, profit figures are adjusted for the expenses of the environmental resources (natural capital) employed.

The 1990s saw a tremendous growth in environmental reporting. However, the practices of environmental accounting and reporting have been inconsistent and varied across industries, regions, and governmental requirements. To improve the situation, the International Chamber of Commerce has developed the Charter for Sustainable Development, which consists of 16 principles for environmental management. The Charter has provided a common basis for improving business environmental performance, thereby minimizing reporting differences. By the end of the 1990s, a majority of large corporations in the United States (more than 50%) and the United Kingdom (more than 75%) issued environmental reports.

Social accounting and reporting began to gain advocates and practitioners a few years after environmental reporting. Social accounting measures the quality of stakeholder relationships and social performance of a company. In 1997, the U.S. Council on Economic Priorities developed a code of conduct named Social Accountability 8000 (SA 8000), which defines both the criteria for workplace conditions and a system of independent verification of factory compliance. Then, in 1999, UN Secretary-General Kofi Annan announced the proposal to create the UN Global Compact at the World Economic Forum in Davos, Switzerland. The Global Compact provides nonbinding recommendations related to corporate social performance. In another effort, the Institute for Social and Ethical Accountability (ISEA), formed in 1995, created accounting and auditing standards in a comprehensive framework that is called AA1000. Companies such as The Body Shop, British Telecom, and Royal Dutch/Shell, together with organizations from the nonprofit sector, joined up to be proactive in implementing the AA1000 standards with independent assurance. These developments suggest that in only a few years social reporting evolved from a marginal to a central activity of many large companies.

One of the major challenges with respect to triple-bottom-line reporting lies in the integration of environmental and social reports in the company's conventional accounting systems. Environmental and social reports are qualitatively different from financial accounting and auditing. In the case of the former two domains, there is currently an absence of standard methodology as they are more open to subjective opinion or interpretation. Some areas of environmental and social performances, such as the level of trust or employee morale, are measured by collecting stakeholders' perceptions of performance. Information is usually collected through interviews, focus groups, surveys, and stakeholder meetings. For example, the AA1000 framework provides guidance on the selection and administration of these data collection techniques. Some other areas of performance, such as sponsorship and gas emissions, can be measured through the use of more "objective" data. In short, economic performance is assessed with standardized systems and protocols, whereas environmental and social accounting systems still suffer from an absence of standard methodology and lack of accounting and auditing experience. Because of this ongoing debate about environmental and social reports, though, it becomes essential for business to assess these domains internally—via regular *responsibility,* or *social audits.*

CRITIQUES

The concept of the triple bottom line has attracted a few critics, who claim that the concept is synonymous with *corporate social responsibility* and is not novel. Furthermore, the aforementioned lack of standardized, aggregate measurement has been criticized. Critics often contrast the triple bottom line with the concept of the financial bottom line, which they consider internally consistent. Yet, as argued by Meyer and Gupta, there is empirical evidence that different measures of economic performance not only *can* contradict each other but also are in fact *likely* to do so. In fact, financial measures may be as prone to measurement error and deliberate distortion as other organizational performance variables. There have been several important developments that represent clear attempts to bring triple-bottom-line measures (e.g., GRI) in line with the concept and thus enhance construct validity. Given the relatively brief history of this comprehensive model of organizational effectiveness, it may be unrealistic to expect perfect measures. Different business contexts militate against a "one-size-fits-all" model of the triple bottom line for any firm of any scale in any industry.

MOTIVATIONS

Since 1997, the concept of the triple bottom line has gained tremendous currency, especially among managers of large international corporations whose reputation is on the line on a daily basis. Of course, companies adopt the triple-bottom-line principles for a variety of reasons. Some do so because their executives believe in and espouse these principles. Other managers embrace the concept (at least publicly) because they are expected to comply with stakeholder values or because they regard this approach as a useful marketing tool. In short, there may be all kinds of "motivations" of triple-bottom-line accounting. As the triple bottom line can be conceptualized as an inherently moral-normative concept, the second-guessing of ulterior business motives is understandable. However, raising questions about company motives is confused for two main reasons. First, some authors regard Elkington's notion of sustainable development as inherently utilitarian. This means it is primarily concerned with business contributions to social value and minimization of environmental impact as two *outcome* measures, or *consequences,* of company performance. Second, more generally, attributing "motivations" to organizations ascribes human features to these social entities at the collective level. Talk of some "corporate motivation" may misapply a fundamentally individual-level concept to higher levels of analysis in social theory. Hence, in the end, such ethical fault-finding in organizational motives might often be counterproductive because, ultimately, motives can only be inferred at individual levels of analysis, whereas outcomes can be measured and evaluated at higher levels.

CONCLUSION

The triple-bottom-line concept, in general, addresses the evolving relationships between business and society. Such relationships involve complex issues of measurement and assessment of a company's performance through three different lenses. It also requires careful consideration of various aspects of stakeholders' perceptions of business processes and outcomes. Therefore, the main challenges continue to lie in the operationalization of the triple bottom line. The implementation of the triple-bottom-line philosophy requires integrative dialogues between stakeholders that seem to be in opposition—for example, companies and environmental groups, shareholders and employees, industries and local communities, and governments and businesses. These stakeholder groups need to develop various partnerships to reconcile tensions between their goals and achieve integration of economic prosperity, environmental quality, and social justice. Some recent empirical research indicates that many of these tensions and oppositions may be dysfunctional social constructions that are, in the final analysis, more apparent than real.

—Marc Orlitzky and Ljiljana Erakovic

214

Further Readings

Elkington, J. (1998). *Cannibals with forks: The triple bottom line of the 21st century.* Oxford, UK: Capstone.

Global Reporting Initiative (GRI) [website]. Retrieved from www.globalreporting.org

Hawken, P., Lovins, A. B., & Lovins, L. H. (1999). *Natural capitalism: The next industrial revolution.* London: Earthscan. Retrieved from www.natcap.org

Holliday, C. O., Schmidheiny, S., & Watts, P. (2002). *Walking the talk: The business case for sustainable development.* San Francisco: Greenleaf.

International Chamber of Commerce. (2005, March 4). *ICC views on economic, environmental and social reporting* (Policy Statement). Retrieved from www.iccwbo.org

Meyer, M. W., & Gupta, V. (1994). The performance paradox. *Research in Organizational Behavior, 16,* 309–369.

Norman, W., & MacDonald, C. (2004). Getting to the bottom of "triple bottom line." *Business Ethics Quarterly, 14*(2), 243–262.

Orlitzky, M., Schmidt, F. L., & Rynes, S. L. (2003). Corporate social and financial performance: A meta-analysis. *Organization Studies, 24*(3), 403–441.

Orlitzky, M., & Swanson, D. L. (2002). Value attunement: Toward a theory of socially responsible executive decision making. *Australian Journal of Management, 27,* 119–128.

Porter, M. E., & van der Linde, C. (1995). Green and competitive: Ending the stalemate. *Harvard Business Review, 73*(5), 120–134.

Wheeler, D., & Elkington, J. (2001). The end of the corporate environmental report? Or the advents of cybernetic sustainability reporting and communication. *Business Strategy and the Environment, 10,* 1–14.

CORPORATE SOCIAL FINANCIAL PERFORMANCE

The relationship between corporate social performance and corporate financial performance is a topic that "business and society" scholars have been debating for several decades. This entry will focus on the empirical evidence that point to complementarities and, thus, a positive correlation between corporate social and financial performance. However, different scholars have also portrayed social and financial performance as two contradictory or independent concepts. Before the arguments for each position are summarized, the definition and consequences of "social responsibility" and "social performance" must be specified a bit more clearly.

Corporate social performance can be defined as an organization's configuration of principles of social responsibility, processes of social responsiveness, and observable outcomes as they relate to the organization's societal relationships. In other words, a socially responsible organization evaluates its impact on society comprehensively and acts on certain principles to protect and improve its social and natural environments. Consequently, such a responsible firm will develop internal structures and processes to respond constructively to concerns ranging from product safety to pollution prevention to employee work-life balance. As such, high corporate social performance is the outcome of a relationship-building process between the organization and all its internal and external stakeholders. Organizational stakeholders include, among others, employees, customers, suppliers, partners, social and environmental activists, governments, local communities, and other groups. It is important to keep these specific, technical definitions of "social responsibility" and "social performance" in mind throughout this entry. (Contrary to this usage of the term in this entry, some economists redefine "business social responsibility" as "profit maximization.")

A COMPLEMENTARY RELATIONSHIP?

According to instrumental stakeholder theory, an organization will be more likely to achieve its economic goals if it tries to satisfy its various stakeholders' needs in a balanced way. Through social performance, an organization may enhance its economic effectiveness because it may have developed a favorable reputation for fair business dealings, which may attract more customers (increase sales revenues) or better and more committed employees (increase labor productivity). Simultaneously, balanced stakeholder management can either reflect organizational learning or build up managerial skills, which can translate into higher financial performance. In turn, higher financial performance may allow organizations to spend more money on social or environmental causes. Such complementarities may result in self-reinforcing cycles of social and financial performance in which both variables are positively correlated.

A CONTRADICTORY RELATIONSHIP?

Some economists and ethicists regard the complementary vision of social and financial performance as utopian and idealistic. For example, economists such as Nobel Prize winner Milton Friedman argue that, by definition, corporate social performance is an altruistic, sacrificial strategy that expends financial and other organizational resources at the expense of the organization's owners. A social responsibility strategy, according to this view, is particularly harmful to a firm's market performance because stakeholder management is performed by executives that have not been elected by the public and generally do not possess the skills (especially compared with the government) to make informed decisions about stakeholders in social and environmental arenas. Overall, advocates of this perspective argue that social performance is a waste of shareholder funds and, thus, hinders rather than enhances an organization's economic performance, which explains and predicts a negative relationship between the two variables.

ARE THESE TWO CONCEPTS INDEPENDENT, AND THUS THE RELATIONSHIP NULL?

A third strand of theorizing postulates a null relationship between social and financial performance. More recently, economists have argued that corporate social responsibility was a normal good whose provision would be determined by the forces of supply and demand. Overall, market forces will cause the overall relationship to be zero, or null, although a number of contingencies (e.g., firm size or innovation) may also cause it to be positive or negative. Furthermore, some business and society scholars postulate that the principles driving instrumental market activities and duty-bound ethical activities are, in fact, very different. These normative incompatibilities may explain why many studies have indicated a null correlation between social and financial performance.

OVERARCHING EMPIRICAL EVIDENCE TO DATE

The Meta-Analytic Technique

Meta-analysis is the way most quantitative sciences (e.g., medicine, physics, psychology) take stock and reach overall conclusions about a research area. It represents an empirical quantitative integration of the findings of previous research and corrects for certain study artifacts that affect any primary study (e.g., sampling error, measurement error, and a few other possible study artifacts). Thus, for reaching conclusions about an entire research program spanning several decades, meta-analysis is a more valid research tool than narrative reviews, which in this research area have typically concluded that there does not appear to be any relationship between the two variables. However, four meta-analyses in this area have shown that overall social performance and financial performance are most likely complementary.

Interpretation of Results

Overall, the award-winning meta-analysis by Orlitzky, Schmidt, and Rynes supports the hypothesis of a positive relationship between social and financial performance. A lot of the variability in findings across studies seems to be due to statistical study artifacts and different research strategies. According to this meta-analysis, sampling and measurement errors accounted, on average, for 24% of the variance across studies; reputation measures of social performance were better predictors of financial performance than social-audit disclosures; and the economic impact of social performance was stronger on accounting measures than market measures of economic return. Orlitzky and his colleagues also addressed concerns regarding availability bias—the possibility that studies that fail to show a relationship between social and financial performance are unlikely to be published. File drawer analysis is a technique useful for assessing this concern. The file drawer analysis indicated that more than 1,000 such unpublished studies excluded from the meta-analysis would be needed to change their overall conclusions.

In addition, according to evidence provided by meta-analysis, corporate social performance and financial performance tend to be mutually reinforcing organizational activities. Through the use of time lags, Orlitzky and his colleagues found that financial performance is a positive predictor of future social performance and that social performance also predicts financial performance. In other words, the meta-analytic findings suggest that a business can develop mutually beneficial relations with stakeholder groups, which can actually pay off surprisingly quickly for the socially responsible firm.

Social performance and financial performance are most likely positively correlated because social performance helps improve managerial competencies and enhance corporate reputations. Through a company's positively constructive (rather than adversarial) relations with stakeholders, its stakeholders may perceive that company favorably. For example, internal stakeholders, such as employees, may become more committed, or external stakeholders, such as customers, may become more willing to buy the company's products or pay a premium for the goods from socially responsible firms. Although the meta-analysis suggested that competency building was a less important factor in the economic-performance-enhancing effects of social responsibility than corporate reputation, corporate social performance might also help organizations develop internal organizational learning mechanisms to deal with the uncertainties presented by its stakeholders.

Social performance may also reduce business risk. Again, these effects are most likely mediated by organizational reputation, as the meta-analytic findings by Orlitzky and Benjamin suggest. By balancing a multitude of stakeholder interests, a firm may increase various stakeholder groups' confidence that the firm will be understanding and nonadversarial in resolving future stakeholder conflicts. In turn, this may reduce the variability of accounting rates of return and share prices because the investment community will not respond to temporary company setbacks by panic selling of its shares, for example.

Organization size does not appear to confound the relationship between social and financial performance. That is, large and—quite unexpectedly—even small companies can reap economic rewards from balanced stakeholder analysis and management. The logic could be illustrated as follows: Small companies that are high in social performance may infuse greater trust into their relationships with allies and reach economically beneficial supply agreements because the company is seen as a more trustworthy and honest partner.

Predating but also narrower in scope than these meta-analyses by Orlitzky and his colleagues, Frooman had shown, in a meta-analysis of event studies only, that irresponsible and illicit corporate actions generally reduced shareholder wealth. This earlier meta-analysis by Frooman is another piece of evidence that suggests that building constructive stakeholder relations serves the enlightened self-interest of companies, their managers, and owners.

Implications for Management

The empirical research accumulated and meta-analytically integrated to date supports the view that, conceptually, corporate social and financial performance are not only compatible with each other in many cases but may also manifest, in tandem, the elusive construct of overall organizational effectiveness. This research program also supports the convictions of some practitioners that a business can maximize its performance when its executives are aware of the multitude of business opportunities that exist in its daily interactions with all its stakeholders. A narrow corporate orientation centered only on shareholder wealth maximization may miss these societal and environmental opportunities and cause the organization to be out of touch with developments in broader society. Ultimately, such an isolation from trends that are broader than market forces and from stakeholder concerns more generally may harm the corporation economically because it may lead to a reactive, rather than proactive, strategic stance.

The promotion of social performance can reflect enlightened self-interest because it may preempt costly defensive actions in lawsuits. By being socially responsible, an organization could be attuned to stakeholder concerns long before they become legal problems. More positively, quantitative literature reviews of this long stream of research on social and financial performance suggest that corporate social performance can be an investment in the long-term economic sustainability of the organization.

The finding that social performance is likely to be a lever of financial performance is not only reassuring, though. It also raises the important point of the effective and efficient *implementation* of this more value- and stakeholder-based management style. For example, there is a dearth of research in human resource management on the type of organizational staffing, pay, or performance-appraisal practices that are most suitable for maximizing social performance while enhancing financial performance. It is important to stress that the economic pay-offs from high social performance are not automatic.

Therefore, business managers and researchers must understand in much greater depth how this potential synergy between social and financial performance can be cultivated in practice. This cultivation may be affected by, and indeed depend on, executives' value orientations and decision making, for example.

The meta-analyses by Orlitzky and colleagues also pointed to a number of challenges in this research area. First, both social performance and financial performance need to be measured with greater reliability. Second, more contingency factors must be considered because, overall, the meta-analysis showed that about 76% of the variability in past findings is *not* explained by the two statistical artifacts of sampling error and measurement error. With respect to several subdimensions of social and financial performance, the relationships were weak, partly due to stakeholder mismatching in prior studies. Stakeholder mismatching occurs when individual studies correlate specific social and financial performance measures that should, in fact, not be correlated (e.g., because researchers provide no theoretical rationale). In addition to these primary-study problems, theoretical contingencies may apply as well. For instance, in empirical research conducted between the late 1960s and the late 1990s, environmental performance was only a weak positive predictor of economic performance, and 60% of its cross-study variance remained unexplained. This finding points to moderators, or contingencies, that future research could explore.

—Marc Orlitzky

Further Readings

Donaldson, T., & Preston, L. E. (1995). The stakeholder theory of the corporation: Concepts, evidence, and implications. *Academy of Management Review, 20,* 65–91.

Friedman, M. (1970, September 13). The social responsibility of business is to increase its profits. *New York Times Magazine,* p. 33.

Frooman, J. (1997). Socially irresponsible and illegal behavior and shareholder wealth: A meta-analysis of event studies. *Business & Society, 36,* 221–249.

Hunt, M. (1997). *How science takes stock: The story of meta-analysis.* New York: Russell Sage Foundation.

Jensen, M. C. (2002). Value maximization, stakeholder theory, and the corporate objective function. *Business Ethics Quarterly, 12*(2), 235–256.

Jones, T. M. (1995). Instrumental stakeholder theory: A synthesis of ethics and economics. *Academy of Management Review, 20*(2), 404–437.

Levitt, T. (1958). The dangers of social responsibility. *Harvard Business Review, 36*(5), 38–44.

McWilliams, A., & Siegel, D. (2000). Corporate social responsibility and financial performance: Correlation or misspecification? *Strategic Management Journal, 21,* 603–609.

McWilliams, A., & Siegel, D. (2001). Corporate social responsibility: A theory of the firm perspective. *Academy of Management Review, 26,* 117–127.

Orlitzky, M. (2001). Does organizational size confound the relationship between corporate social performance and firm financial performance? *Journal of Business Ethics, 33*(2), 167–180.

Orlitzky, M. (2006). Links between corporate social responsibility and corporate financial performance: Theoretical and empirical determinants. In J. Allouche (Ed.), *Corporate social responsibility. Vol. 2: Performances and stakeholders.* London: Palgrave Macmillan/European Foundation for Management Development.

Orlitzky, M., & Benjamin, J. D. (2001). Corporate social performance and firm risk: A meta-analytic review. *Business & Society, 40*(4), 369–396. (Won 2001 Best Article Prize awarded by the International Association for Business and Society (IABS) in association with *California Management Review.*)

Orlitzky, M., Schmidt, F. L., & Rynes, S. L. (2003). Corporate social and financial performance: A meta-analysis. *Organization Studies, 24*(3), 403–441.

Strand, R. (1983). A systems paradigm of organizational adjustment to the social environment. *Academy of Management Review, 8,* 90–96.

Swanson, D. L. (1995). Addressing a theoretical problem by reorienting the corporate social performance model. *Academy of Management Review, 20,* 43–64.

Swanson, D. L. (1999). Toward an integrative theory of business and society: A research strategy for corporate social performance. *Academy of Management Review, 24,* 506–521.

Ullmann, A. (1985). Data in search of a theory: A critical examination of the relationship among social performance, social disclosure, and economic performance. *Academy of Management Review, 10,* 540–577.

Waddock, S. A., & Graves, S. B. (1997). Quality of management and quality of stakeholder relations: Are they synonymous? *Business & Society, 36*(3), 250–279.

Wood, D. J. (1991). Corporate social performance revisited. *Academy of Management Review, 16,* 691–718.

Wood, D. J., & Jones, R. E. (1995). Stakeholder mismatching: A theoretical problem in empirical research on corporate social performance. *International Journal of Organizational Analysis, 3,* 229–267.

CORPORATE SOCIAL RESPONSIBILITY AS PROFIT MAXIMIZATION

The claim that the social responsibility of business is to increase its profits is associated with the late Milton Friedman and is the title of a famous article he published in 1970. The article is a devastating critique of the popular idea that corporations have social responsibilities that trump profit maximization. It has proved to be prophetic. The article was written, as it states, against a background of "widespread aversion to 'capitalism,' 'profits,' [and] the 'soulless corporation.'" At the time, Friedman further noted, managers would often disguise actions that were really intended to increase profits in the cloak of corporate social responsibility (CSR). But today, in a remarkable reversal, Friedman's doctrine of shareholder value is triumphant, and managers often use the rhetoric of profit maximization as a cloak for actions that are, in part at least, really driven by considerations of CSR.

The doctrine of CSR teaches that corporations have responsibilities to promote certain social goals, even at the expense of their own profitability. CSR requires more than simply playing by the rules—that is, engaging in free and open competition without deception or fraud. It imposes on corporations affirmative obligations to play their part in solving social problems and righting social wrongs. At the time the article was written, corporations were exhorted to help fight inflation and high unemployment among inner-city youth. Today, corporations are urged to combat global warming, help solve the AIDS crisis, alleviate poverty at home and abroad, and much more.

The argument of Friedman's article is actually less a case for profit maximization than it is a demolition of the case for CSR. And Friedman's position is more complex and nuanced than is suggested by the polemical title of his article. The critical passage in his article is as follows:

> In a free-enterprise, private-property system, a corporate executive is an employee of the owners of the business. He has direct responsibility

to his employers. That responsibility is to conduct the business in accordance with their desires, which generally will be to make as much money as possible while conforming to the basic rules of the society, both those embodied in law and those embodied in ethical custom.

It is apparent that Friedman's objection to CSR is not that it leads to spending money on social goals but that it does so *without the consent of a corporation's owners.* Managers have accepted a fiduciary obligation to manage the corporation in accordance with the desires of its owners, and CSR would permit or require them to violate that obligation. As Friedman notes, things would be quite different if the managers had promised something else. If a group of people established a corporation for a charitable purpose, such as building a hospital or a school, then the manager of that corporation would have a fiduciary duty to carry out that objective.

It is also an entirely different matter, Friedman says, if the manager chooses to devote some of his *own* money or time or energy to help achieve a social objective, because in that case "he is acting as a principal, not an agent; he is spending his own money or time or energy, not the money of his employers or the time or energy he has contracted to devote to their purposes." If managers disagree with a corporation's priorities, then of course they are free to "refuse to work for particular corporations."

There are other objections to CSR. First, it empowers managers to spend other people's money for a general social interest. That is objectionable because it usurps a function of government: It means that managers are in effect "imposing taxes, on the one hand, and deciding how the tax proceeds shall be spent, on the other." It places public decision making in private hands and bypasses the traditional checks and balances of our political system. Second, nothing in the training or experience of managers qualifies them to make public policy—they are "experts at making money, not social policy." Third, CSR harms the foundations of our free society by reinforcing the idea that profits are wicked and so must be controlled. From that idea, it is a short step to the detailed regulation of the economy by "the iron fist of Government bureaucrats."

Friedman makes a final point that has passed relatively unnoticed: Not only is CSR undesirable, but it is probably *unworkable* too. That is because the manager who strays too far from minding the bottom line will likely be fired by the shareholders—"either the present ones or those who take over when his actions in the name of social responsibility have reduced the corporation's profits and the price of its stock." The market for corporate control strictly limits the scope for managers to engage in CSR (unless of course it is profitable).

Friedman's *positive* case for seeing profit maximization as business's social responsibility is really the subject of two other classic works—*Capitalism and Freedom* (1961) and *Free to Choose* (1980). There, Friedman lays out the case that individual freedom can thrive only where markets are substantially free. This is because the freedom to determine one's own economic choices (including whether or not to seek to make a profit) is both an important element of individual freedom in itself *and* a necessary condition for political freedom. Economic freedom and political freedom are linked because political freedom is illusory if one's livelihood is under the control of the government. History attests that there have been no free societies without free markets. (Unfortunately, the reverse does not hold: Relatively free economies have coexisted with tyrannies.)

Friedman's thesis has scandalized many critics, particularly because it appears to celebrate the profit motive at the expense of the common weal. Many of these criticisms are wide off the mark or simply based on misreadings of Friedman's article. Space limitations permit only a superficial review. First, it is wrong to say that Friedman celebrates self-interest. As we have seen, he doesn't object to managers contributing to worthy public purposes; he just wants them to contribute their own money, time, or effort. Second, Friedman's case for profit maximization does not rest on the supposed greater efficiency of market economies. The goal of efficiency is a distant second to Friedman's concern to secure our freedom. Third, it is false to claim that Friedman's position privileges shareholders at the expense of "stakeholders." The corporation's stakeholders all voluntarily acquiesce in this arrangement or the corporation could not exist. Employees freely choose to work for corporations because they offer favorable wages and conditions. Consumers purchase from them because they offer better products, and so on. Fourth, the frequent charge that corporations don't "give back" to society is mystifying. Corporations pay market prices for their inputs, and they pay taxes. In fact, as is well known, the owners of corporations—the shareholders—are subject to double taxation on their shares of corporate profits. The corporation's shareholders make numberless other contributions to society. Advocates of CSR have failed to offer a convincing explanation for why shareholders should be expected to give back yet again, this time under the rubric of CSR.

There are, however, some more damaging criticisms of Friedman's thesis. One can best be suggested by an example. What should a manager do if he or she discovers that one of the corporation's plants is emitting a dangerous chemical into the atmosphere but that a loophole in the law would permit it to go on doing so? For the British economics writer Samuel Brittan, the answer is obvious: "The absence of effective legislation should not excuse a chemical company for polluting the air." However, it is not clear what Friedman's position would be. He might take a hard line and argue, as he does elsewhere in the article, that the manager should not make "expenditures on reducing pollution beyond the amount that is in the best interests of the corporation or that is required by law in order to contribute to the social objective of improving the environment." (Assuming that the government is unaware of the loophole, would the manager have a duty to bring it to the government's attention?) Or he might invoke the passage quoted earlier, which requires the manager to conform to the basic rules of society, both legal and *ethical*. That is to say, Friedman might argue that the manager has an ethical responsibility to stop the pollution. Neither answer is satisfactory. The first is blind to the fact that there are always gaps in the laws that may have to be filled by business's sense of responsibility. The second won't do because the clause about ethical custom should probably be disregarded as an embarrassing loose end in an otherwise tightly constructed argument. On many issues, there simply is no canonical "ethical custom," and Friedman points us to no source for one. Critics have predictably seized on the clause to argue that CSR is part of society's ethical custom, thus negating Friedman's thesis. The first answer—that the manager has no duty to do more than the law requires—is probably more consistent with the position Friedman has staked out in the article and elsewhere.

A final criticism is that much of the debate over CSR versus profit maximization is moot. One reason is that, as Friedman himself has explained, the market for corporate control severely limits the scope for managers to exercise social responsibility. However, that assumes that there is (and will continue to be) a functioning market for corporate control. To the extent that, say, state antitakeover statutes weaken the market, the legitimacy of CSR may become a live issue once again. Another reason why the debate over CSR may be moot is that virtually all shareholders today had notice of corporations' CSR policies when they purchased stock in them. Arguably, by purchasing the stock, they consented to at least the existing level of CSR. That removes Friedman's main objection to much of contemporary CSR.

—Ian Maitland

Further Readings

Birsch, D. (1990). The failure of Friedman's agency argument. In J. R. DesJardins & J. J. McCall (Eds.), *Contemporary issues in business ethics* (2nd ed., pp. 12–21). Belmont, CA: Wadsworth.

Carson, T. L. (1993). Friedman's theory of corporate social responsibility. *Business and Professional Ethics Journal, 12,* 3–32.

Friedman, M. (1961). *Capitalism and freedom.* Chicago: University of Chicago Press.

Friedman, M. (1970, September 13). The social responsibility of business is to increase its profits. *New York Times Magazine,* p. 32.

Friedman, M., & Friedman, R. (1980). *Free to choose: A personal statement.* New York: Harcourt Brace Jovanovich.

Henderson, D. (2002). *Misguided virtue: False notions of corporate social responsibility.* London: Institute of Economic Affairs.

Hooker, J. (2004). The case against business ethics education: A study in bad arguments. *Journal of Business Ethics Education, 1,* 75–88.

Reason Online. (2005). *Rethinking the social responsibility of business* (A Reason debate featuring Milton Friedman, Whole Foods' John Mackey, and Cypress Semiconductor's T. J. Rodgers). Retrieved from www.reason.com/news/show/32239.html

APPENDIX A

Problematic Practices

SUGGESTED PAIRINGS TABLE*

Problematic Practices	Related Entries
Love Canal	Corporate Social Responsibility Corporate Social Responsiveness Corporate Public Affairs
Merck & Co., Inc.	Corporate Social Responsibility Corporate Social Performance
Enron Corporation	Corporate Social Responsibility Corporate Governance
Nike, Inc.	Corporate Social Responsibility Global Corporate Social Responsibility
Martha Stewart	Corporate Social Responsibility Public Relations
Tylenol Tampering	Corporate Social Responsibility Corporate Social Responsiveness

*This correlation table provides suggested pairings between the problematic practices that follow and the entries that appear throughout the text, so that instructors have an idea of which concepts are illustrated in the problematic practices entries.

LOVE CANAL

Love Canal, a small community near Niagara Falls, New York, entered into our national memory starting with a front-page story in the *New York Times* on August 1, 1978. In that story, it was noted that Hooker Chemical Company had dumped toxic wastes into the ground up until 1953. The article addressed the incidence of birth defects in children in the area. Lois Gibbs, a resident, became a national spokesperson for all those who lived in Love Canal.

Love Canal was named after a Mr. William Love, who attempted to build a canal connecting two levels of Niagara Falls in 1890. His plan ultimately failed, and the only actual accomplishment was the building of a canal about 1 mile long, 15 feet wide, and 10 feet deep. The City of Niagara Falls began using it to dump chemical wastes as early as 1920, and the U.S. Army used the site to bury wastes from chemical warfare experiments. In 1942, Hooker Chemical Company (an arm of Occidental Petroleum) expanded the use of the site and, in 1947, bought the land for its own use. By 1952, the site was filled to capacity with approximately 21,800 tons of toxic wastes.

The local school board was seeking out new land for school buildings as a consequence of population growth. The school board pressed Hooker for the property and the firm refused on several occasions. The community threatened to take over the land by eminent domain and the firm finally agreed to sell the property for $1. The company warned the community of the dangers of the site, of the risks involved with the toxic wastes, and included a 17-line explanation in the agreement outlining the dangers and transferring all liability for the site to the City of Niagara Falls. This transfer of liability has often been ignored in public comment and debate. In the building of the school, the cap directly on top of the waste site was broken through (several drill bits were broken in the process). This breaking of the cap allowed water to seep into the site and toxic chemicals to leach out into the surrounding area.

Starting in 1978, Lois Gibbs, the then president of the Love Canal Homeowners' Association, led the community effort to obtain information about health concerns and to get redress for the situation. The association was opposed by Occidental and by government at all levels. Eventually, in 1980, as a result of extraordinary publicity, President Jimmy Carter declared it a federal emergency and had the residents evacuated from Love Canal. More than 800 families were eventually relocated and reimbursed for their residences. Occidental Petroleum spent more than $200 million on the cleanup.

This incident was used to further national public interest in hazardous waste sites and led to the passage of federal legislation, commonly referred to as the Superfund, to clean up toxic and hazardous waste sites nationwide.

—John F. Mahon

Further Readings

Gibbs, L. M. (1982). *Love Canal: My story.* Albany: State University of New York Press.

Tesh, S. N. (2000). *Uncertain hazards: Environmental activists and scientific proof.* Ithaca, NY: Cornell University Press.

Zuesse, E. (1981). Love Canal: The truth seeps out. *Reason Online.* Retrieved June 4, 2006, from http://reason.com/8102/fe.ez.the.shtml

MERCK & CO., INC.

Merck & Co. Inc., a large U.S. public pharmaceutical company, has faced several important ethical and social responsibility tests over the years. Established in 1891, Merck discovers, develops, manufactures, and markets vaccines and medicines in more than 20 therapeutic categories. The company has approximately 60,000 employees and sells products in approximately 150 countries. Worldwide sales in 2005 were more than $22 billion. The firm has always had a "patient first" approach to doing business as indicated by George Merck, the son of the founder, who stated that Merck tries never to forget that medicine is for the people, not for the profits. This view is currently reflected in the company's values, which states that Merck's business is preserving and improving human life. Although the firm has faced many challenges, two of the more significant ethical and social responsibility issues confronted by Merck include whether to produce and distribute a drug to help cure river blindness and whether to recall its arthritis drug Vioxx.

In terms of the first major issue faced by Merck, river blindness is an eye and skin disease caused by a worm that is transmitted to humans through the bite of a fly. The baby or larval worms then move through the body migrating in the skin and the eye causing itching, severe skin disease, and after repeated years of exposure, blindness. Merck researchers discovered that it was highly likely that by spending tens of millions of dollars they could develop the cure for river blindness. The problem was that the millions of people afflicted by the disease lived in parts of the world (primarily Africa) where they could not afford to pay for the drug. Other pharmaceutical companies, foundations, governments, and health organizations were not interested in paying for the development of the drug. Other concerns related to the risk of side effects for humans that might then affect the sales of Merck's animal drug, or that the human drug might be diverted into the black market, undercutting sales of the animal drug. The company also risked creating a precedent both internally among its researchers and externally among the public that might be difficult to meet in the future in terms of developing other important drugs with little or no financial return expected.

Despite the costs and the risks, Merck, through the leadership of its CEO Roy Vagelos, decided to spend the money. The drug, known as Mectizan, was not only developed but also distributed by Merck for free for years beginning in 1987. The decision did end up having indirect financial benefits for the firm, which according to Dr. Vagelos related primarily to the recruitment of top researchers. In December 2002, the World Health Organization declared river blindness virtually eradicated as a world disease, with the program reaching 40 million people annually in more than 30 countries.

The second major ethical and social responsibility issue places Merck in a potentially more negative light. The issue involves what has been perceived as Merck's delayed decision to recall its arthritis drug Vioxx, despite apparent knowledge of numerous deaths caused by the drug. Merck pulled its $2.5 billion-a-year drug off the market on September 30, 2004, when a study indicated that it doubled the risk of heart attack and stroke in patients who took the drug for more than 18 months. The issue appears similar to that faced by A. H. Robins Company, which was eventually forced into bankruptcy in the mid-1980s after facing lawsuits due to its allegedly defective Dalkon Shield intrauterine birth control device.

Plaintiffs claim that Merck knew of the additional risk of heart attacks based on previous clinical studies, but failed to warn doctors and consumers of the risk. From 1999 to 2004, more than 20 million Americans took Vioxx. By the end of 2005, Merck faced close to 10,000 lawsuits in the United States. The firm is also being sued in Europe, Australia, Brazil, Canada, Israel, and Turkey. As of April 2006, Merck had already spent hundreds of millions of dollars to defend four cases, with two wins and two losses (with judgments against Merck for $253 million in Texas and $13.5 million in New Jersey). The company continues to refuse to pursue a global settlement and is appealing the cases it has lost. Some estimate that the company may have to defend more than 100,000 Vioxx lawsuits leading to possible liability of up to $50 billion (U.S.) for Merck, since epidemiologists estimate that 100,000 people might have suffered heart attacks because of the drug. It is still unclear how Vioxx will ultimately affect the future prospects of Merck, and whether Merck will be able to withstand the current legal assault.

—Mark S. Schwartz

Further Readings

Berenson, A. (2006, April 12). Merck jury adds $9 million in damages. *New York Times*. Retrieved from www.nytimes.com/2006/04/12/business/12vioxx.html

Bollier, D., Weiss, S., & Hanson, K. O. (1991). *Merck & Co. Inc.: Addressing Third World needs (A and B)*. Boston: Harvard Business School Press.

Merck Corporate. [website]. *The Merck mectizan donation program.* Retrieved from www.merck.com/about/cr/policies_performance/social/mectizan_donation.html

Merck Corporate. [website]. *VIOXX information center.* Retrieved from www.merck.com/newsroom/vioxx_withdrawal

Velasquez, M. G. (2006). *Business ethics: Concepts and cases* (6th ed.). Upper Saddle River, NJ: Prentice Hall.

ENRON CORPORATION

E nron Corporation's December 2, 2001, Chapter 11 reorganization filing was the largest bankruptcy in history, until it was exceeded in 2002 by WorldCom. Enron, headquartered in Houston, Texas, had grown quickly into a superficially giant and well-regarded company. It rapidly collapsed following the sudden disclosure of massive financial misdealing, which revealed the company to be a shell rather than a real business. During 2001, Enron stock fell to about $0.30—an unprecedented collapse for a blue-chip stock.

The Enron scandal helped propel passage of the McCain-Feingold Bipartisan Campaign Reform Act of 2002 (March). While Enron was neither the biggest nor the most important source of political funds, it had been active in making political contributions and attempting to influence legislators. Part of the Enron scandal involved political connections to President George W. Bush (former governor of Texas) and Vice President Dick Cheney (formerly CEO of a Texas-headquartered company). In May 2005, a U.S. appeals court dismissed a related lawsuit against the vice president on the grounds that an administration must be free to seek confidential information (including Enron) concerning energy policy.

Enron, quickly followed by WorldCom, helped propel the Sarbanes-Oxley Act of 2002 (July), the most significant change in U.S. securities laws since the early 1930s. As shocking as the sudden bankruptcy of a blue-chip company was, the subsequent revelations were worse: The traditional U.S. corporate governance watchdogs—attorneys, auditors, and directors—had either aided and abetted the responsible executives or had been grossly negligent in the supervision of those executives. The United States and several other countries were rocked by multiple revelations of corporate scandals that ultimately also included analysts; auditors; banks; brokerages; mutual, hedge, and currency trading funds; and the New York Stock Exchange.

ARROGANCE, CORRUPTION, GREED, AND RUTHLESSNESS

Enron was not the first nor the last nor the largest of the corporate scandals in recent years. Nevertheless, Enron became, above all other companies, the emblem for management fraud, director negligence, and adviser misconduct. Enron is easily the most widely studied and best documented of the recent corporate frauds. Enron was a prolonged media event.

The high education levels and intelligence of Chairman Kenneth L. Lay (PhD in economics), CEO Jeffrey K. Skilling (Harvard MBA and top 5% Baker Scholar), and CFO Andrew Fastow (Northwestern MBA) raised serious questions about business school treatment of ethics and law. In January 2005, the documentary movie *Enron: The Smartest Guys in the Room,* based on Bethany McLean and Peter Elkind's 2003 bestseller of the same name, premiered at the Sundance Film Festival in Utah. Spring 2005 releases took place in Austin and then Houston. The theme of the book and the movie is that smart guys can outsmart themselves as well as everyone else.

The most astonishing aspect of the Enron scandal was that a significant number of executives had engaged in improper actions despite the company having in place the key elements and best practices of a comprehensive ethics program. There was a detailed 64-page "Code of Ethics" with an introductory letter from Chairman Ken Lay and a "Statement of Human Rights Principles" together with a sign-off procedure on the code for each employee, an internal reporting and compliance system, visible posting of corporate values (banners in the headquarters building, signs in the parking garage, and so forth), and an employee-training video—*Vision and Values*—discussing ethics and integrity. Enron issued a 2000 annual report on corporate responsibility. The "Code of Ethics," like other Enron paraphernalia, was later auctioned on eBay. The Smithsonian Institution reportedly obtained a copy of the code for its permanent collection.

The publicized "values" of Enron were respect, integrity, communication, and excellence. The real "ethical" climate at Enron was a combination of arrogance (or hubris), corruption, greed, and ruthlessness. The gap between words and deeds at Enron was dramatic. This gap suggests that it is not particular corporate governance devices that matter most but the probity and integrity of individuals in relationship to the ethical climate within a company.

The executives were arrogant in attitude and conduct. The company strategy was one of revolutionizing trading by breaking traditional rules. The "vision" at Enron was to become the world's leading energy company—in reality, by any means necessary. There were rumors of sexual misconduct by executives. Expensive vehicles and power-oriented photogenic poses were commonplace.

The weight of evidence suggests that the lure of wealth had suborned the corporate governance watchdogs. It turned out that the directors must have been asleep at the switch or mesmerized by the rising stock price. It turned out that the external attorneys and auditors could not afford to lose such a successful client. Enron executives did not hesitate to bully the external safeguards, such as analysts, when and if necessary. A corruption machine was at work, whether intentionally or inadvertently.

In the 1987 film *Wall Street,* the character named Gordon Gekko announces that greed is good. Enron—whose logo became known as "the Crooked E"—epitomized that slogan. Greed is a morally disturbing paradox at the heart of the market economy. Bernard Mandeville, in the *Fable of the Bees, or Private Vices, Publick Benefits* (1714), argued that individual vices and not individual virtues produce public benefits by encouraging commercial enterprise. An economic actor engages in selfish calculation of interest or advantage. This consequentialist perspective emphasizes outcomes over intentions or means. The Enron executives carried this perspective to its logical extreme. Adam Smith's telling criticism in *The Wealth of Nations* of the East India Company's personnel suggests that he would hardly be surprised.

The company culture embodied ruthlessness toward outsiders and insiders alike. Skilling emphasized a process of creative destruction within the company. The rank and yank system of employee evaluation by peer review, reportedly installed by CEO Skilling, annually dismissed the bottom 20% of the employees—and perhaps corruptly rather than objectively. It has been reported that traders were afraid to go to the bathroom because someone else might steal information from their trading screen. In such a culture, no one would report bad news. In such a culture, individual achievement was everything and teamwork was nothing. Enron culture emphasized bonuses, hardball, take no prisoners, and tacit disregard for ethics and laws.

THE RISE OF ENRON

Ken Lay, then CEO of Houston Natural Gas, formed Enron in 1985 by merger with InterNorth. Lay had worked in federal energy positions and then in several energy companies. He was an advocate of free trade in energy markets and had experience in political influence peddling. Enron was originally involved in transmission and distribution of electricity and natural gas in the United

States. It also built and operated power plants and gas pipelines, and similar industrial infrastructure facilities, globally. Allegedly, bribes and political pressure tainted contracts around the world—most notoriously a $30 billion contract with the Maharashtra State Electricity Board in India.

Jeff Skilling was a senior partner at McKinsey & Co. and in the later 1980s worked in that capacity with Enron. Skilling joined Enron in 1990 as chairman and CEO of Enron Capital & Trade Resources. In 1996, he became president and COO of Enron. The company morphed into an energy trading and communications company that grew to some 21,000 employees, and its stock price rose to about $85. Enron grew to the seventh largest publicly listed company in the United States. Strategy emphasized bold innovation in trading of power and broadband commodities and risk management derivatives—including highly exotic weather derivatives. Trading business involved mark-to-market accounting in which revenues were booked, and bonuses awarded, on the basis of effectively Enron-only estimates of the value of contracts. *Fortune* magazine named Enron "America's Most Innovative Company" for five consecutive years (1996–2000). Enron made *Fortune*'s "100 Best Companies to Work for in America" list in 2000. The company's wealth was reflected in an opulent office building in downtown Houston. Business school cases on Enron's business practices and culture were circulated for teaching purposes. Skilling served briefly as CEO of Enron from February to August 2001. Then, he abruptly resigned from Enron and Lay took over as CEO.

THE FALL OF ENRON

Following the bankruptcy filing, there were multiple investigations, including one commissioned by the Enron board of directors and directed by William C. Powers Jr., dean of the University of Texas at Austin's law school. The U.S. Department of Justice announced (January 9, 2002) a criminal investigation of Enron, and various congressional hearings began (January 24, 2002). The hearings also revealed the role of Sherron Watkins, a certified public accountant, who had warned Lay about Fastow's offshore devices after Skilling suddenly resigned. Watkins's experience helped propel into law the whistle-blower protection elements of the Sarbanes-Oxley Act. The investigations emphasized two key matters, revealing how Enron had been built as an empty house of cards.

Enron was deeply involved in manipulating the California energy crisis. John Forney, a former energy trader, was indicted in December 2002 on

11 counts of conspiracy and wire fraud and pled guilty. Tape recordings revealed Enron traders on the phone asking California power plant managers to get a little creative in shutting down plants for repairs. Forney was a *Star Wars* fan. His "Death Star" strategy involved shuffling energy around the California power grid to generate state payments relieving congestion. Death Star deliberately created congestion. He named other devices JEDI (Joint Energy Development Investments) and Chewco (after the character of Chewbacca).

The other key revelation concerned CFO Andrew Fastow's creative use and alleged partial ownership of offshore special purpose entities (SPEs) or limited partnerships. These devices separated debt from revenues and kept market-to-market losses off Enron's books temporarily. Fastow had been a *CFO Magazine* award for excellence winner. Fastow was indicted (November 1, 2002) on 78 counts, including fraud, money laundering, and conspiracy. He and his wife, Lea Fastow, former assistant treasurer of Enron, accepted a plea agreement (January 14, 2004) in exchange for testifying against other Enron defendants. Mr. Fastow received a 10-year prison sentence and a loss of $23.8 million; Mrs. Fastow received (for income tax evasion charges in concealing Mr. Fastow's gains) a 5-month prison sentence and 1 year of supervised release, including 5 months of house arrest. The Enron board had waived conflict of interest rules in its own Code of Conduct to permit Fastow to oversee some of these SPEs. Most important were the "Raptors" (after *Jurassic Park* creatures) or "LJM1" and "LJM2," named for Fastow's wife and two children. It was alleged that Fastow had engaged in unauthorized self-dealing and benefited directly from these supervised devices.

The Enron bankruptcy resulted in the criminal conviction for obstruction of justice and, thus, forced auditing license surrender of its auditor Arthur Andersen, which collapsed. The audit partner assigned to Enron, David Duncan, pled guilty to ordering large-scale destruction of work documents. Some 28,000 Arthur Andersen employees had to find other employment. On May 31, 2005, the U.S. Supreme Court unanimously overturned the firm's conviction on grounds that the trial judge's jury instructions were too vague and broad. Federal prosecutors decided in November 2005 not to retry the case. Duncan was allowed to withdraw his guilty plea, although other charges could be filed against him.

As of July 2005, there had been 16 guilty pleas and six convictions (one thrown out) in the Enron cases. Former Merrill Lynch bankers and Enron executives were convicted in the Nigerian barge trial. (One executive was found innocent.) Nonexistent barges (to be built) were flipped between Enron and Merrill Lynch to generate paper profits and bonuses. In July 2005, three former executives of Enron Broadband Services (EBS) were acquitted of some charges; the jury deadlocked on other charges against them and two other defendants. The charges had argued intentional overpromotion of EBS's value. The judge dismissed the remaining charges against all defendants. In November 2005, a special grand jury issued three streamlined indictments against the five codefendants. Skilling was indicted in February 2004 and Lay in July 2004, both on multiple counts. Both pled not guilty; their trials had not commenced as of November 2005. The prosecution wanted to try, with Lay and Skilling, the former chief accounting officer of Enron Rick Causey. He had pled not guilty to more than 30 charges of fraud. He was indicted in January 2004.

EMPLOYEES AND SHAREOWNERS

Enron's bankruptcy had serious effects for many individuals and organizations. The Houston Astros paid Enron $5 million to rename Enron Field as Astros Field, subsequently changed to Minute Maid Park. *Playboy* (August 2002) featured a pictorial "The Women of Enron." David Tonsall, former Enron employee, became rapper "N Run" (i.e., Enron and "never run") on a December 2003 CD *Corporate America.*

Shareowners lost virtually everything. Several employees lost their jobs and their life savings that they had invested in Enron stock. Like former Arthur Andersen employees, former Enron employees may have damaged résumés. The Enron bankruptcy reorganization was a lengthy affair under a new management and bankruptcy examiner. The state of California is attempting recovery of monies from various parties. Eventually, shareowners and employees may begin partial financial recoveries from various parties, including banks and insurance companies. As of November 2005, Citigroup had settled for $2 billion, J. P. Morgan Chase for $2.2 billion, and the Canadian Imperial Bank of Commerce for $2.4 billion. These figures represent the largest securities class-action settlement on record, and there are still a number of other prominent defendant banks remaining. The U.S. bankruptcy court finalized a settlement in May 2005 of about $3,500 on average for more than 20,000 current and former employees (about $69 million total). Civil lawsuits are still proceeding against Lay, Skilling, Enron, and others. The directors of Enron (and WorldCom) personally paid damages.

—Duane Windsor

Further Readings

Berenson, A. (2003). *The number: How the drive for quarterly earnings corrupted Wall Street and corporate America.* New York: Random House.

Brewer, L., & Hansen, M. S. (2002). *House of cards: Confessions of an Enron executive.* College Station, TX: Virtualbookworm.com.

Bryce, R. (2002). *Pipe dreams: Greed, ego, and the death of Enron.* New York: PublicAffairs.

Cruver, B. (2002). *Anatomy of greed: The unshredded truth from an Enron insider.* New York: Carroll & Graf.

Eichenwald, K. (2005). *Conspiracy of fools: True story of the Enron scandal.* New York: Broadway Books.

Enron traders caught on tape [Electronic version]. (2004, June 1). *CBS Evening News.* Retrieved from www.cbsnews.com/stories/2004/06/01/eveningnews/main620626.shtml

Fox, L. (2003). *Enron: The rise and fall.* New York: Wiley.

Fusaro, P. C., & Miller, R. M. (2002). *What went wrong at Enron: Everyone's guide to the largest bankruptcy in U.S. history.* New York: Wiley.

Holtzman, M. P., Venuti, E., & Fonfeder, R. (2003). Enron and the raptors [Electronic version]. *CPA Journal.* Retrieved from www.nysscpa.org/cpajournal/2003/0403/features/f042403.htm

Jaedicke, R. K. (2002). The role of the board of directors in Enron's collapse. In *Hearing before the House Committee on Energy and Commerce, Subcommittee on Oversight and Investigation.* 107th Congress, testimony of R. K. Jaedicke, Enron Board of Directors, Chairman of Audit and Compliance Committee.

McLean, B., & Elkind, P. (2003). *The smartest guys in the room: The amazing rise and scandalous fall of Enron.* New York: Portfolio.

Persons of the year—The whistleblowers: Cynthia Cooper of WorldCom, Coleen Rowley of the FBI, Sherron Watkins of Enron. (2002, December 30, to 2003, January 6). *Time, 160*(27).

Rapoport, N. B., & Dharan, B. G. (Eds.). (2004). *Enron: Corporate fiascos and their implications.* New York: Foundation Press.

Smith, R., & Emshwiller, J. R. (2003). *How two Wall Street Journal reporters uncovered the lies that destroyed faith in corporate America.* New York: HarperBusiness.

Swartz, M. (with Watkins, S.). (2003). *Power failure: The inside story of the collapse of Enron.* New York: Doubleday.

Watkins, S. S. (2003). Ethical conflicts at Enron: Moral responsibility in corporate capitalism. *California Management Review, 45*(4), 6–19.

NIKE, INC.

Nike, Inc. is a high-profile sporting goods and apparel company that engages in the design, development, and marketing of footwear, equipment, and accessory products worldwide under brand names such as NIKE, Cole Haan, Converse, Starter, Hurley, and Bauer. The company, which is headquartered in Beaverton, Oregon, sells its products through a mix of independent distributors, licensees, and subsidiaries in approximately 120 countries worldwide. Nike has experienced substantial financial and marketing success since its founding in the 1960s and is now the largest sporting goods company in the world (in terms of market capitalization). Despite its success, the company has been the target of much criticism in recent years for alleged abusive or "sweatshop" labor practices in its subcontractors.

Nike was founded as an athletic shoe company by Phil Knight and Bill Bowerman in 1962 under the name Blue Ribbon Sports. In 1972, the company changed its name to Nike, after the Greek goddess of victory. Knight had been a track athlete and business student at the University of Oregon, where Bowerman was his coach. While getting his MBA at Stanford, Knight devised a strategy for the manufacturing of athletic shoes overseas that would take advantage of lower-cost off-shore production capabilities. The plan was for Nike to be essentially a design, marketing, and distribution company with all the production performed by subcontractors operating overseas.

This strategy proved highly successful. Nike started subcontracting in Japan and then moved its sourcing operations to South Korea and Taiwan to take advantage of lower cost of production in these locations. As the economies of South Korea and Taiwan developed, Nike continued to move its sourcing operations to even cheaper locations such as China, Indonesia, and Vietnam.

In the fiscal year 2005, Nike had revenues of $13.7 billion and employed about 24,000 people directly and another 650,000 in more than 800 supplier factories worldwide. The company has operations in several locations including Oregon, Tennessee, North Carolina, and the Netherlands in addition to its Niketown and Nike Factory Store retail outlets. It has several subsidiaries: Cole Haan (casual luxury footwear and accessories), Bauer Nike Hockey

(hockey equipment), Hurley International (teen-oriented sports apparel for surfing, skateboarding, and snowboarding), Converse (athletic footwear), Nike IHM, Inc. (cushioning components used in Nike footwear), and Exeter Brands Group, which includes Starter and licenses other Nike brands. Nike became a publicly traded company in 1980, and its New York Stock Exchange ticker symbol is NKE.

One of the key components of Nike's strategy has been the use of celebrity athletes as endorsers for its products. Its endorsers have included some of the biggest names in sports such as Michael Jordan (after whom the famed "Air Jordan" shoes were named), Lance Armstrong, Tiger Woods, Kobe Bryant, and Jerry Rice.

In the late 1980s, Nike found itself at the center of controversy brewing over alleged sweatshop labor working conditions in its subcontractor factories in developing countries. Critics alleged that a number of labor-oriented problems existed in these factories including (1) wage and salary concerns—both the payment of low wages and the use of various schemes to cheat workers out of the wages to which they were entitled, (2) unsafe/unhealthy working conditions, (3) excessive working hours and forced overtime, (4) harsh and abusive disciplinary tactics, (5) the use of child labor, and (6) active opposition to unionization efforts by the workers. According to some critics, such as labor activist Jeff Ballinger, the opposition to unionization was the key concern because, it was reasoned, with effective union representation the other issues could be resolved.

Several incidents contributed to the notoriety Nike quickly acquired on these issues. There were several worker fatalities reported in Nike subcontractor factories in the early 1990s. In addition, reports started circulating of Nike's involvement with the use of child labor in its subcontractor factories. A picture purported to be of a child worker in a Nike subcontractor factory in Pakistan sewing soccer balls appeared in *Life* magazine in 1996. It was later learned that the photo was staged (soccer balls are sewn before they are inflated but the ball the child was holding had already been inflated). Nevertheless, Nike was perceived by the general public as a leading culprit in the exploitation of child labor. The company was lampooned in comic strips such as Doonesbury and by late night talk show hosts such as Jay Leno and David Letterman (e.g., one of the top 10 signs you are at a bad summer camp: you spend all day sewing swooshes on Nike sneakers). Critics also parodied Nike's "Just Do It" slogan by suggesting that Nike "Just Stop It."

There are several ironies related to Nike's strategy that contributed to the publicity this controversy received. The fact that Nike's shoes were high-prestige luxury items sold to well-to-do children (and sometimes not-so-well-to-do children) in the United States and other western countries contrasted sharply with working conditions being portrayed in the media and the perceived exploitation of child labor.

In addition, Jeff Ballinger, who had been working to organize Nike subcontractor factories in Indonesia in the late 1980s and early 1990s, was able to point out the disparity in the money Nike paid celebrity endorsers versus what workers were paid to make Nike shoes. In the August 1992 issue of *Harper's* magazine, Ballinger was quoted as saying that an Indonesian worker making Nike shoes in Java would have to work 44,492 years to make what Nike paid Michael Jordan in one year. This criticism was an example of how Ballinger and other critics were able to use Nike's celebrity endorsement strategy against the company. Although Ballinger would later concede that Nike was no worse than other firms in the industry, Nike's name became synonymous with the term *sweatshop labor* in the eyes of much of the general public.

Labor-affiliated critics of Nike's overall strategy and labor practices were concerned both with the loss of jobs to overseas production and what they referred to as a "race to the bottom." According to this line of argument, the exploitation of low-paid workers overseas in harsh working conditions put downward pressure on wages and working conditions of workers in the United States. Thus, it was both a matter of labor solidarity and self-interest that led union activists to criticize Nike's labor practices and to call for reforms.

The criticisms of Nike got traction on the nation's college campuses where chapters of Students Against Sweatshops began to form. Students and faculty involved began demanding to know who was making the college-branded gear (e.g., hats, sweatshirts, T-shirts) being sold in the college bookstores and under what conditions they were being made. About the same time, the mid-1990s, a boycott of Nike products over sweatshop labor concerns began to pick up steam.

Both critics and supporters of Nike concede that Nike's problems were exacerbated by its initial response to the criticism. This was to disavow any responsibility for labor problems in its subcontractor facilities on the grounds that it did not make the shoes—they are made by its subcontractors. Nike subsequently enlisted former Atlanta Mayor and UN Representative Andrew Young to investigate its subcontractor factory operations in Vietnam. When a generally upbeat report was issued, Young was criticized for bias and sloppy research methods.

In November 1997, the *New York Times* stated that in an inspection report that was prepared for the company's internal use only, Ernst & Young wrote that workers at the factory near Ho Chi Minh City were exposed to carcinogens that exceeded local legal standards by 177 times in parts of the plant and that 77% percent of the employees suffered from respiratory problems. The article leaked several excerpts from this report that detailed the unsafe and unhealthy working conditions in Nike's factories.

While Nike was at the center of the controversy over alleged sweatshop labor practices, other firms and parties became embroiled in it as well. When morning talk show host Kathie Lee Gifford's line of clothing was criticized for being made with abusive labor practices, she investigated the allegations herself and confirmed some of the charges. Ms. Gifford then became an advocate for improving working conditions in the apparel industry.

As the criticism mounted regarding the use of sweatshop labor in the apparel and footwear industries, the federal government got involved. During the Clinton Administration, the White House convened a meeting of industry, labor, and activist representatives to address issues of sweatshop labor in the apparel industry. Originally called the Apparel Industry Partnership, this group came to be known as the Fair Labor Association whose purpose was to promote adherence to international labor standards and improve working conditions worldwide.

A turning point in Nike's response to critics was Phil Knight's appearance at the National Press Club in May 1988. In his speech, Knight conceded that Nike bore responsibility for conditions in its subcontractors' factories and that many of the critics' complaints about those factories were valid. Furthermore, he pledged to reform Nike's labor practices with respect to child labor, worker development, and safe working conditions. More specifically, Knight promised to raise the minimum age of all sneaker workers to 18 and apparel workers to 16, adopt clean air standards, advance microloans to workers, and expand its monitoring program. Following this speech Nike undertook a number of institutional changes to carry out Knight's promises. Notably, Nike changed its response to this controversy from defensive to proactive and began to take the lead in efforts to reform working conditions in poor countries. In addition, Nike has become more proactive in addressing criticisms of the company. Nike representatives have participated in forums at professional associations such as the Academy of Management and the International Association of Business and Society. Nike has also welcomed researchers into its factories and it has hosted college study abroad groups visiting countries in which its subcontractors operate. How much of this response was due to a sincere belief that the company had acted wrongly in the treatment of its subcontractor workers and how much was due to business expediency to silence the critics is uncertain.

Nike is one of the first companies to publicly publish a list of its active subcontractors/suppliers in an effort to establish transparency and also to gain efficiency for monitoring and inspections by collaborating with other companies who use the same subcontractors. As of May 2005, Nike is also recognized by four institutions that gauge according to their own specific criteria whether a company should be considered a socially responsible investment. These are *FTSE4Good Index Series, Dow Jones Sustainability Index, Ethibel Investment Register,* and *KLD Broad Market Social*^{SM} *Index.*

Furthermore, Nike has also published a 113-page Corporate Responsibility Report FY04 freely available on its website. While the company painstakingly details its efforts at engaging its five most important stakeholders, namely consumers, shareholders, business partners, employees, and the community, it recognizes that for the future they need to focus on the following priority issues with respect to workers and factories: freedom of association; harassment, abuse, and grievance procedures; payment of wages; hours of work; environment; and safety and health. The report notes that its biggest challenge is in China, which accounts for 180,000 contract workers in more than 110 factories. China accounts for 36% of its manufactured footwear and has a large and fast-growing domestic market for Nike goods. However, upholding its code of conduct in China is a difficult problem for Nike due to local laws that prevent independent labor organizing. Several other problems exist, such as the lack of clarity about the law and its monitoring, falsification of information related to wages by factories, and social problems caused by temporary migration of workers from rural China to manufacturing provinces. Nike believes that engagement with its stakeholders, including the Chinese government, and building partnerships in China is the long-term solution to improving labor conditions there.

Because Nike has been so closely tied to the sweatshop labor controversy, the underlying debate about the ethics of sweatshop labor is particularly relevant to the Nike case. Many critics have argued that companies like Nike have a responsibility to see to it that their subcontractors provide better than market-derived or legally mandated wages and working conditions in their operations in developing countries. Others though have argued that if such companies were to do so, there would be less incentive to invest in these developing countries and the benefits of economic growth would be forfeited.

As of this writing, critics and supporters of Nike are still very far apart on the quality of working conditions and the extent of labor abuses in Nike subcontractor factories. However, there does seem to be fairly widespread agreement that the criticisms leveled against the company have brought about an improvement in these conditions since the controversy started.

—Richard E. Wokutch and Manisha Singal

Further Readings

Arnold, D. G., & Bowie, N. E. (2003). Sweatshops and respect for persons. *Business Ethics Quarterly, 13*(2), 221–242.

Ballinger, J. (1992, August). The new free trade heel: Nike's profits jump on the backs of Asian workers. *Harper's Magazine, 285,* 46–47.

Maitland, I. (1997). The great non-debate over international sweatshops. *British Academy of Management Annual Conference Proceedings, September,* 240–265.

Nike homepage. Retrieved November 28, 2005, from www.nikebiz.com

Spar, D. L. (2002). *Hitting the wall: Nike and international labor practices.* Boston: Harvard Business School. (Original work published 2000)

Greenhouse, S. (1997, November 8). Nike shoe plant in Vietnam is called unsafe for workers. *New York Times,* p. A1.

Wokutch, R. E. (2001). Nike and its critics. *Organization & Environment, 14*(2), 207–237.

MARTHA STEWART (1941–)

Martha Stewart was a very popular and influential American celebrity in the late 1990s and early 2000s, a virtual media icon who ran afoul of the law and served prison time. Stewart was born on August 3, 1941, in Jersey City, New Jersey, and when she was 3 years old, her parents, Edward and Martha Kostyra, moved her and her five siblings to Nutley, New Jersey. Because of her legendarily strong work ethic and character, she received a partial scholarship to Barnard College in New York City. To pay the remainder of her tuition, she worked as a model for television commercials and magazines. At Barnard College, she met her husband Andrew Stewart, and they married during her sophomore year in 1961, just before she graduated with a bachelor's degree in European history and architectural history. In 1965, she had her daughter Alexis, and within 2 years she became a stockbroker. When recession hit Wall Street in 1973, Stewart decided to leave the brokerage and move to Westport, Connecticut, with her husband and daughter.

Stewart became a writer and columnist for the magazine *House Beautiful,* while simultaneously serving in a similar capacity for the *New York Times.* In 1982, she coauthored her first book, *Entertaining,* and shortly thereafter she started publication of her own magazine, *Martha Stewart Living.* By this time, she was a regular guest on the morning network talk shows, and she even appeared on *The Tonight Show* and *Late Night with David Letterman.* In 1993, she began her own syndicated television program, *Martha Stewart Living,* and she became a well-known and much-loved celebrity, her empire capped by the creation of Martha Stewart Living Omnimedia, Inc. She was the American guru of housekeeping, cooking, gardening, decorating, crafts, and holiday parties.

However, her period of prosperity lasted only about a decade. In 2004, at age 62, Martha Stewart stood trial on charges of conspiracy, obstruction, securities fraud, and lying to investigators in connection with the sale of her stock in ImClone, a biotechnology company. Standing trial alongside Stewart was her former stockbroker, 41-year-old Peter Bacanovic, who faced the same charges in addition to perjury and falsifying documents. Stewart's troubles stemmed from her sale of shares of ImClone on December 27, 2001, one day before the FDA announced it had rejected the application for approval of ImClone's cancer drug, Erbitux—news that caused the company's stock prices to plummet.

It was Stewart's response to the subsequent federal probe that ultimately proved incriminating as prosecutors claimed that she not only conspired with Bacanovic to cover up evidence concerning the sale but also lied publicly about her involvement in the scandal to protect the stock price of her own company, Martha Stewart Omnimedia. Bacanovic claimed he and Stewart sold her ImClone stock after having a "selling conversation" on December 20, 2001, a week before the sale was executed. During that conversation, Bacanovic said he and Stewart reviewed her entire portfolio, not just her shares of ImClone, and agreed to sell her shares in the company if the price sunk to $60.

Although she made $51,000 by selling her shares in advance of the announcement, Stewart was never charged with insider trading. Stewart, ever the domestic diva, even while facing a maximum of 30 years in prison, would join her daughter Alexis every morning before court to have their hair and makeup done. Stewart was convicted in March 2004 of lying to investigators and conspiring with Bacanovic to cover up the circumstances surrounding the stock trade during the federal probe that followed. On July 16, 2004, Martha Stewart was sentenced to 5 months behind bars and 5 months house arrest, with an additional 2 years probation and $30,000 fine.

Stewart issued statements proclaiming her innocence before, during, and after the trial. Her supporters criticized the investigation as being sexist, saying that federal agents unfairly targeted one of the richest women in the world (whose wealth directly resulted from her reputation, the public perceptions of her) while ignoring far worse criminals. In a sense, one's perceptions of and attitudes about this case reflect the mind-set, background, and perspective of the perceiver as much if not more than the facts about Martha Stewart and her fall from the pinnacle of American society.

—Dirk C. Gibson, Rebecca Warin, and Robert McClain Gassaway

Further Readings

Academy of Achievement. (2005, March 4). *The Catherine B. Reynolds Foundation and Exxon Mobile.* Retrieved from www.achievement.org/autodoc/page/steObio-1

Cohen, D. (2002). *Biography on Martha Stewart.* Retrieved from http://lala.essort ment.com/biographyonmar_rino.htm

The reinvention of Martha Stewart. (2006, November 6). *BusinessWeek Online.* Retrieved from www.businessweek.com/magazine/content/06_45/b4008076 .htm?campaign_id=rss_daily

TYLENOL TAMPERING

One of the most significant examples of business ethics and corporate crisis management involved the actions of Johnson & Johnson (J&J) during the Tylenol tampering crisis. In the fall of 1982, a subsidiary of United States–based J&J, McNeil Consumer Products, learned that seven people in Chicago had died from taking Extra Strength Tylenol capsules that had been laced with cyanide. The management was convinced that the tampering did not occur at its plants, meaning that it must have taken place once the product had reached Illinois. J&J faced a dilemma, how best to handle the crisis without damaging the reputation of the company, when the company had quickly established that it could not be held liable for the tampering.

Reports on the firm's decision-making process during the crisis indicate that the company placed the safety of its customers first, before considering profit implications. A nationwide voluntary recall took place, involving approximately 31 million bottles of Tylenol, representing more than $100 million in sales. Consumers were told not to use any type of Tylenol product until the cause of the tampering had been established. Production and advertising of Tylenol ceased. The company offered to exchange all Tylenol capsules that had been purchased for Tylenol tablets. Relations were quickly established with the Chicago police, the FBI, and the Food and Drug Administration (FDA). A toll-free crisis phone line was set up for concerned consumers. Senior executives, including CEO James Burke, were readily accessible to the media. As part of a longer-term response, the company reintroduced Tylenol capsules with new triple-seal tamper-resistant packaging. Despite the firm having its market share drop from 33% to 18%, it wasn't too long before the company was able to recover its position. Following a second tampering incident in 1986, J&J made the decision to offer Tylenol in a caplet form, as opposed to a capsule form. No one was ever convicted of the tampering incidents and subsequent deaths.

Probably the most significant aspect of how J&J handled the crisis was the apparent corporate culture that existed at the time. According to J&J executives, turning to the firm's credo enabled the firm to make the right early decisions that led to the comeback phase. The credo, initially written in 1943, stated that the firm had obligations to society beyond merely profit maximization or enhancing shareholder value.

As a direct consequence of the Tylenol murders, U.S. Congress approved in 1983 a new Tylenol Bill that made maliciously tampering with consumer products a federal offense. In 1989, the FDA set national requirements for all over-the-counter products to be tamper-resistant.

Unlike many other firms, which often fail to react quickly on discovering potential danger to their stakeholders, J&J is remembered as a company that possessed an ethical corporate culture enabling the firm to handle the Tylenol tampering crisis quickly, openly, and honestly. By doing so, J&J was able to protect and enhance its corporate reputation into the future.

—Mark S. Schwartz

Further Readings

Hartley, R. F. (2005). Johnson and Johnson's Tylenol scare: The classic example of responsible crisis management. In R. F. Hartley (Ed.), *Business ethics: Mistakes and successes* (pp. 303–314). Hoboken, NJ: Wiley.

Johnson, C. H. (1989). A matter of trust. *Management Accounting, 71*(6), 12–13.

Kaplan, T. (2006). The Tylenol crisis: How effective public relations saved Johnson and Johnson. In J. W. Weiss (Ed.), *Business ethics: A stakeholder and issues management approach* (pp. 89–96). Mason, OH: Thomson/South-Western.

Snyder, L., & Foster, L. G. (1983). An anniversary review and critique: The Tylenol crisis/reply. *Public Relations Review, 9*(3), 24–35.

APPENDIX B

DIRECTORY OF CSR-RELATED ORGANIZATIONS AND INTERNET LINKS

African Institute of Corporate Citizenship, http://www.aiccafrica.org/

The African Institute of Corporate Citizenship (AICC) is a non-governmental organisation committed to promoting responsible growth and competitiveness in Africa by changing the way companies do business in Africa.

Aspen Institute Business and Society Program (formerly Aspen ISIB), http://www.aspen institute.org/isib/

The Business and Society Program is an independently funded policy program at the Aspen Institute, dedicated to increasing the supply of business leaders who understand and seek to balance the complex relationship between business success and social and environmental progress.

Association for Independent Corporate Sustainability and Responsibility Research, http://www.csrr-qs.org/

A new European standard (CSRR-QS 1.0) has been drawn up with the objective of promoting confidence in those Groups performing Corporate Sustainability and Responsibility Research (CSRR). CSRR-QS 1.0 is the first quality standard conceived and worked out at sector level in the field of CSR and SRI research and analysis. The project was initiated, supported and funded by the European Commission, Employment and Social Affairs DG.

As You Sow Foundation, http://www.asyousow.org/

As You Sow is a non-profit organization dedicated to promoting corporate social responsibility.

Beyond Grey Pinstripes, http://www.beyondgreypinstripes.org/

Beyond Grey Pinstripes highlights the most innovative MBA programs and faculty infusing environmental and social impact management into the business school curriculum.

Business Alliance for Local Living Economies (BALLE)

Building Economies for the Common Good, http://www.livingeconomies.org/BALLE/

BALLE Mission: To create, strengthen and connect local business networks dedicated to building strong Local Living Economies.

BALLE Vision: We envision a sustainable global economy as a network of Local Living Economies. Living economies sustain community life and natural life as well as long-term economic viability.

Business for Social Responsibility (BSR), http://www.bsr.org/

Business for Social Responsibility (BSR) is a global nonprofit organization that helps member companies achieve commercial success in ways that respect ethical values, people, communities and the environment. BSR member companies have nearly $2 trillion in combined annual revenues and employ more than six million workers around the world.

Business in the Community, http://www.bitc.org.uk/

Business in the Community is a unique movement of companies across the UK committed to continually improving their positive impact on society, with a core membership of 700 companies, including 80% of the FTSE 100.

Business Roundtable Institute for Corporate Ethics, http://www.businessroundtable .org/also at: http://www.darden.edu/corporate-ethics/

This Institute is a bold investment that will bring together the best educators in the field of ethics, active business leaders and business school students to forge a new and lasting link between ethical behavior and business practices.

Canadian Business for Social Responsibility (CBSR), http://www.cbsr.ca/

Founded in 1995, CBSR is a non-profit, business-led, national membership organization of Canadian companies that have made a commitment to operate in a socially, environmentally and financially responsible manner, recognizing the interests of their stakeholders, including investors, customers, employees, business partners, local communities, the environment and society at large.

Caux Round Table, http://www.cauxroundtable.org/

The Caux Round Table (CRT) is a group of senior business leaders from Europe, Japan and North America who are committed to the promotion of principled business leadership. The CRT believes that business has a crucial role in identifying and promoting sustainable and equitable solutions to key global issues affecting the physical, social and economic environments.

Centre for Business Relationships, Accountability, Sustainability and Society (BRASS), http://www.brass.cf.ac.uk/

The ESRC Centre for Business Relationships, Accountability, Sustainability and Society exists to understand and promote the key issues of sustainability, accountability and social responsiveness, through research into key business relationships.

Center for Corporate Change, http://www.vailleadership.org/programs/index.htm

The Center for Corporate Change, a component of the Vail Leadership Institute, was established out of a concern for the state of corporate ethics. It is based on the premise that business is not a game but an integral component of our nation's democratic capitalistic society.

Center for Corporate Citizenship at Boston College, http://www.bcccc.net/

The Center for Corporate Citizenship is a leading resource on corporate citizenship, providing research, executive education, consultation and convenings on citizenship topics. Our mission is to establish corporate citizenship as a business essential, with the goal that all companies act as economic and social assets by integrating social interests with other core business objectives.

Center for Corporate Citizenship (U.S. Chamber of Commerce), http://www.uschamber .com/ccc/

The Center for Corporate Citizenship is a business service organization of the U.S. Chamber of Commerce. It exists to enable and facilitate corporate civic and humanitarian initiatives particularly in terms of civic engagement, economic development, economic security, and disaster management/economic recovery.

Centre for Corporate Social Responsibility, http://www.centreforcsr.org.sg/

The Centre for CSR, an independent not-for-profit organisation, was set up on 17th April 2003 by a group of like-minded and civic-conscious individuals and seeks to raise the awareness of the community at large about the importance of Corporate Social Responsibility (CSR). . . . The Centre for CSR aims to be a national platform for the discussion and understanding of CSR and to be a leading Centre for CSR globally and more particularly in the Asia Pacific.

Center for Economic and Social Justice, http://www.cesj.org/

The Center for Economic and Social Justice (CESJ), established in 1984, promotes a free enterprise approach to global economic justice through expanded capital ownership. CESJ is a non-profit, non-partisan, ecumenical, all-volunteer organization with an educational and research mission.

Center for Ethical Leadership, Seattle, http://www.ethicalleadership.org/

The Center motivates people to practice ethical leadership, inspires institutions to create cultures of integrity and gathers the community to animate cultural change, all for the common good.

Center for Public Integrity, http://www.publicintegrity.org/

The mission of the Center for Public Integrity is to provide the American people with the findings of our investigations and analyses of public service, government accountability and ethics related issues.

CEOs for Cities, http://www.ceosforcities.org/

CEOs for Cities is a national bipartisan alliance of mayors, corporate executives, university presidents and other nonprofit leaders. Its mission is to advance the economic competitiveness of cities. Its national meetings and research products underscore the organization's basic tenet, which is that urban economies are strengthened when public and private sectors come together to collaborate on economic development policy-making and practice.

CERES Network for Change, Coalition for Environmentally Responsible Economies, http://www.ceres.org/

Today, it is often difficult for corporations, activists and socially responsible investors to have honest, meaningful dialogue on corporations' environmental and social practices. CERES provides an innovative forum for this kind of exchange and a unique opportunity for real accountability and real results.

Community Business Limited, http://www.communitybusiness.org.hk/

Community Business Limited is committed to working with companies on corporate social responsibility in Hong Kong.

Conversations with Disbelievers, http://www.conversations-with-disbelievers.net/

Welcome to the Conversations with Disbelievers website, which for the first time brings together much of the available quantitative evidence that addressing social challenges can help businesses improve their financial bottom lines. . . . The website is designed to be used by business managers, nonprofit leaders, consultants and public policy makers alike to provide practical guidance on how best to use the available evidence in encouraging businesses to address social objectives.

Corporate Citizenship Unit, http://users.wbs.warwick.ac.uk/group/ccu/

The Corporate Citizenship Unit (CCU) aims to become a globally recognised centre of excellence in the area of research and teaching in corporate citizenship by bringing together diverse people from business, government, and civil society organisations to examine changes in the relationship between corporations, states and communities.

Corporate Culture, http://www.communicatingforgood.co.uk/

This website is the definitive online resource of customer-led CSR communications.

Corporate Responsibility, http://www.corporateresponsibility.nl/

This website is designed to function as a platform for the dissemination of information on the subject of Corporate [Social] Responsibility.

Corporate Social Responsibility Forum (part of the Prince of Wales Business Leaders Forum), http://www.csrforum.com/

The Prince of Wales Business Leaders Forum is an international charity which was founded in 1990 to promote socially responsible business practices that benefit business and society, and which help to achieve socially, economically, and environmentally sustainable development. The Forum works at the very highest levels in 60 of the world's leading multinational companies, and is active in some 30 emerging and transition economies.

Corporate Social Responsibility Forum, http://www.csrforum.com/

The International Business Leaders Forum is an international educational charity set up in 1990 to promote responsible business practices internationally that benefit business and society, and which help to achieve social, economic and environmentally sustainable development, particularly in new and emerging market economies.

Council for Ethics in Economics, http://www.businessethics.org/

The Council for Ethics in Economics is a worldwide association of leaders in business, education, and other professions working together to strengthen the ethical fabric of business and economic life. The Council identifies and responds to issues important for ethical economic practices and assists in the resolution of these issues.

CR Academy, http://www.csracademy.org.uk/

The CR Academy aims to promote CSR learning through the first dedicated CSR Competency Framework. It is for companies of all sizes as well as for UK educational institutions.

CSR Australia, http://www.csra.com.au/

Founded in 2003, Corporate Social Responsibility Australia, Inc., is a national not-for-profit-membership-based Incorporated Association. Its mission is to help business achieve profitability, competitiveness and sustainable growth through the continuous improvement of skills, knowledge, and ethical behaviour and by applying the principles of Corporate Social Responsibility.

CSR Europe, http://www.csreurope.org/

CSR Europe is the business-to-business network for Corporate Social Responsibility in Europe. We are a membership-based organization. Our mission is to help companies achieve profitability, sustainable growth and human progress by placing Corporate Social Responsibility (CSR) in the mainstream of business practice.

CSR Meetup Groups, http://csr.meetup.com/

Meet other local people interested in implementing or learning about corporate, values-based decision making.

CSR Watch, http://www.csrwatch.com/

Your eye on the anti-business movement.

EMPRESA, http://www.empresa.org/

EMPRESA is an American alliance of CSR-based business organizations that promotes corporate social responsibility (CSR) throughout the Americas.

Equal Exchange, http://www.equalexchange.com/

Equal Exchange was founded in 1986 to create a new approach to trade, one that includes informed consumers, honest and fair trade relationships, and cooperative principles. As a worker-owned co-op, we have accomplished this by offering consumers fairly traded gourmet coffee direct from small-scale farmer co-ops in Latin America, Africa and Asia.

EU Multi-Stakeholder Forum on CSR, http://forum.europa.eu.int/irc/empl/csr_eu_multi_stakeholder_forum/info/data/en/csr%20ems%20forum.htm

The European Multi-Stakeholder Forum on Corporate Social Responsibility (CSR EMS Forum), chaired by the Commission, brings together European representative organisations of employers, business networks, trade unions and NGOs, to promote innovation, convergence, and transparency in existing CSR practices and tools. The Forum's mandate was approved at the launch on 16th October 2002.

CSR Final Report, http://europa.eu.int/comm/enterprise/csr/documents.htm

European Academy of Business in Society, http://www.eabis.org/

The European Academy of Business in Society (EABIS) is a unique alliance of academic institutions, companies, and other stakeholders committed to integrating business in society into the heart of business theory and practice in Europe.

European Business Campaign on CSR, http://www.csrcampaign.org/

The European Business Campaign on Corporate Social Responsibility has set itself the goal of mobilising 500,000 business people and partners to integrate CSR into their core business by 2005.

European Business Ethics Network, http://www.eben.org/

The European Business Ethics Network, EBEN, is the only International network dedicated wholly to the promotion of business ethics in European private industry, public sector, voluntary organizations, and academia.

European Union's CSR website, http://europa.eu.int/comm/employment_social/soc-dial/csr/csr_index.htm

Useful CSR Internet Links: http://europa.eu.int/comm/employment_social/soc-dial/csr/csr_links.htm

Foundation for Global Community—Business and Sustainability, http://www.global community.org/business/index.shtml

The Foundation for Global Community's Business and Sustainability Group (BSG) focuses on educating local companies about the principles of sustainable development and promoting a broader measurement of business success, namely the Triple Bottom Line.

Global Exchange, http://www.globalexchange.org/

Global Exchange is a human rights organization dedicated to promoting environmental, political, and social justice around the world. Since our founding in 1988, we have been striving to increase global awareness among the U.S. public while building international partnerships around the world.

Global Reporting Initiative (GRI), http://www.globalreporting.org/

Recognized by the recent UN World Summit on Sustainable Development, the Global Reporting Initiative (GRI) is an independent global institution which is developing a generally accepted framework for sustainability reporting. The aim of the GRI Guidelines is to enable companies and other organizations to prepare comparable triple bottom line reports on their economic, environmental, and social performance.

Global Sullivan Principles of Social Responsibility, http://globalsullivanprinciples.org/

The objectives of the Global Sullivan Principles are to support economic, social, and political justice by companies where they do business; to support human rights and to encourage equal opportunity at all levels of employment, including racial and gender diversity on decision making committees and boards; to train and advance disadvantaged workers for technical, supervisory, and management opportunities; and to assist with greater tolerance and understanding among peoples; thereby, helping to improve the quality of life for communities, workers and children with dignity and equality.

Group of 77 at the United Nations[1], http://www.g77.org/

As the largest Third World coalition in the United Nations, the Group of 77 provides the means for the developing world to articulate and promote its collective economic interests and enhance its joint negotiating capacity on all major international economic issues in the United Nations system, and promote economic and technical cooperation among developing countries.

Heartland Institute, http://www.thoughtleadergathering.com/

Founded in 1995 by Craig and Patricia Neal, Heartland Institute creates Essential Conversations among individuals and within organizations to help bring about the systemic change needed in these extraordinary times. . . . Our programs are anchored in the belief that essential conversations among leaders will transform our organizations and the world.

ILO Tripartite Declaration of Principles Concerning MNEs and Social Policy, http://www.ilo.org/public/english/standards/norm/sources/mne.htm

Institute for Global Ethics, http://www.globalethics.org/

Mission: To promote ethical behavior in individuals, institutions, and nations through research, public discourse, and practical action.

Interfaith Center on Corporate Responsibility, http://www.iccr.org/

For thirty years the Interfaith Center on Corporate Responsibility (ICCR) has been a leader of the corporate social responsibility movement. ICCR's membership is an association of 275 faith-based institutional investors, including national denominations, religious communities, pension funds, endowments, hospital corporations, economic development funds and publishing companies. ICCR and its members press companies to be socially and environmentally responsible.

International Association for Business and Society (IABS), http://www.iabs.net/

IABS is a learned society devoted to research and teaching about the relationships between business, government, and society.

International Business Ethics Institute, http://www.business-ethics.org/

Fostering global business practices to promote equitable economic development, resource sustainability and just forms of government.

International Business Leaders Forum, http://www.iblf.org/, http://www.iblf.org/csr/ csrwe bassist.nsf/content/f1.html

The IBLF is an international educational charity set up in 1990 to promote responsible business practices internationally that benefit business and society, and which help to achieve social, economic, and environmentally sustainable development, particularly in new and emerging market economies.

International Centre for Business Performance and Corporate Responsibility, http:// mubs.mdx.ac.uk/Research/Research_Centres/icbpcr/

The Centre is located at Middlesex University's Business School, and aims to be an internationally-renowned Centre of Excellence in the promotion of corporate responsibility and its relationship to business performance in both financial and non-financial dimensions.

International Centre for Corporate Social Responsibility, http://www.nottingham.ac.uk/ business/ICCSR/

The ICCSR engages in mainstream teaching and research in the broad area of corporate social responsibility.

International Institute for Sustainable Development, http://www.iisd.org/

The International Institute for Sustainable Development contributes to sustainable development by advancing policy recommendations on international trade and investment, economic policy, climate change, measurement and indicators, and natural resources management.

Japan for Sustainability, http://www.japanfs.org/en/business/reports.html

Here are links to environmental/sustainability reports of Japanese companies. The reports disclose their policies, strategies and perfor-mance in environmental, social, and/or sustainability management.

LifeWorth, http://www.lifeworth.com/

As more of us work on corporate responsibility, sustainable business and responsible investment, we are forming a new profession and a new social movement. . . . We support this new movement and pro-fession by bringing together people and organizations with common values.

Net Impact, http://www.net-impact.org/

Net Impact is a powerful and influential network of over 10,000 MBA students and professionals committed to using the power of business to create a better world. Through education, career resources, events, and access to an international network, Net Impact helps members to utilize their business skills for positive social change.

New Academy of Business, http://www.new-academy.ac.uk/

The New Academy of Business was founded in 1995 by Anita Roddick to provide entrepreneurs, managers, and organisational leaders with the insights and capacities necessary to respond progressively to the emerging challenges of sustainability and organisational responsibility.

Nordic Partnership, http://www.nordicpartnership.org/

The Nordic Partnership is an NGO-business network founded in 2001 by the World Wide Fund for Nature (WWF), Danish media centre Monday Morning, and key corporate players operating in the Nordic region. . . . Using a partnership approach, the members of the Nordic Partnership work together to find new ways of making sustainable initiatives more attractive and rewarding to business. By doing this, we aim to provide fresh perspectives, challenges, and recommendations to the rules of the game that relate to sustainable development.

Organization for Economic Co-operation and Development (OECD), http://www.oecd .org/department/0,2688,en_2649_33765_1_1_1_1_1,00.html

The emergence of private initiatives for corporate responsibility— including the development of codes of conduct, management systems for improving compliance with these codes, and non-financial reporting standards—has been an important trend in international business over the last 25 years. The Investment Committee's work in this area is part of its broader efforts to support implementation of the OECD Guidelines for Multinational Enterprises and to enhance the contribution of international investments to sustainable development.

Procott, http://www.procott.org/

A procott (flipside of boycott) is a movement educating and organizing around conscious consumer efforts to support the production and purchase of earth/justice-friendly goods and services.

Project Sigma, http://www.projectsigma.com/

Project SIGMA aims to provide clear, practical advice to organisations to help them make a meaningful contribution to sustainable development.

Public Citizen, http://www.citizen.org/

Public Citizen is a national, nonprofit consumer advocacy organization founded by Ralph Nader in 1971 to represent consumer interests in Congress, the executive branch and the courts.

We fight for openness and democratic accountability in government, for the right of consumers to seek redress in the courts; for clean, safe, and sustainable energy sources; for social and economic justice in trade policies; for strong health, safety, and environmental protections; and for safe, effective and affordable prescription drugs and health care.

Social Venture Network, http://www.svn.org/

Founded in 1987 by some of the nation's most visionary leaders in socially responsible entrepreneurship and investment, Social Venture Network (SVN) is a nonprofit network committed to building a just and sustainable world through business.

Society for Business Ethics, http://www.societyforbusinessethics.org/

The Society for Business Ethics (SBE) is an international organization of scholars engaged in the academic study of business ethics and others with interest in the field.

Spirit in Business, http://www.spiritinbusiness.org/

Mission: To connect leaders in a global community of inquiry, learning and action, to release the creative power of individuals and organizations for the benefit of the whole.

Sustainable Business Institute, http://www.sustainablebusiness.org/

The Sustainable Business Institute (SBI) is a non-profit, non-partisan organization dedicated to bringing about increased understanding of, and commitment to, the concept of sustainability within business and communities worldwide.

Sustainability Education Center, http://www.sustainabilityed.org/

The Sustainability Education Center (SEC) was created in 1995 in response to the growing need for educational materials and professional development focused on sustainability.

Tomorrow's Company, http://www.tomorrowscompany.com/

Tomorrow's Company represents a practical future of sustainable success which makes sense to shareholders and to society. The Centre for Tomorrow's Company is a think-tank and catalyst, researching and stimulating the development of a new agenda for business. Our purpose is to create, with business, a future for business which makes equal sense to staff, shareholders, and society.

UN Global Compact Principles, http://www.unglobalcompact.org/

Through the power of collective action, the Global Compact seeks to advance responsible corporate citizenship so that business can be part of the solution to the challenges of globalisation.

UN Millennium Development Goals, http://www.un.org/millenniumgoals/

By the year 2015, all 191 United Nation Member States have pledged to meet these goals.

Win-Win Partners, http://winwinpartner.com/

Win-Win Partners are companies and organizations achieving competitive advantage through community investment.

World Business Council for Sustainable Development, http://www.wbcsd.org/

The World Business Council for Sustainable Development (WBCSD) is a coalition of 160 international companies united by a shared commitment to sustainable development via the three pillars of economic growth, ecological balance, and social progress.

World Resources Institute, http://www.wri.org/

World Resources Institute is an independent nonprofit organization with a staff of more than 100 scientists, economists, policy experts, business analysts, statistical analysts, mapmakers, and communicators working to protect the Earth and improve people's lives.

NOTE

1. "The G77 (the descendent of the former nonaligned countries) accounts for nearly 80 percent of the world's population," Noam Chomsky, The Crimes of "Intcom," *Foreign Policy*, September/October 2002, pp. 34–35.

APPENDIX C

DIRECTORY OF ONLINE CSR
INFORMATION SOURCES AND PUBLICATIONS

Brooklyn Bridge Newsletter—TBLI Group, http://www.tbli.org/index-newsletter.html

Brooklyn Bridge publishes a digital Newsletter on SRI/CSR every month.

Business and Human Rights Resource Centre, http://www.business-humanrights.org/

The Business & Human Rights Resource Centre is an independent, international, nonprofit organisation, in a collaborative partnership with Amnesty International sections and leading academic institutions. Our online library covers over 1,800 companies, over 160 countries, over 150 topics.

Business and Society, http://www.sagepub.com/journalManuscript.aspx?pid=131

Business & Society publishes the most outstanding scholarship on social issues and ethics, and their impact and influence on organizations. In this fast-growing, ever-changing, and always challenging field of study, *Business & Society* is the only peer-reviewed scholarly journal devoted entirely to research, discussion, and analysis on the relationship between business and society.

Business Ethics Magazine, http://business-ethics.com/

The mission of *Business Ethics* is to promote ethical business practices, to serve that growing community of professionals striving to work and invest in responsible ways.

Business Ethics Magazine's Corporate Social Responsibility Report, 100 Best Corporate Citizens, http://www.business-ethics.com/whats_new/100best_2005.html

Business Ethics Quarterly, http://www.societyforbusinessethics.org/beq.htm

Business Ethics Quarterly (BEQ) is the journal of the Society for Business Ethics. BEQ publishes scholarly articles and book reviews on all aspects of ethics in business, especially those that raise conceptual, methodological, practical, or theoretical issues.

Chronicle of Philanthropy, http://philanthropy.com/

The Chronicle of Philanthropy is the newspaper of the nonprofit world. It is the No. 1 news source, in print and online, for charity leaders, fund raisers, grant makers, and other people involved in the philanthropic enterprise.

Common Dreams News Center, http://www.commondreams.org/

Breaking news and views for the progressive community.

CSR Online Survey, http://www.csr-survey.org/

How companies communicate CSR to customers and shareholders, is vital. It says as much about their brand as do their products and services. It will affect not only their reputation in the city, but also with their customers. The aim of this survey was to look at how well— or badly—Britain's top companies are communicating their CSR activities.

CSR Wire—Corporate Social Responsibility Newswire Service, http://www.csrwire.com/

CSRwire seeks to promote the growth of corporate responsibility and sustainability through solutions-based information and positive examples of corporate practices.

CSR Wire—CSR Directory, http://www.csrwire.com/directory/

CSRwire and the SRI World Group technical team have developed this searchable, online version of the CSR Directory as a free service to the CSR community.

Electronic Journal of Business Ethics and Organization Studies, http://ejbo.jyu.fi/index.cgi?page=cover

Electronic Journal of Business Ethics and Organization Studies, the aim of which is to promote research and practise of business and organization ethics.

Ethical Corporation Magazine, http://www.ethicalcorp.com/

Ethical Corporation Magazine is an independent business publication for corporate responsibility, producing 12 issues per year.

Ethical Performance, http://www.ethicalperformance.com/

Ethical Performance is a monthly newsletter for professionals with a corporate social responsibility or socially responsible investment brief. It is the only independent business newsletter to cover trends in

- social reporting
- corporate governance
- ethical codes of practice
- socially responsible investment
- risk and reputation management
- supply chain monitoring.

Ethics in Economics Quarterly, http://www.businessethics.org/ethicsq.htm

The quarterly publication of the Council for Ethics in Economics.

ETHICOMP Journal, http://www.ccsr.cse.dmu.ac.uk/journal/

The *ETHICOMP Journal* aims to further the work of the conference series—recognised as one of the premier international events on computer ethics and social responsibility attended by delegates from all over the world.

EurActiv.com (Corporate Social Responsibility page), http://www.euractiv.com/Section?idNum=3750340

EurActiv.com is now the leading online media on European Union policies.

Faith in Business quarterly, http://www.fibq.org/

> *Faith in Business* is a quarterly journal relating Christian faith and
> values to the business world.

Global Corruption Report, http://www.globalcorruptionreport.org/

> *The Global Corruption Report* . . . is the new publication of Transparency
> International (TI), the leading global anti-corruption NGO. It provides an
> overview of the state of corruption around the globe.

Greenbiz.com, http://www.greenbiz.com/

> The nonprofit, nonpartisan GreenBiz.com works to harness the
> power of technology to bring environmental information, resources,
> and tools to the mainstream business community.

GreenMoney Journal, http://www.greenmoneyjournal.com/

> *The GreenMoney Journal* encourages and promotes the awareness of
> socially & environmentally responsible business, investing, and con-
> sumer resources in publications & online.

Journal of Business Ethics, http://www.kluweronline.com/issn/0167–4544

> The *Journal of Business Ethics* publishes original articles from a
> wide variety of methodological and disciplinary perspectives con-
> cerning ethical issues related to business.

Journal of Corporate Citizenship, http://www.greenleaf-publishing.com/jcc/jcchome.htm

> *The Journal of Corporate Citizenship* (JCC) aims to publish the best
> ideas integrating the theory and practice of corporate citizenship in a
> format that is readable, accessible, engaging, interesting, and useful for
> readers in business, consultancy, government, NGOs and, academia.

mallenbaker.net, http://www.mallenbaker.net/csr/

> This site is part of the personal site of Mallen Baker—Development
> Director for Business in the Community. It is an expression of my
> own interest and concern in how companies respond to the agenda for
> corporate citizenship—the growing need to manage issues that affect

their business reputation—and to respond to the growing needs and concerns of a range of different stakeholders.

New Academy Review, http://www.new-academy-review.com/

The International Journal of Corporate Social Responsibility, Sustainability, Leadership and Ethics.

Nonprofit Management Educational Resources, http://www.uwex.edu/li/index.html

The Learner Resource Center provides you with a number of resources on the web that could provide you with assistance in a variety of nonprofit management and leadership issues.

NonProfit Times, http://www.nptimes.com/

The leading business publication for nonprofit management.

NPT Top 100

The leading in-depth study of America's Top 100 Nonprofits.

OneWorld.net, http://www.oneworld.net/

The OneWorld network and portal brings you the latest news, action, campaigns and organisations in human rights and global issues across five continents and in 11 different languages, published across its international site, regional editions, and thematic channels.

Simon Zadek, http://www.zadek.net/

This site is a resource area for people concerned with improving the social, environmental, and economic performance of business.

Socialfunds.com, http://www.socialfunds.com/

SocialFunds.com features over 10,000 pages of information on SRI mutual funds, community investments, corporate research, share-owner actions, and daily social investment news.

Socially Responsible Investing (SRI) Compass, http://www.sricompass.org/

The SRI Compass is the first European online resource featuring all existing green and ethical retail funds and indices in Europe. The SRI

Compass is the result of a joint initiative by CSR Europe and the SiRi Group with the support of Euronext.

Spirit in Business, http://www.spiritinbusiness.org/

Spirit in Business is for business people who care.
Spirit in Business is about an economy that works for everyone.

Stanford Social Innovation Review, http://www.ssireview.com/?stanford

Discover powerful insights from leading executives and world-class faculty. *Stanford Social Innovation Review* presents the best ideas in nonprofit management, philanthropy, and corporate citizenship. Find out what works and what doesn't. And how to strengthen your social impact.

SustainableBusiness.com, http://www.sustainablebusiness.com/

Vision: A world where human activities live in harmony with earth's carrying capacity.

Worthwhile Magazine, http://www.worthwhilemag.com/

The editorial mission of *Worthwhile* is to put purpose and passion on the same plane as profit. *Worthwhile* offers a roadmap for business success that is more personally fulfilling and socially responsible. We live by the motto that it is impossible to have a meaningful life without meaningful work.